Colonial Delaware Wills and Estates to 1800: An Index

Donald O. Virdin

HERITAGE BOOKS
2008

HERITAGE BOOKS
AN IMPRINT OF HERITAGE BOOKS, INC.

Books, CDs, and more—Worldwide

For our listing of thousands of titles see our website at

www.HeritageBooks.com

Published 2008 by
HERITAGE BOOKS, INC.
Publishing Division
100 Railroad Ave. #104
Westminster, Maryland 21157

International Standard Book Numbers
Paperbound: 978-0-7884-0020-9
Clothbound: 978-0-7884-7036-3

Contents

Introduction

This book is an index to colonial Delaware wills and estates to 1800 and includes the wills and estates that could be located in published works concerning Kent County, Sussex County, and New Castle County. However, as a general rule, the compiler has been able to obtain from published sources only a list of wills for New Castle County.

In some periods of the history of Delaware, the law did not require probated wills to be recorded. Sometimes individuals using the original wills took them home with them. Many wills have deteriorated as a result of too much use.

The author has alphabetized wills and estates to provide a basic book for anyone interested in Delaware genealogy or families who lived on the Delmarva Peninsula in its early history. The author hopes that his effort will be useful to genealogists and others searching for family connections.

November 1993 Donald Odell Virdin

INDEX

DATE	NAME	COUNTY	BOOK & PAGE
1799	Aaron, Daniel	N	0.451
1790	Abbott, John	S	A57-8/9
1790	Abbott, Richard	S	D.271/2
1702	Abbott, Robert	S	A.40/3
1782	Abbott, Susannah	S	C.294/5
----	Abbott, Temperance	S	A57-24
1776	Abbott, William, Sr.	S	C.24/6
1798	Abbott, William	S	A57-26
1785	Abdell, Littleton	S	A57-31
1784	Ackroyd, John	K	M.29
1785	Adair, John	N	M.94
1788	Adama, Alexander	N	M.321
1787	Adams, Abraham	S	D.139/40
1775	Adams, George	N	K.248
1799	Adams, George	S	A88-182
1731	Adams, James	K	H.24
1793	Adams, James, Sr.	N	N.308
1766	Adams, Leven	N	L.18/19
1782	Adams, Nannie	S	C.288/9
1781	Adams, Nathan	K	L.229
1758	Adams, Peter	S	B.169/71
1778	Adams, Richard	S	C.148/50
1766	Adams, Roger	S	A57-91
1786	Adams, Roger, Jr.	S	D.120
1727	Adams, Thomas	K	F.10
1763	Adams, William	K	1.763
1764	Adderson, Jacob	S	A57-107
1783	Adkins, Daniel	S	A57-199
1788	Aiken, Fanny	N	M.320
1747	Aiken (Eaken), Robert	N	G.43
1798	Ake, Riley	S	E.155
1766	Akin (Ecan), Allen	K	L.21
1790	Akins, William	K	M.253
1761	Akles, John	K	1.45
1767	Albany, John	K	L.26
1758	Alberry (Norberry), Benjamin	K	K.177
1784	Alcock, John	K	M.30

1773	Aldricks, Peter	N	K.82
1787	Alee, John	K	M.132
1700	Aleefe, Joseph	S	A.30/32
1781	Alexander, Francis	N	L.229
1785	Alexander, Isaac	N	M.162
1717	Alexander, James	N	C.103
1784	Alford, Charity	K	M.20
1784	Alford, Charity	K	M.18/19
1748	Alford, George	N	G.201
1759	Alford, Mary	K	K.263/4
1762	Alford, Mary	K	K.271
1762	Alford, Thomas	K	K.271
1778	Alfree, Mary	N	L.24
1746	Aliff, Joseph	S	A.377/8
1762	Alle, Jacob, Jr.	K	K.278
1795	Allcbond, Thomas	K	N.108
1770	Allee, Abraham, Sr.	K	L.83
1766	Allee, Abraham, Jr.	K	L.12
1768	Allee, Abraham, Jr.	K	L.45
1778	Allee, Abraham, Jr.	K	L.207
1766	Allee, Jacob	K	L.19/20
1769	Allee, John, Jr.	K	L.54
1775	Allee, Jonathn	K	L. 171
1782	Allee, Presley	K	L.208
1789	Allee, Sarah	K	M.206
1754	Allen, Charles	K	K.93
1720	Allen, James	K	D.30
1757	Allen, John	K	K.158
1757	Allen, John	K	K.172
1767	Allen, John	S	B.324/6
1773	Allen, John	N	K.66
1774	Allen, Joseph	S	C.85/6
1774	Allen, Joseph	K	L.150
1791	Allen, Robert	N	N.227
1757	Allen, Sarah	K	K.172
1726	Alles, John	K	F.21
1721	Allett, Thomas	N	C.324
1718	Alley, John	K	D.7/8
1767	Allford, Thomas	K	L.30
1787	Allison, Sarah	N	M.245
1761	Allman, John	N	H&I.528

1794	Allman, Mary	N	N.450
1785	Allmond, William	N	M.166
1775	Allston, Arthur	N	K.255
1760	Allston, Israel	K	K.247
1746	Allston, Thomas	K	I.129/130
1772	Allston, Thomas	K	L.120
1797	Almond, Thomas	N	0.218
1764	Alrich, Peter Sigfredus	N	N.230
1779	Alrichs, Hannanus	N	I.173
1694	Alrichs, Peter	N	——
1716	Alrichs, Sigfreedus	N	C.40
1780	Alrichs, Sigfriedes	N	L.205
1789	Alricks, Benjamin	N	N.75
1741	Alsop, Benjamin	K	I.106
1795	Alston, Abner	N	0.63
1794	Alston, Israel	K	N.110
1772	Alston, Randal	K	N.113
1794	Alston, Thomas	K	N.119
1736	Alstone, Arthur	K	H.133
1777	Alexander, Margaret	K	L.191
1794	Alexander, Philip	K	N.77
1777	Alexander, Richard	K	L.191
1774	Amor (Amour), John	K	L.149
1796	Amos, Elizabeth	K	N.147
1738	Amos, Henry	K	H.148
1795	Amous, James	K	N.127
1798	Amous, James	K	N.220
1799	Amur, John	K	N.236
1779	Anderson, Christianea	N	L.133
1701	Anderson, Cornelius	S	A.35/6
1773	Anderson, Elijah	K	L.130
1786	Anderson, Elijah	K	A1.151
1777	Anderson, Elizabeth	K	L.191
1779	Anderson, Erick	N	L.160
1793	Anderson, Ezekiel	K	N.57/8
1777	Anderson, Francis	N	Misc. 1.1
1708	Anderson, Frank	K	B.61
1751	Anderson, Jacob	K	K.41
1793	Anderson, Jacobus, Sr.	N	N.354
1762	Anderson, James	K	K.282
1780	Anderson, James	K	L.270

1791	Anderson, James	K	M.267/8
1794	Anderson, James	K	A1.178
1795	Anderson, James	K	N.135
1717	Anderson, James	N	C.86
1785	Anderson, James	N	M.143
1797	Anderson, James	N	O.275
1686	Anderson, John	N	A.79
1747	Anderson, John	K	I.200
1750	Anderson, John	K	K.39
1773	Anderson, John	K	L.140
1775	Anderson, John	N	K.266
1784	Anderson, Mary	N	M.27
1750	Anderson, Peter	N	G.405
1738	Anderson, Thomas	K	H.148
1718	Anderson, Urian	N	----
1777	Anderson, William	N	K.350
1778	Anderson, William	N	L.62
1735	Anderton (Anderson), Edward	K	H.92
1772	Anderton, John	K	L.122/3
1709	Andree, Peter	N	B.200
1750	Andrews, Miriam	N	G.419
1750	Andrews, Robinson	S	A.435/6
1793	Andrews, Sarah	N	N.387
1779	Andrews, Thomas	S	C.215/7
1748	Andrews, William	N	G.109
1744	Anit (Amyatt), John	K	I.98
1715	Annand, William	K	L.42
1791	Appleton, Robert	K	M.275
1784	Appleton, Robert	K	M.36
1777	Argo, Alexander	S	C.115/8
1794	Argo, Moses	S	A.57-180
1785	Armstrong, Ann	N	M.98
1799	Armstrong, Ann	N	O.499
1775	Armstrong, Archibald	N	K.229
1797	Armstrong, Robert	N	O.295
1774	Armstrong, William	N	K.181
1775	Armstrong, William	N	K.271
1792	Armstrong, William	N	N.303
1781	Arnet, John	K	L.230
1784	Arnet, Thomas	K	M.20
1776	Arnett, Isabella	S	A.57-153

1749	Arnett, James	K	K.7
1779	Arnold, William	S	A.57-189
1770	Arnoll, Samuel	S	B.382/3
1783	Aron, Michael	K	M.13
1781	Aron, William	K	L.276
1766	Arrowsmith, Thomas	K	L.11
1774	Arrowsmith, Thomas	K	L.151
1770	Art, Jacob	S	A57.192/3
1763	Arthur, Robert	K	K.282
1794	Arthur, William	K	N.76
1788	Ash, Josiah	N	M.300
1705	Ashberry, Joseph	k	B.53
1736	Ashborn (Ashburn), Martain	K	H.130
1762	Ashee, Eleanor	K	A.2-9
1796	Ashford, Mary	K	N.146
1706	Ashton, Robert	N	B.123
1721	Askey, James	S	A.153/4
1752	Askie, Grace	S	B.40/1
1701	Asueress (Asuerus, Asuersee), Hendrick	S	A.18/19
1799	Atkins, Elijah	S	A.57-202
1746	Atkins, John	S	A.377/8
1793	Atkins, John Hancock	S	A.57/209
1792	Attax, Aquilla	K	N.16
1796	Auston, Isaac	S	A.57-227
1797	Autrim, John	N	O.287
1685	Avery, John	S	——
1778	Aydekott, Henry	S	C.143/44
1783	Aydelott, Jespos	S	D.7
1799	Aydelott, John	S	E.242/3
1791	Aydelott, John. Sr.	S	D.330
1791	Aydelotte, Frances	S	A.57-233/4
1797	Ayler, James	K	L.263
1719	Ayliff, William	S	A.108/9
1786	Ayres, Abraham	K	M.113/4
1793	Ayres, James	K	N.40
1795	Ayres, James	K	N.121
1795	Ayres, James	K	A2.39
1795	Ayres, Simon	K	N.117

- B -

1748	Babb, Thomas	N	G.484
1788	Babb, Thomas	N	M.358
1751	Babb, Thomas, Sr.	N	G.4854
1784	Bacon, Dodson	S	D.45/6
1795	Bacon, George	S	E.61/3
1778	Bacon, Jacob	K	L.197
1796	Bacon, John	S	E.108/9
1790	Bacon, Levin	S	D.280
1763	Badger, Edmund	K	K.327/8
1679	Badger, John	S	AM2013.88
1770	Bagswell, Thomas	S	B.396/8
1721	Bagwell, Frances	S	A.145/6
1799	Bagwell, John	S	E.226/7
1770	Bagwell, Thomas	S	B.286/8
1773	Bagwell, William	S	A.58-61
1787	Bagwell, William	S	A.58-60&62
1745	Bailey, James	S	A.392/3
1782	Bailey, Nathaniel	S	C.310
1777	Bailey, Robert	N	K.338
1778	Bailey, Edmond	K	L.200
1797	Bailey, Edmond	K	N.170
1727	Bailey, Elias	K	F.33
1791	Baily, John	S	A.58-72
1789	Baily, John	K	M.212
1748	Baily, Jonathan	S	A.394/5
----	Baily, Stephen	S	A.58-96
1775	Bainum, Eleanor	S	C.11/12
1791	Bainum, Isaac	S	A.58-103/4
1741	Baird, Rebecca	N	Misc.2.8
1696	Baker, Ambrose	N	B.57
1796	Baker, Elias	S	A.58-108/9
1787	Baker, George	K	M.160
1695	Baker, George	N	B.36
1790	Baker, Hugh	S	A.18
1772	Baker, Joshua	N	K.33
1796	Baker, Mary	S	E.78
1794	Baker, Thomas	S	A.58-141
1772	Baker, William	K	L.189
1785	Baker,William	K	M.37

1783	Baker, William	S	A.58-142
1783	Baldwin, Eli	N	L.395
1790	Baldwin, Elizabeth	N	N.100
1785	Baldwin, Francis	N	M.148
1745	Baldwin, John	N	Misc.2.12
1746	Baldwin, John	N	Misc.2.14
1786	Baley, Jonathan	S	D.118/9
1747	Ball, James	N	G.56
1695	Ball, John	N	B.30
1780	Ball, Martha	N	L.187
1709	Ball, William	N	B.195
1747	Ball, William	N	G.41
1783	Balton, James	K	M.16
1725	Bamton, John	K	F.5
1798	Baning, james	K	N.197
1791	Baning, Phineas	K	M.271
1742	Baning, Richard	K	I.61
1750	Bannet, William	N	G.368
1766	Barber, Abraham	K	L.14
1775	Barber, Abraham	K	L.160
1793	Barber, Francis	K	N.62
1794	Barber, Francis	K	N.86
1755	Barber, James	N	Misc.1.23
1794	Barber, Joseph	K	N.86
1794	Barber, Mary	K	N.47
1793	Barcus, Rachel	K	N.41/2
1730	Barger, James	K	H.7
1787	Barker, Ann	S	A.58-91
1789	Barker, Annie (Ann)	S	A58.174/5
1798	Barker, Eley (Eli)	S	E.149/50
1749	Barker, Job	S	A.402/3
1789	Barker, Leatherberry	S	D.231/2
1786	Barker, Perry	S	A.58-192
1759	Barker, Thomas	K	K.202
1773	Barker, William	K	L.143
1796	Barker, Zadak	S	A.58-193/4
1791	Barlow, Josiah	N	N.208
1684	Barnes, John	N	A.60
1790	Barnes, Robert	S	D.298/9
1767	Barnet, John	K	L.25
1790	Barnet, John	K	M.246

1748	Barnet, John	K	I.222
1764	Barnet, Moses	K	K.347
1756	Barnet, Samuel	K	K.138/9
1790	Barnet, Solomon	K	M.250
1790	Barnet, Thomas	K	K.129/30
1759	Barns, Ann	K	K.208
1761	Barns, Ann	K	K.266
1790	Barns, Ezekiel	K	M.229
1789	Barns, George	S	A.58-202
1794	Barns, James	K	N.86
1726	Barns, John	K	F.11/12
1695	Barns, John	K	A.77
1738	Barns, John	K	I.5
1770	Barns, John	K	A.2-220
1788	Barns, John	K	M.179
1767	Barns, John	K	L.23/4
1770	Barns, John, Jr.	K	L.73
1789	Barns, Mary	S	A.48-206
1791	Barns, Sarah	K	N.7
1759	Barns, Stephen	K	K.205
1767	Barns, Stephen	K	L.23
1797	Barns, Stephen	K	N.173
1753	Barns, William	K	K.85
1758	Barns, William	K	A.2-231
1768	Barns, William	K	A.2-232
1778	Barns, William	N	L.117
1785	Barns, William	K	M.67
1789	Barns, William	K	M.183
1727	Barnseley, Thomas	K	G.8/9
1742	Barr, Adam	K	I.77
1785	Barr, James	S	A.58-212/3
1786	Barr, John	S	A.58-250
1760	Barr, Robert	N	Misc.24-25
1784	Barr, William	S	A.58-215
1751	Barratt, Benjamin	K	K.40
1726	Barratt, Humphrey	K	F.14
1772	Barratt, John	K	L.104
1797	Barratt, Nathaniel	K	N.184/5
1784	Barratt, Philip	K	M.33/35
1734	Barratt, Phoebe	K	H.81
1760	Barrett, Benjamin	K	K.223

1795	Barrett, Roger	K	N.97
1783	Barrot, Roger	K	M.17
1785	Barrow, Gilbert	K	M.42/3
1714	Bartleson, Bartle	N	C.24/25
1689	Bartlet, Nicholas	K	AM2013.112
1757	Bartlet, Samuel	K	K.163
1781	Bartlett, Elijah	K	M.119
1774	Bartlett, Jane	N	K.141
1762	Bartlett, William	S	B.254/7
1787	Barton, Joseph	K	M.131
1790	Barton, William	S	D.311/2
1790	Basnett, Sarah	S	D.175/6
1799	Basset, Benjamin	K	N.238
1790	Basset, John	N	N.126
1707	Bassett, Bartholomew	N	Misc.1.3
1752	Bassill, Robert	K	K.78
1783	Batchelor, Cornelius	N	L.372
1791	Batson, Thomas	S	D.345/6
1792	Battell, Elizabeth	K	N.32/3
1794	Battell, Elizabeth	K	N.80
1792	Battell, French	K	N.32
1782	Battell, French	K	L.230
1794	Battell, French	K	N.80
1794	Battell, John Fench	K	N.80
1799	Bayard, Thomas	K	N.227
1751	Bayley, James	N	G.469
1781	Bayley, John	N	L.238
1791	Bayley, Clement Lee	S	D.347/8
1795	Bayly, John L.	S	E.40/1
1787	Baynard, Elizabeth	K	M.165
1787	Baynard, Elizabeth	K	M.127
1786	Baynard, Thomas	K	M.112/3
1774	Beakham, Francis	K	L.153/4
1761	Beard, Ann	K	K.266
1797	Beard, Duncan	N	O.257
1779	Beard, John	K	L.213
1787	Beard, Moses	K	M.163
1799	Beathards, Elizabeth	K	N.230/1
1777	Beaty, Elizabeth	N	K.349
1795	Beauchamp, David	K	N.107/8
1781	Beauchamp, Grace	K	L.236/7

1794	Beauchamp, Isaac	K	N.107
1774	Beauchamp, John	K	L.166
1788	Beauchamp, John	K	M.164/5
1788	Beauchamp, John	K	M.178
1795	Beauchamp, John	K	N.107
1771	Beauchamp, Marcy	K	L.104
1795	Beauchamp, Marcy	K	N.107
1788	Beauchamp, Mary	K	M.178/9
1775	Beauchamp, Robert	K	L.172
1740	Beauvett, Peter	K	I.29
1781	Beavens, William, Sr.	S	C.227/8
1747	Beavis, Francis	N	G.89
1787	Becket, Bede	S	A.65-4
1743	Becket, William	S	A.350/2
1757	Bocket, William	K	K.162
1797	Beckworth, William	K	N.168
1789	Bedford, William	N	N.84
1785	Bedlow, William	K	M.73
1792	Bedwell, Agnes	K	N.15
1786	Bedwell, Ezekiel	K	N.122
1698	Bedwell, Henry	K	B.28
1771	Bedwell, James	K	L.91
1686	Bedwell, Robert	K	AM2013-66
1765	Bedwell, Robert	K	L.2
1794	Bedwell, Thomas	K	N.84/5
1717	Bedwell, Thomas	S	A.95/6
1788	Beeson, Edward	N	M.309
1790	Beeson, Thomas	N	N.117
----	Belch, Joseph	K	N.82
1781	Belew, Jacob	N	L.253
1783	Belew, Sarah	N	L.383
1787	Bell, John	K	M.132/3
1788	Bell, John	S	A.59-53
1729	Bell, John	K	G.33/4
1791	Bell, John	K	M.277
1793	Bell, John	K	N.47
1795	Bell, John	N	O.65
1797	Bell, Nancy	K	N.172
1774	Bell, Richard	N	K.155
1760	Bell, Robert	K	K.220
1784	Bell, Stephen	S	A.59-62

1774	Bell, Thomas	K	L.149
1790	Bell, Thomas	S	A.59-64/5
1789	Bell, Thomas, W.	S	D.209
1795	Bellach, James	K	N.137
1793	Bellach, James	K	N.68/72
1770	Bellach, John	K	L.86
1794	Bellach, Thomas	K	N.73
1690	Bellamy, John	S	AM2013-131
1729	Bellarby, Isaac	N	C.288
1790	Bellew, Thomas	N	----
1795	Belloch, Elizabeth	K	N.136
1694	Bembrick, Edward	S	AM2013-158
1776	Benn, James	K	L.181
1777	Bennet, Andrew	K	L.193
1756	Bennet, Elinor	K	K.152
1761	Bennet, Nicholas	N	Misc.1.30
1778	Bennet, Nicholas	N	L.116
1779	Bennet, Thomas	N	L.164
1777	Bennett, John	S	C.93/4
1786	Bennett, John	K	M.112/3
1748	Bennett, John	K	I.245/6
1786	Bennett, Purnell	S	D.94/6
1753	Bennett, Stephen	S	B.43/5
1794	Bennum (Bannum), George	S	E.17/18
1749	Benson, Daniel	K	I.257
1786	Benson, Daniel	K	M.110/11
1773	Benson, James	S	A.59-133
1763	Benson, Jonathan	K	K.305
1789	Benson, Nancy	K	M.187
1748	Benson, Thomas	K	I.245/6
1751	Benston, Daniel	K	A.3-234
1787	Benston, Daniel	K	A.3-235
1783	Benston, Elisha	K	L.27
1751	Benston, John	K	A.3-238
1788	Benston, Levin	K	M.172
1794	Bentley, James	N	N.434
1786	Berchine, Joseph	K	M.124
1732	Bermingham (Birmingham), John	K	H.54&60
1796	Berry, Benjamin	K	N.148
1792	Berry, Charles	K	N.19
1725	Berry, Edward	K	F.7

1785	Berry, Elijah	K	M.90
1769	Berry, James	K	L.62/3
1773	Berry, Joseph	K	L.137
1743	Berry, Samuel	K	I.108
1774	Berry, Thomas	K	A.9
1694	Berry, William	K	K.9
1799	Berry, William	K	N.229
1712	Best, Humphrey	N	B.179
1752	Beswick, George	K	K.79
1771	Beswick, John	K	L.104
1750	Beswick, William	K	K.5
1797	Betheards, William G.	K	N.165
1799	Betheards, William G.	K	N.230
1698	Betts, John	K	A.22
1710	Betts, Mary	K	C.85/6
1727	Betts, Robert	K	G.5/6
1759	Betts, Ruth	K	K.211
1740	Betts, William	K	I.33
1784	Betts, William	K	M.20
1798	Bevans (Bivans), Mary	S	E.165
1783	Bevins, James	S	A.59-158
1795	Bevins, James	S	E.26/7
1762	Bibbin, John	K	K.273
1749	Bickley, Samuel	N	G.318
1755	Bicknall (Bignall), John	S	B.86/9
1771	Bicknell, Sarah	S	B.409/11
1785	Bicknell, William	S	A.59-177/8
1778	Biddle, Augustine	K	L.201
1772	Bigs, David	N	Misc.1.34
1791	Bilderback, Joseph	N	N.183
1706	Biles, John	K	B.57
1791	Bileter, Daniel	K	N.1/2
1742	Billiter, Sarah	K	M.102
1754	Bird, John	N	Misc.1.22
1776	Bird, John, Jr.	N	K.322
1781	Bird, Joseph	K	M.102
1789	Bird, Rachel	N	N.34
1726	Bird, Thomas	N	Misc.1.6
1778	Bird, Thomas, Sr.	N	L.35
1745	Bird, William	K	I.110/11
1782	Bird, William	N	L.218

1793	Birk, Charles	K	N.45/6
1757	Bisbin, John	K	K.168/70
1750	Bishop, Hester	N	G.426
1747	Bishop, John	K	I.169/70
1745	Bishop, Nicholas	N	Misc.2.11
1790	Bishop, Risdon	K	N.12
1770	Bishop, Samuel	K	L.79
1694	Bishop, Sarah	K	A.7
1699	Bishop, Thomas	K	B.33
1783	Black, Ann	S	D.14/16
1724	Black, James	K	D.66
1775	Black, James	S	A.59-190
1794	Black, James	N	O.24
1795	Black, James	N	O.54
1720	Black, John	K	D.23
1784	Black, John	S	A.59-191
1789	Black, John	K	M.208
1789	Black, Mary	K	M.211
1782	Black, Mitchell	S	A.58-198
1775	Black, Sarah	S	B.536/7
1781	Black, Stephen	K	L.229
1782	Black, Stephen, Jr.	K	L.231
1783	Black, Stephen	K	L.231
1789	Black, Stephen	K	M.211
1762	Black, Thomas	K	K.289
1777	Black, Thomas	N	Misc.11.35
1786	Black, Thomas	K	M.104/5
1774	Black, William	N	K.183
1770	Blackburn, William	N	K.75
1785	Blackiston, Benjamin	K	M.59
1778	Blackiston, George	K	L.205/6
1789	Blackiston, John	K	M.208
1795	Blackiston, John	K	N.127
1758	Blackiston, William	K	K.180
1762	Blacks, Samuel	K	K.289
1764	Blacksare (Blacksheare), Ebenezer	K	K.339
1772	Blackshare, George	K	L.106
1772	Blackshare, Jane	K	L.109
1767	Blackshare, John	K	L.21
1790	Blackshare, Morgan	K	M.250
1791	Blackshare, Morgan	K	A.4-96

1798	Blackshare, Randal	K	N.220
1778	Blackshare, Robert	K	L.199
1793	Blackshare, Robert	K	N.37
1790	Blackshare, Sarah	K	M.246
1790	Blackshare, Thomas	K	M.234/6
1767	Blackshear, Eve	K	L.20
1757	Blackshear, Randel	K	K.159
1768	Blackshear, Thomas	K	L.41
1797	Blackstone, John	K	N.183
1695	Blake, Edward	N	B.42
1790	Blandon, George	K	M.234
1789	Blizzard, William, Sr.	S	D.238/9
1768	Bloom, Peter	K	L.46
1791	Bloxom, Elijah	S	A.59-225/6
1795	Bluxum (Bloxsom, Blocksom), Hannah	S	E.63/4
1793	Bloxom, Richard	S	A.59-238
1783	Bloxom (Bloxsom, Blocksom), William	S	D.21/2
1748	Bluett, Thomas	K	K.1
1775	Blundel, Susanna	K	L.161
1770	Blundell, James	K	L.73
1794	Blundell, Sarah	K	N.82
1758	Blunt, Levy	K	K.185
1727	Boak, Benjamin	K	F.33/4
1727	Boak, Joan	K	G.15
1784	Boddy, Benjamin	N	L.415
1765	Boggs, John	K	L.8
1785	Boggs, Joseph	K	M.82
1790	Boggs, Joseph	K	A.4-178
1798	Boggs, Joseph	K	A.4-179/80
1773	Boggs, Matthew	K	L.126/7
1774	Boggs, Matthew	K	L.149
1765	Bohannan, Robert	K	L.2
1767	Bohannen, Robert	K	L.31/2
1775	Bohannon (Buckhannon), Robert	K	L.160
1793	Boice, Alexander	K	A.4-191
1785	Bolden, Elizabeth	N	M.91
1796	Boldin, Bethiah	N	O.195
1714	Bolton, John	N	C.22
1741	Bonbonous, John	N	Misc.2.4
1794	Bond, John	N	N.447
1692	Bonde (Bowde, Barode), Isaac	S	AM2013-136

1778	Bonham, Hannah	N	L.93
1780	Bonine, Abel	K	L.217
1796	Bonsall, Vincent	N	O.136
1737	Boog, John	K	L.105
1771	Boogs, William	K	L.105
1795	Boon, Thomas	K	N.127
1682	Booth, Edward	S	A.1/2
1782	Booth, Isaac	K	L.230
1790	Booth, John	S	D.285/6
1751	Booth, John	K	K.34
1732	Booth, Joseph	K	H.109
1732	Booth, Joseph	K	H.65
1736	Booth, Joseph	K	H.119/20
1747	Booth, Joseph	K	I.176
1753	Booth, John, Sr.	K	K.83
1769	Booth, Peter	K	L.62/3
1756	Booth, Thomas	K	K.129/30
1774	Boram, Aaron	N	K.146
1768	Bostick, Abraham	K	L.46
1768	Bostick, James	K	L.31
1795	Bostick, James	K	N.97
1779	Bostick, John	K	L.70
1795	Bostick, Noah	K	N.128
1787	Bostick, Robert	K	M.133/4
1792	Bostick, Sarah	K	N.19
1768	Bostick, William	K	L.40
1747	Bostick, William	K	I.162
1784	Boulden, James, Sr.	N	M.7
1729	Boulton, John	N.	Misc.1.5
1781	Bound, Joseph	K	L.229
1787	Bounds, Jesse	S	A.60-31
1790	Bounds, Jesse	S	A.60-32/3
1698	Bourdet, Peter	K	B.32
1749	Bourgardin, John	N	Misc.1.17
1797	Boushelle, Sleighter	N	O.233
1685	Bowcomb, Peter	K	AM2013-53
1767	Bowden, Ezekiel	K	L.30
1722	Bowden, Ezekiel	K	D.60
1781	Bowen, Jesse	N	L.197
1790	Bowen, John	N	N.91

1791	Bowen, John	K	N.12/13
1798	Bowen, John	K	N.197
1784	Bowen, Nathan	K	M.23
1798	Bowen, Sarah	K	N.197
1747	Bowen, Solomon	K	I.167
1795	Bowen, William	K	N.135
1799	Bowing, William, Sr.	K	A.5-36
1762	Bowman, Henry	K	K.284
1755	Bowman, John	S	B.98/100
1773	Bowman, John	K	L.128
1795	Bowman, John	K	N.131
1766	Bowman, John	K	L.12/13
1718	Bowman, John	K	D.3
1760	Bowman, Miriam	K	K.235
1740	Bowman, Nathaniel	K	I.24
1796	Bowman, Nathaniel	K	N.137
1728	Bowman, Peter Peterson	K	G.17/18
1741	Bowman, Sarah	K	I.42
1771	Bowman, Thomas	K	L.90
1789	Bowman, Thomas, Sr.	K	M.187
1789	Boyce, Alexander	K	M.209
1774	Boyce, John	K	L.157
1778	Boyce, Joseph	S	C.188/91
1789	Boyce, Joseph, Sr.	S	D.238/9
1783	Boyce, Mary	N	L.316
1779	Boyce, Robert	N	L.138
1789	Boyce, Sarah	N	N.23
1768	Boyde, John	S	B.343/4
1741	Boyer, Daniel	K	I.36
1790	Boyer, James	K	M.234
1790	Boyer, Littleton	K	M.216
1786	Boyer, Richard	K	M.124
1798	Boyer, William	K	N.196
1755	Boyle, William	K	K.108/9
1749	Bracken, William	N	G.359
1779	Brackin, Henry, Sr.	N	L.156
1753	Bradey, Philip	K	K.64
1741	Bradey, Samuel	K	I.56
1789	Bradford, Catharine	N	N.232
1792	Bradford, Isaac	K	N.15
1791	Bradford, Nathaniel	S	A.60-127

1763	Bradford, Samuel	N	H&I.190
1774	Bradford, Samuel	N	K.166
1744	Bradley, Henry	K	I.843
1795	Bradley, Isaac	S	A.60-94
1799	Bradley, John	S	E.225/6
1742	Bradley, Josiah	K	I.72
1748	Bradley, Josiah	K	A.5-114
1767	Bradley, Josiah	K	L.35/6
1797	Bradley, Peggy	S	A.60-108
1787	Bradley, Thomas	S	A.60-110/2
1784	Bradley, William	S	D.66/7
1760	Bradley, William	K	K.221
1798	Bradley, William	K	N.220
1797	Bradly, Nathan	K	N.170
1745	Bradshaw, John	K	I.116
1697	Bradshaw, Thomas	K	A.19
175-	Brady, Absolom	K	K.44
1708	Brady, Benjamin	K	A.5-146/7
1790	Brandel, George	K	A.5-146/7
1786	Bratcher, Nathan	K	M.100
1793	Bratten, John	N	N.384
1780	Brattin, James	N	L.191
1792	Bratton, Joseph	S	A.60-133/4
1748	Bready, Solomon	K	I.239
1792	Bready, Solomon	S	A.60-135
1755	Brereton, Henry, Sr.	S	B.93/5
1786	Brereton, John	S	A.60-145
1715	Brewster, Job	N	C.30
1719	Brewster, John	N	C.158
1745	Briar, Alexander	K	I.110/11
1786	Brice, Benedict	K	M.115
1796	Brice, Benedict	K	N.148
1767	Brickle, Curtis	K	L.2
1796	Bright, Jonathan	K	N.138
1752	Brimberg, Christian	N	Misc.2.18
1754	Brinckle, Daniel	K	K.97
1771	Brinckle, Daniel	K	L.89
1733	Brinckle, Elizabeth	K	H.107/8
1754	Brinckle, Esther	K	K.136
1763	Brinckle, Esther	K	A.5-169

1740	Brinckle, Hester	K	I.19
1764	Brinckle, John	K	K.348/9
1764	Brinckle, John	K	K.1/2
1749	Brinckle, John, Sr.	K	I.263
1769	Brinckle, John	K	L.68
1782	Brinckle, John	K	L.230
1777	Brinckle, Joseph	K	L.192
1725	Brinckle, Margaret	K	F.8
1728	Brinckle, Pater	K	G.10
1765	Brinckle, Peter	K	L.4/5
1759	Brinckle, Richard	K	A.5-203
1766	Brinckle, Richard	K	A.5-204
1794	Brinckle, Richard	K	N.111
1741	Brinckle, Thoma	K	I.38
1722	Brinckle, William	K	D.52/4
1764	Brinckley, Benjamin	K	K.344/5
1778	Brinckley, Mary	K	L.200
1723	Brincklow, Elizabeth	K	D.62/3
1748	Brinkle, William	K	I.238/9
1742	Brinett, Paul	K	I.51
1751	Brion (Bryon), ohn	K	K.35
1779	Britahan, Ann	N	L.131
1798	Britt, Daniel	N	O.335
1757	Brittain, William	N	Misc.2.25
1789	Broadway, James	K	M.209
1789	Broadway, Ambrose	K	M.208
1787	Broadway, Ambrose	K	M.162
1776	Brobson, William	N	K.304
1733	Brock, Richard	K	H.103/4
1789	Brokfield, Urich	S	D.207/9
1792	Brookfield, Ann	S	A.60-153/4
1789	Brookfield, Azariah	S	A.60-155
1786	Brookfield, Eli	S	A.60-157
1770	Brooks, Arthur	K	L.83/4
1733	Brooks, Benjamin	K	H.75/6
1727	Brooks, James	K	F.29
1760	Brooks, John	K	K.228
1791	Brooks, John	K	M.277
1761	Brooks, Jonathan	K	K.268
1761	Brooks, Martha	K	K.268

1741	Brooks, Matthew	K	I.54
1791	Brooks, Nicholas	K	M.277
1785	Brooks, Sarah	N	M.130
1731	Brooks, Samuel	K	H.19
1791	Broom, James	N	O.14
1749	Broom, Thomas	N	G.352
1788	Brotherer, Joseph	S	D.200
1789	Brown, Aaron	K	M.184
1796	Brown, Abraham	N	O.172
1761	Brown, Ann	K	K.258
1769	Brown, Benjamin	K	L.69
1787	Brown, Benjamin	K	M.134
1778	Brown, Benjamin	K	L.206
1769	Brown, Benjamin, Sr.	K	L.50/1
1793	Brown, Charles, Sr.	S	A.60-170/1
1760	Brown, Christian	N	Misc.1.26
1773	Brown, Christian	K	L.128
1725	Brown, Daniel	K	F.3
1749	Brown, Daniel	K	I.266
1779	Brown, Edward	N	L.175
1773	Brown, Elizabeth	K	L.147
1791	Brown, Elizabeth	K	M.277
1797	Brown, Ezekiel	S	E.126/7
1771	Brown, George	K	L.104
1773	Brown, George	K	L.128
1796	Brown, Humphreys	S	A.60-190/3
1792	Brown, Israel	S	A.60-155
1704	Brown, James	S	A.46/7
1761	Brown, James	K	K.266
1798	Brown, James	S	A.60-201/2
1794	Brown, James, Sr.	S	E.12/3
1774	Brown, James	K	L.151
1755	Brown, James	K	K.102
1708	Brown, John	K	B.64
1733	Brown, John	K	H.68
1749	Brown, John	K	I.260
1758	Brown, John	K	A.6-51/2
1769	Brown, John	K	L.57
1774	Brown, John	K	L.155
1773	Brown, John	K	L.127
1781	Brown, John	K	L.225

1795 Brown, John K N.137
1789 Brown, John K M.186
1790 Brown, John K M.250
1794 Brown, John S E.6
1794 Brown, John N N.444
1774 Brown, Joseph K L.149
1762 Brown, Joshua K K.293
1766 Brown, Margaret K L.15
1777 Brown, Mary S C.209
1744 Brown, Pemberton K I.97
1759 Brown, philip K K.207
1788 Brown, Stephen K M.174
1799 Brown, Thomas K N.233
1798 Brown, Thomas S A.60-227
1782 Brown, Tilgham S A.60-228/9
1778 Brown, William K L.200
1791 Brown, William K M.261/2
1793 Broxon, John K N.38
1785 Bruce, Alexander S A.60-237
1791 Bruce, Esther S A.60-238
1784 Bruce, Magdaline S A.60-241
1786 Bryam, James K M.124
1760 Bryanm Alexander N Misc.1.28
1750 Bryan, Andrew N G.390
1777 Bryan, Andrew N L.5
1787 Bryan, Bennett S D.156/7
1794 Bryan, Betsy S A.60-247
1771 Bryan, John K L.89
1789 Bryan, Jonathan S A.60-249
1789 Bryan, Jonathan S D.231/2
1791 Bryan, Rachel S A.61-6
1764 Bryan, Robert N Misc.1.31
1786 Bryan, Robert N M.174
1775 Bryan, Thomas S A.61-10
1778 Bryan, Timothy L L.208
1749 Bryers, Alexander K A.46-113
1789 Buchanan, James S D.215/6
1796 Buck, James K N.158
1753 Buckanan, William N Misc.1.20
1799 Buckhanan (Buchanan), Betsy S E.238/40
1775 Buckingham, Howell K L.171

1787	Buckingham, Isaac	K	M.140/1
1774	Buckingham, Isaac	N	K.132
1793	Buckingham, James	N	N.323
1789	Buckingham, William	N	N.65
1760	Buckley, Adam	N	———
1784	Buckley, Adam	N	M.33
1791	Buckley, Arnold	K	M.275
1763	Buckley, James	K	L.45
1786	Buckmaster, Esther	K	M.97/8
1768	Buckmaster, William	K	L.4/5
1781	Bulger, Peter	K	L.230
1787	Bullen, John	K	M.166
1768	Bullet, Mary	K	———
1790	Bullock, Ezekiel	K	N.237
1777	Bullock, Richard	K	L.189
1748	Bullock, Thomas	N	G.90
1796	Bunker, Benjamin	N	O.142
1793	Burbage, Thomas	S	D.403/4
1761	Burch, George	N	Misc.1.29
1788	Burch, Rachel	K	M.168
1799	Burcher, William	S	A.61-26
1799	Burchinal, Jeremiah	K	N.227
1794	Burchinal, Joseph	K	A.6-195/8
1778	Burgess, Herbert	N	L.80
1788	Burgess, William	N	M.303
1794	Burgin, Benjamin	N	O.23
1775	Burgin, John	N	K.240
1748	Burklow, Harman	K	I.214/5
1747	Burnet, John	N	Misc.1.24
1748	Burns, Gilbert	K	I.226/7
1744	Burns, James	K	I.85
1797	Burns, William	K	N.166
1785	Burroughs, Charles	S	A.61-56
1785	Burroughs, Mary	S	A.61-57
1796	Burroughs, William	S	A.61-62/3
1788	Burrows, Ebenexer	K	.169
1709	Burrows, Edward	K	L.7-82
1785	Burrows, Elijah	K	M.50
1797	Burrows, Elizabeth	K	N.183
1782	Burrows, James	K	L.232
1795	Burrows, James	K	N.122

1785	Burrows, Jesse	K	M.44
1762	Burrows, John	K	K285
1789	Burrows, John	K	M.211
1790	Burrows, Nehemiah	K	M.245
1799	Burrows, Nehemiah	K	N.229
1788	Burrows, Sarah	K	M.177
1768	Burrows, Thomas	K	L.47/8
1782	Burrows, William	K	L.265
1785	Burrows, William	K	M.55
1798	Burrows, William	K	N.191/2
1788	Burt, Henry	K	M.183
1794	Burton, Ann Catherine	S	D.415
1790	Burton, Anne	S	A.61-73
1783	Burton, Benjamin	S	D.24/6
1798	Burton, Benjamin	S	E. 183/4
1798	Burton, Elizabeth	S	A.61-130
1750	Burton, John	S	A.428/30
1706	Burton, John	K	B.54
1708	Burton, John	K	B.73
1788	Burton, Joseph	S	A.124/6
1757	Burton, Joseph	S	B.131/3
1797	Burton, Joseph	S	A.61-204/5
1793	Burton, Mary	S	A.61-223
1753	Burton, Richard	S	B.48/9
1725	Burton, Robert	S	A.187/90
1724	Burton, Robert, Jr.	S	A.184/6
1788	Burton, Robert, Sr.	S	D.191/2
1796	Burton, Sarah	S	E.94/5
1798	Burton, Stratton	S	A.62-20/1
1790	Burton, William	S	D.294/5
1797	Burton, William	S	E.145/7
1795	Burton, William	S	E.39/40
1777	Burton, William	S	C.98/100
1730	Burton, Woolery	S	A.231/4
1730	Burton, Woolsey	S	B.1/4
1764	Busby (Bushban), James	K	K.348
1698	Busby, Richard	K	B.26
1781	Bush, Abraham	K	L.230
1793	Bush, David, Sr.	N	N.325
1790	Busse, Samuel	K	M.246
1796	Butcher, Frances	S	E.71/2

1796	Butcher, Frances	S	A.62-73
1774	Butcher, John	N	K.174
1760	Butcher, John	K	K.248
1772	Butcher, Magdelane	N	K.3
1750	Butcher, Michael	N	G.380
1749	Butcher, Moses	K	K.2/3
1731	Butcher, Robert	K	H.23/4
1733	Butcher, Robert	K	H.77
1763	Butcher, Robert	S	B.268/70
1785	Butcher, Robert	S	A.109-48
1782	Butcher, William	S	C.286/288
1785	Butcher, Wm.	S	A.109-48
1783	Butler, Andrew	K	L.271
1748	Butler, Edmond	K	I.228/9
1793	Butler, Elizabeth	K	N.54
1789	Butler, Esther	K	M.208
1799	Butler, Isaac	K	N.223
1789	Butler, James	K	M.185
1799	Butler, Jonathan	K	N.240
1749	Butler, Peter	K	K.36
1799	Byars, Samuel	N	O.484
1758	Bydndelin, John Rudolphus	K	K.188
1794	Byrnes, Caleb	N	N.398

- C -

1683	Cabley, John	K	AM2013/16
1797	Cacey, Elijah	K	N.169
1783	Cade, John	S	A.62-93
1778	Cade, Mary	S	A.62-99
1797	Cade, Thomas	S	E.127
1796	Cade, Richardson	S	E.75
1760	Caffee, William	K	K.218/9
1783	Caffey, Ezskiel	K	M.18
1786	Cahoon, Frances	S	D.121
1747	Cahoon, James	K	I.175
1797	Cahoon, James	K	N.176
1797	Cahoon, Lydia	K	N.186
1777	Cahoon, Mark	K	L.194

1744	Cahoon, Marmaduke	K	I.88
1783	Cahoon, Mary	K	M.48/49
1785	Cahoon, Sampson	S	A.62-110
1770	Cahoon, Thomas	K	L.72
1784	Cahoon, Thomas	K	M.21
1786	Cahoon, Thomas	K	M.112
1796	Cahoon, Thomas	K	N.147
1774	Cahoon, William	K	L.153
1768	Cahoon, William	K	L.40
1795	Cahoon, William	K	N.130
1748	Cain, Daniel	K	I.192
1784	Cain, Daniel	K	M.24
1764	Cain, Francis	K	K.340/1
1795	Cain, Francis	K	N.125/6
1797	Cain, Francis	K	N.168
1771	Cain, James	K	L.105
1794	Cain, John	K	N.88
1793	Cain, Othaniel	K	N.48
1741	Cain, Owen	K	I.126
1782	Cain, Owen	K	L.233
1760	Cain, Rachel	K	K.234
1760	Cain, Rachel	K	A.79
1788	Cain, Thomas	K	M.167
1799	Cain, Thomas	K	N.246/7
1751	Caldwell, Andrew	K	K.35
1775	Caldwell, Andrew	K	L.162/6
1790	Caldwell, Andrew	K	M.231
1790	Caldwell, Andrew	K	M.260
1791	Caldwell, Andrew	K	M.273
1792	Caldwell, David	N	N.262
1795	Caldwell, David	N	O.67
1782	Caldwell, Hannah	K	L.231
1783	Caldwell, James	K	M.18
1742	Caldwell, James	K	I.61&67
1782	Caldwell, James	K	L.234
1783	Caldwell, John	K	L.270
1790	Caldwell, John	K	M.249
1786	Caldwell, Jonathan	K	M.121
1781	Caldwell, Jonathan	K	L.237/8
1791	Caldwell, Jonathan	K	M.272
1786	Caldwell, Margaret	K	M.121

1786	Caldwell, Margaret	K	M.124
1791	Caldwell, Mary	K	M.273
1787	Caldwell, Mary	K	M.145/6
1791	Caldwell, Mary	K	M.277
1783	Caldwell, Neven	N	M.287
1790	Caldwell, Robert	K	M.222
1790	Caldwell, Robert	K	M.260
1791	Caldwell, Robert	K	M.272
1790	Caldwell, Sarah	K	M.212/3
1794	Caldwell, Sarah	K	N.68
1785	Caldwell, Timothy	K	M.83
1790	Caldwell, Timothy	K	M.217
1798	Caldwell, Timothy	K	N.220
1795	Caldwell, Train	K	N.122
1736	Caldwell, William	K	H.124
1728	Cale, John	K	G.10
1768	Callahan, Edward	K	L.46
1783	Callaway, Benjamin	S	D.30/1
1789	Callaway, Ebenezer	S	D.234/5
1796	Callaway, Ebenezer	S	E.71/2
1790	Callaway, Ebenezer	S	A.62-123
1791	Callaway, Ebenezer	S	D.223/4
1795	Callaway, Eli	S	A.62-138
1787	Callaway, Elizabeth	S	D.156
1793	Callaway, Elilsha	S	D.395/6
1783	Callaway, James	S	A.62-152/3
1782	Callaway, John, Sr.	S	C.297
1775	Callaway, Joshua	S	A.62-162
1784	Callaway, Levin	S	A62.166/7
1790	Callaway, Matthew	S	D.313
1790	Callaway, Peter	K	M.228
1788	Callaway, William	S	A.62-177
1793	Callaway, William	S	D.395/6
1769	Calloway, James	K	———
1769	Calloway, Peter	K	L.80/1
1795	Calloway, Sarah	K	N.117
1796	Calvert, Eleanor	N	O.210
1782	Cambel, Joseph	K	L.250/1
1782	Cambel, William	K	L.268
1778	Cameron, James	N	L.67
1766	Cammell (Campbell), James	K	L.15

1757	Campbell, George	S	B.156/8
1773	Campbell, John	S	C.31/2
1794	Campbell, John	S	A.62-198
1767	Campbell, John	N	H&I.204
1798	Campbell, Joseph	K	N.217
1773	Campbell, NathN	S	A.62-204
1797	Campbell, Nicholas	N	O.250
1774	Campbell, Samuel	S	A.62-212
1749	Campion, James	N	G.314
1732	Campling, Edward	K	H.105
1791	Canby, Benjamin	N	N.185
1747	Candey, Robert	K	I.162/3
1772	Candy, Cashenna	K	L.121
1798	Cannady, Nathaniel	N	O.307
1792	Cannon, Absulom	S	D.373/4
1796	Cannon, Absolom	S	A.62-217
1694	Cannon, Ann	K	A.2
1775	Cannon, Charles	N	K.263
1777	Cannon, Constantine	S	A.62-243/4
1781	Cannon, Eleanor	N	L.248
1783	Cannon, Henry	S	C.307
1780	Cannon, Jacob	S	C.246/8
1790	Cannon, James	S	A.63-63
1789	Cannon, James, Sr.	S	D.214/5
1790	Cannon, Jeremiah	S	A.63-64
1790	Cannon, Jesse	S	D.316/7
1788	Cannon, John	S	A.63
1799	Cannon, Joseph, Sr.	S	F.446/8
1793	Cannon, Joseph	N	N.343
1786	Cannon, Levin	S	A.63-101/2
1798	Cannon, Levin	S	A.63-103
1784	Cannon, Newton	S	A.63-118/9
1739	Cannon, Patrick	N	Misc.1.41
1785	Cannon, Sarah	S	D.70/1
1793	Cannon, Stephen, Sr.	S	D.406
1791	Cannon, Thomas	S	A.63-139/40
1783	Cannon, William	S	D.18/9
1795	Cannon, Willia, Sr.	S	E.35/6
1793	Cannon, Wingate	S	A.63-52
1685	Cantwell, Edmund	N	A.78
1716	Cantwell, Richard	N	C.77

1741	Cope, Joseph	K	I.34
1796	Capelle, Joseph	N	O.199
1778	Capron, Jarrad	K	L.198
1760	Carbin, James	K	K.235
1795	Cardeen, Daniel	K	N.140
1778	Cardeen, William	K	L.212
1787	Cardiff, Christopher	S	D.154
1799	Carey, Elizabeth	S	E.214/5
1774	Carey, John	S	A.64-52
1756	Carey, Samuel	S	B.128/31
1756	Carey, Thomas	S	B.119/31
1790	Carey, Thomas	S	D.300/1
1744	Carey, William	S	A.369/70
1796	Carey, William	K	N.151
1762	Carl, Thomas	K	A.7-216
1722	Carleton, Edward	K	D.55
1794	Carlisle, John	S	A.63-162/3
1788	Carlisle, William	S	D.183/5
1797	Carlton, Richard	K	N.179
1794	Carman, James	K	N.121
1763	Carman, Joseph	K	K.311
1796	Carman, Joseph	K	A.7-225
1773	Carmon, Rachel	K	L.147
1740	Carpenter, Affiance	S	A.320/1
1783	Carpenter, Benjamin	S	A.63-220
1786	Carpenter, George	S	A.63-223
1738	Carpenter, James	S	A.302/4
1777	Carpenter, James	S	A.63-230
1790	Carpenter, James Cannon	S	D.312
1752	Carpenter, John	K	K.63
1770	Carpenter, John	K	L.70
1782	Carpenter, John	K	L.230
1777	Carpenter, Loben (Laban)	S	C.64/5
1776	Carpenter, Luke	S	C.52/3
1754	Carpenter, Mary	K	K.93/4
1799	Carpenter, Nephtali	S	A.60-250/1
1778	Carpenter, Samuel	N	L.55
1784	Carpenter, Sarah	S	A.64-9
1798	Carpenter, William	N	O.347
1770	Carpenter, William	S	B.366/7
1786	Carpenter, William, Sr.	K	M.92/4

1774	Carr, Arthur	N	K.152
1776	Carr, John	K	L.177
1724	Carr, Robert	K	D.68
1782	Carson, Richard	N	L.298
1763	Carson, William	N	Misc.1.60
1794	Carter, Daniel	K	N.84
1740	Carter, Robert	K	I.74
1796	Carter, Samuel	K	L.177
1799	Carter, Susannah	K	N.248
1796	Carter, Thomas	N	O.198
1748	Carter, William	K	I.241
1764	Carter, William	K	L.7/8
1760	Carter, William	K	K.229/30
1760	Carter, William	K	A.8-44
1759	Cartmill, Thomas	N	Misc.1.51
1713	Cartwright, Abraham	N	C.10
1789	Cartwright, Isaac	N	N.52
1789	Cartwrite, Jacob	N	N.82
1790	Carty, Isaac	K	M.240/1
1762	Carty, Sarah	K	K.281/2
1791	Carvil, Isaac	K	N.4
1792	Cary, Amos	S	A.64-20/3
1761	Cary, Ann	S	A.64-24
1767	Cary (Cairy), Bowin	K	L.28/9
1758	Cary, Ester	S	B.166/9
1795	Cary, John	K	N.126
1723	Cary, John	S	A.169/70
1796	Cary, Nelly	S	A.64-83
1797	Cary, Samuel	S	A.64-94/5
1767	Cary, Thomas, Sr.	S	B.326/9
1795	Cary, Thomas, Jr.	S	E.50/1
1795	Cary, Thomas, Sr.	S	E.56/8
1782	Casson, John	K	L.253/4
1787	Casson, John	K	A.7-246
1791	Catlin, Joseph	K	N.4
1793	Catlin, Joseph	K	N.50
1798	Catlin, Polly (Mary)	K	N.292
1773	Catlin (Cattlin), Robert	K	L.132
1744	Caton, John, Sr.	K	I.80/1
1769	Caton, John	K	L.63/4
1772	Cattlin, Robert	K	1.110

1772	Catts, James	K	L.110
1774	Catts, John	K	L.151
1748	Catts, Stephen	K	I.233/4
1799	Catts, Thomas	K	N.226
1774	Catts, Vincent	K	L.151
1769	Catts, William	K	L.53
1774	Catts, William	K	L.151
1785	Caulk, Benjamin	N	M.168
1785	Caulk, Jacob	N	M.88
1785	Caulk, Lambeth	S	A.64-116
1778	Caulk, Richard	N	L.22
1788	Causey, Priscilla	K	M.173
1788	Cavender, Arthur	S	D.193
1792	Cavender, James, Sr.	S	D.376/7
1761	Cavender, Jane	K	K.262
1788	Cavender, William	K	M.168
1790	Cayton, Mary	K	M.217
1778	Cazier, John	N	L.104
1779	Cazier, Rachel	N	L.146
1795	Cazier, Sarah	N	O.72
1768	Chadwick, James	K	L.41/2
1768	Chadwick, Thomas	K	L.39
1785	Chambers, Elizabeth	N	L.339
1799	Chambers, Frank	K	N.229
1789	Chambers, Harry	K	K.105
1793	Chambers, James	S	A.64-122
1792	Chambers, John	S	A.64-123
1789	Chambers, Joseph	K	M.212
1774	Chambers, Robert	N	K.189
1772	Chambers, William	K	L.113
1769	Chamis, John	K	L.53
1774	Champbell (Campbell), Sarah	K	L.158
1773	Chance, Alexander	N	K.57
1774	Chance, Alexander	K	I.86
1775	Chance, Elijah	K	L.173
1783	Chance, Elijah	K	L.269
1785	Chance, Elijah	K	L.269
1785	Chance, Elijah	K	M.55
1697	Chance, Elizabeth	K	A.23
1760	Chance, John	K	K.232
1729	Chance, John	K	G.27

1786	Chance, John	S	A.64-124/5
1782	Chance, Mary	S	A.64-126
1772	Chance, Spencer	S	A.64-128
1769	Chandler, Ann	N	H&I.280
1799	Chandler, Ann	N	O.470
1775	Chandler, Caleb	N	K.270
1798	Chandler, Elizabeth	N	O.333
1781	Chandler, Isaac	N	L.254
1779	Chandler, Isaac, Jr.	N	L.166
1782	Chandler, Thomas	N	L.286
1697	Chant, John	K	A.21/22
1698	Chant, John	K	——
1780	Chase, Isaac	S	A.64-130
1790	Chase, William	S	D.305
1790	Chase, William	S	A.65-2
1790	Cheffins, James	K	M.234
1733	Cherry, John	K	H.50/1
1747	Chew, Mary	K	I.137
1744	Chew, Samuel	K	I.86
1747	Chew, Samuel	K	I.136/7
1734	Chhant, William	S	A.275/7
1741	Chicken, John	K	I.35
1793	Chicken, John	K	N.49
1796	Chicken, John	K	N.157
1772	Chicken, Martha	K	L.107
1798	Chicken, Rachel	K	N.244
1696	Child, Thomas	N	B.61
1793	Chipley, James	K	N.39
1772	Chipman, Benjamin	K	L.114
1779	Chipman, Benjamin	K	L.209
1757	Chipman, James	S	B.143/5
——	Chipman, Mary	K	L.181
1781	Chipman, Paris	S	C.269/70
1772	Chipman, Stephen	K	L.114
1793	Chipman, Stephen	K	N.37
1789	Chipman, Thomas	K	M.201/2
1789	Chittington, James	K	M.212
1764	Chrispin, Sylas	K	K.341
177-	Chrispen, Tabitha	K	L.186
1788	Christopher, Benjamin	S	A.64-154
1773	Christopher, Thomas	K	A.8-197

1777	Cirwithan, John	S	C.96/8
1750	Cirwithian, Caleb	S	A.421/3
1791	Cirwithian, Caleb	S	D.327/8
1794	Cirwithian, Isaac	S	A.64-160/7
1794	Cirwithian, John	S	A.64-171
1798	Cirwithian, John	S	A.64-172
1744	Claghorn, Shusan	N	G.137
1763	Clampett, John, Jr.	K	K.309
1756	Clampit, Ezekiel	K	K.153
1789	Clampit, Jonathan	K	M.207
1763	Clampitt, John	K	K.317
1785	Clark, Ann	N	M.121
1796	Clark, Benjamin	K	N.145
1732	Clark, Catheren	K	H.39
1785	Clark, Charles	K	M.68
1766	Clark, David	N	Misc.1.62
1792	Clark, David	N	N.306
1769	Clark, Francis	N	M.213
1792	Clark, Gideon	K	N.164
1797	Clark, Henry	K	N.168
1755	Clark, Hugh	N	Misc.1.49
1787	Clark, James, Jr.	K	M.149
1789	Clark, James	K	M.188
1789	Clark, James	K	M.206
1796	Clark, Jane	K	N.148
1729	Clark, John	K	H.74/5
1765	Clark, John	S	A.64-184
1789	Clark, John	K	M.186
1754	Clark, John	N	Misc.1.50
1782	Clark, John	K	L.255/6
1791	Clark, John	N	N.197
1798	Clark, John	K	N.193
1795	Clark, John Arthur	N	O.100
1799	Clark, John	S	A.64-185/6
1733	Clark, Jonathan	K	H.71
1783	Clark, Jonathan	K	M.16/17
1796	Clark, Joshua	K	N.139/40
1799	Clark, Mary	K	N.234
1781	Clark, Nehimiah	K	L.222
1789	Clark, Rachel	K	M.201
1702	Clark, Richard	N	C.34

1778	Clark, Richard	N	L.73
1796	Clark, Robert	K	N.149/50
1772	Clark, Sarah	K	L.108
1743	Clark, Thomas	K	I.73
1763	Clark, Thomas	K	K.326/7
1748	Clark, Wenlock	K	I.209
1776	Clark, William	N	K.298
1783	Clark, William	N	L.311
1785	Clark, William	S	A.64-199/200
1785	Clark, William	N	M.99
1786	Clark, William	N	M.223
1789	Clark, William	K	M.209
1786	Clark, William	N	M.207
1705	Clarke, William	S	A.2/3
1779	Clarkson, Abraham	S	D.3/4
1788	Clarkson, Benniah	S	D.176/7
1796	Clarkson, Joseph	S	A.64-211
1796	Clarkson, Margaret	S	E.112
1786	Clarkson, Mary	S	A.64-213
1775	Clarkson, Richard	S	C.16/18
1780	Clarkson, Richard	S	A.64-215/7
1782	Clarkson, Richard	S	A.64-216
1796	Clarkson, Robert	S	E.112/3
1798	Clarkson, Thomas	S	E.161/2
1789	Clarkson, William	S	D.160/1
1753	Clary, John	K	K.84
1774	Clatkson, William	S	A.64-222
1789	Clay, Ann	N	N.42
1738	Clay, John	K	H.153
1763	Claypoole, George	S	A.64-226
1798	Claypoole, George	S	E.193
1745	Claypoole, Jeremiah	S	A.374/5
1777	Claypoole, John	S	C.120/2
1688	Claypoole, Norton	S	———
1783	Clayton, Elizabeth	S	D.19/20
1697	Clayton, James	K	A.19
1761	Clayton, James	K	K.262
1718	Clayton, John	K	D.5
1720	Clayton, John	K	D.18
1759	Clayton, John, Sr.	K	K.203
1724	Clayton, John	K	D.69

1789	Clayton, John	K	M.195
1748	Clayton, Jonathan	K	I.234
1796	Clayton, Joseph	N	O.135
1798	Clayton, Joshua	N	O.374
1760	Clayton, Joshua	K	K.326/7
1766	Clayton, Sarah	K	L.18
1785	Clayton, Thomas	K	M.61
1767	Cleane, Joseph	K	L.38
1795	Clemens, Edward	K	N.122
1698	Clemenson, Jacob	N	B.74
1760	Clement, Jane	N	Misc.1.59
1783	Clements, Samuel	N	L.381
1710	Clementson, Clement	N	B.203
1767	Clemmons, Thomas	K	L.22
1751	Clendan(i)el, John	S	A.419/217
1790	Clendaniel, William	S	A.65-2
1788	Clendaniel, Luke	S	D.166/8
1745	Clendaniel, William	S	A.356/7
1792	Clifford, Daniel	K	N.19
1698	Clifford, Thomas	K	A.25
1703	Clifford, Thomas	K	B.49
1747	Clifford, Thomas	K	I.149/50
1791	Clift, Joseph	K	N.1
1740	Clifton, Absolom	K	I.17
1787	Clifton, Benjamin	S	D.134/5
1786	Clifton, Daniel	S	D.107/8
1789	Clifton, Jonathan	S	D.256
1792	Clifton, Jonathan	S	A.65-18
1789	Clifton, Levin	S	D.256
1798	Clifton, Major	S	A.65-24/7
1797	Clifton, Matthew	S	A.64-133
1720	Clifton, Robert	S	A.136/8
1725	Clifton, Robert	S	A.190/2
1785	Clifton, Thomas	K	M.69/71
1796	Clifton, Thomas	K	N.144
1796	Clifton, Tabitha	S	D.173/4
1708	Clifton, Thomas	S	A.64/5
1734	Clinton, Christopher	K	H.88
1792	Cloak (Cloke), Ebenezer	K	N.20
1791	Clothier, John	K	M.267
1717	Cloud, Eliz.	N	G.375

1717	Cloud, Jeremiah	N	C.118
1790	Cloud, john	N	N.122
1793	Cloud, John, Sr.	K	N.63
1745	Cloud, Joseph	N	Misc.1.44
1748	Cloud, William	N	G.150
1788	Clow, China, Jr.	K	M.166
1770	Clowes, David	S	B.389/91
1790	Clowes, John	S	D.288/9
1738	Clubb, Richard	K	H.152
1777	Cobb, Hannah	N	K.354
1782	Cochran, James	N	L.302
1795	Cochran, Thomas	N	O.74
1785	Cockerel, John	K	M.89
1767	Cockran, Agnes	K	L.24
1744	Cockran, Christopher	K	I.85
1748	Cockran, Christopher	K	I.240
1767	Cockran, Mary	K	L.67
1729	Cockrell, Elizabeth	K	G.25
1724	Codd, Berkeley	S	A.167/9
1717	Coe, John	K	K.189
1741	Coe, Mary	K	I.55
1721	Coe, Timothy	S	A.139/40
1720	Coe, William	K	D.24/5
1728	Coe, William	K	G.18/19
1776	Coffan, John	S	C.57
1757	Coffey, Hugh	K	A.9-185
1776	Coffin, John, Jr.	S	A.65-82
1794	Coffin, William	S	A.65-90/2
1755	Coffy, Hugh	K	K.109
1710	Coggeshall, Isaac	S	A.58/9
1787	Cole, Cuthbert	K	N.184
1719	Cole, Edward	N	C.176
1797	Cole, Edward	K	N.184
1782	Cole, John	N	Misc.66
1784	Cole, Matthias	S	A.65-116
1792	Cole (Coole), Rebecca	K	N.19
1792	Cole, Rebecca	K	N.27
1794	Cole, Rebecca	K	N.76
1758	Cole, Sarah	K	K.187
1772	Cole, Spencer	K	L.120
1725	Cole, Thomas	S	A.195/7

1747	Cole, William	K	I.162
1788	Coleburn, Priscilla	S	A.65-105
1784	Coleburn, William	S	A.65-114
1778	Colegate, Bridget	N	L.29
1738	Colehale, William	K	H.150
1791	Coleman, James	K	N.10/11
1796	Coleman, Sarah	K	N.157
1797	Colesberry, Jacob	N	O.272
1783	Colesbury, William	N	L.397
1793	Coley, Daniel	K	N.50
1790	Colgan, James	K	M.217
1777	Colgan, John	K	L.189
1749	Collee, John (Caller, John Lewes)	K	I.255
1799	Colier, Thomas	K	N.234
1742	Collet, James	S	A.330/1
1789	Collier, Henry	K	M.209
1797	Collier, James	S	E.153/4
1773	Collings, Andrew	S	D.125
1772	Collings, Ezekiel	S	A.65-161
1776	Collings, George	S	A.65-161
1776	Collings, Jonathan	K	L.176/7
1788	Collings, Thomas	S	A.66-30/1
1774	Collings, William	S	B.530/32
1775	Collings, William	S	B.553/6
1784	Collins, Andrew	S	A.65-129
1785	Collins, Andrew	S	A.65-131/3
1783	Collins, Catherine	N	L.389
1783	Collins, George	S	D.14
1789	Collins, George	K	M.195
1782	Collins, Hancock	S	A.65-160/7
1782	Collins, Isaac	S	C.298/9
1772	Collins, James	K	L.118
1776	Collins, John	S	C.60/2
1782	Collins, John	S	A.65-184
1787	Collins, John	S	D.145/7
1787	Collins, John	S	D.149
1790	Collins, John	S	D.268/9
1793	Collins, John	S	A.65-188/9
1795	Collins, Joseph	S	A.65-217
1793	Collins, Levi	S	A.65-221
1785	Collins, Mary	S	D.86/7

1791	Collins, Mathias	S	A.66-1/2
1791	Collins, Tabitha	S	A.66-24
1782	Collins, Thomas	N	L.262
1789	Collins, Thomas	k	M.215
1741	Collins, William	K	I.55
1746	Collins, William	K	I.135
1770	Collins, William	K	L.79
1773	Collins, William	S	A.63-44
1786	Collison, George	S	A.66-47
1731	Colter, James	K	N.10
1714	Colvert, Rachel	N	C.20
1791	Comerford, Peter	K	N.10
1768	Commings (Cuming), Delectum	K	L.43
1777	Conaway, James	N	K.364
1796	Conaway, John	S	E.101
1797	Conaway, John	S	E.118/9
1792	Conaway (Conway), Philip	S	D.378/80
1780	Concelio, William	K	L.216
1794	Connarroe, Thomas	N	N.392
1785	Connaway, Hannah	S	A.66-55
1779	Connaway, William	S	A.66-76
1735	Connell, William	K	H.88
1772	Connelly, Patrick	N	K.26
1793	Conner, Abraham	K	N.38
1790	Conner, Dennis	K	M.240
1788	Conner, John	K	M.173
1777	Conner, Patrick	N	K.379
1746	Conner, Samuel	K	I.132/3
1796	Conner, Thomas	N	O.156
1763	Connolly, William	K	K.316
1790	Connor (Conwell), Benedict	S	A.66-88/90
1796	Connor, Daniel	S	A.66-93/4
1777	Connor (Conar), Peter	N	K.402
1789	Connor, Ratliff	S	A.66-92
1758	Conolly, Thomas	K	K.193/4
1726	Consela, Thomas	K	F.14
1739	Conselach, Thomas	K	I.11
1767	Consiglio, Jean	K	L.42/3
1748	Constantine, Augustine	N	G.189
1797	Conwell, Abraham	S	A.66-93/4
1794	Conwell, Charles	S	A.66-95

1778	Conwell, David	S	A.66-96
1782	Conwell, Elias	S	C.308/10
1796	Conwell, Elias	S	E.70/1
1780	Conwell, Elizabeth	S	C.220/1
1773	Conwell, George	S	A.66-108
1773	Conwell, Jeremiah	S	A.66-114/5
1782	Conwell, John	S	C.304/6
1781	Conwell, Samuel	S	A108.192
1782	Conwell, William	S	C.295/7
1787	Cooch, Thomas	N	M.353
1786	Cooch, Thomas	N	M.78
1732	Cook, Andrew	K	A10-105
1720	Cook, Arthur	K	K.24/5
1720	Cook, Arthur	K	G.16
1719	Cook, John	K	D.14
1790	Cook, John	K	M.215
1740	Cook, John	K	I.32/3
1794	Cook, Mark	S	A.66-157
1726	Cook, Mary	K	F.16
1748	Cook, Mickale	K	I.217
1712	Cook, Margaret	K	----
1788	Cook, Michael	K	M.168
1793	Cook, Michael	K	N.59/60
1795	Cook, Michael	K	M.135
1730	Cook, Robert	K	H.107
1734	Cook, Thomas	K	H.81
1733	Cook, William	K	H.108
1783	Cooley, Daniel	K	H.108
1799	Coombc, Benjamin	K	N.247
1742	Coombs, James	K	I.61/2
1799	Cooper, Elizabeth	K	N.246
1787	Cooper, George, Sr.	K	N.106/7
1799	Cooper, John	K	N.247
1784	Copes, Robert	K	M.23
1791	Coppage, John	K	M.263
1798	Coppage, Peter	K	N.220
1763	Copper, Cornelius	K	K.306/7
1764	Copper, Cornelius	K	K.352
1719	Corbet, Mathew	N	C.180
1794	Corbin, Stephen	S	D.417
1789	Corbit, Ann	N	N.27

1755	Corbit, Daniel	N	O.563
1774	Corbit, Daniel, Sr.	N	K.128
1789	Corbit, Israel	N	N.31
1767	Cord, Hezekiah	S	B.321/3
1751	Cord, John	S	A.66-183
1774	Cord, John	S	A.64-52
1738	Cord, Joseph	S	A.298/301
1785	Cord, Rhoda	S	D.78/9
1687	Corderus, Hans	N	A.81
1782	Cordery, Noble	K	L.268
1787	Cordrey, Jacob	S	A.66-202
1783	Cordry, John	S	D.9
1758	Corker, Dennis	K	K.175
1798	Corker, John, Jr.	K	N.203
1789	Cornelius, George	K	M.212
1684	Cornelius, Harmon	S	A2013-04
1770	Cornish, Dyia	S	B.408/9
1796	Cornwall, John, Jr.	S	A.66-229
1728	Cornwallice, William	S	A.225/7
1747	Cornwallis, Rebekah	S	A.386/7
1691	Cornwell, Francis	S	A2013-135
1798	Cornwell (Conwell), Francis	S	E.188/9
1775	Corrans, John	N	K.257
1744	Correy, John	K	I.90
1767	Corry (Corney), John	N	Misc.1.164
1786	Corse, George	K	M.92
1782	Corse, James	K	L.232
1790	Corse, James	K	M.224
1784	Corse, Susannah	K	M.27
1785	Corse, William	K	M.79/82
1788	Corse, William	K	M.179
1777	Costen, Benton	S	C.105/8
1784	Coston, Director	S	D.55
----	Coston, Nathias	S	A.67-13
1792	Coston, Somerset	S	A.67-14/7
1798	Cottingham, Charles	S	E.153/4
1769	Cottingham, Thomas	K	L.63
1799	Couch, James	K	N.246
1784	Couch, Joseph	S	A.67-32/3
1747	Coudrat, Daniel	k	I.185
1747	Coudrat, Peter	K	I.189

1694	Coudrey (Cowthry), William	S	AM2013.1 & 157
1787	Coulbourn, Stephen	S	D.136/7
1755	Coulter, Charles	S	B.91/3
1785	Coulter, Esther	S	A.67-40
1785	Coulter, James	S	A.67-43
1754	Coulter, John	S	B.150/3
1761	Coulter, John	S	B.166/9
1786	Coulter, John	S	D.257/8
1791	Coulter, Joseph	S	A.98-103
1789	Coulter, Margaret	S	D.251/2
1795	Coulter, Robert	S	A.67-65
1768	Coulter, Samuel	S	B.328/9
1793	Counsil, John	N	N.345
1695	Courtney, Peter	K	I.189
1735	Courtney, Thomas	K	H.141/2
1795	Coverdale, Israel	S	E.15/6
1764	Coverdale, John, Sr.	S	B.276/8
1787	Coverdale, John	S	D.158/9
1772	Coverdale, Susannah	S	A.67-103
1796	Coverdill, Richard	S	E.101
1737	Covington, Samuel	K	A.11-67
1772	Cowdratt, John	K	L.116
1772	Cowdratt, Peter	K	L.117
1764	Cowgill, Clayton	K	K.253
1764	Cowgill, Clayton	K	K.346
1792	Cowgill, Ezekiel	K	N.33
1731	Cowgill, John	K	H.20
1752	Cowgill (Cowgle), John	K	K.60/1
1781	Cowgill, John, Jr.	K	L.230
1790	Cowgill, John	K	M.256
1764	Cowgill, Martha	K	K.352
1750	Cowgill, Sarah	K	K.22
1743	Cowgle, Ebenezer	K	I.45
1749	Cowgle, Thomas	K	K.4
1778	Cowing, Elizabeth	S	C.157/9
1756	Cowle, Spencer	K	K.127/8
1750	Cox, Catharine	N	G.407
1799	Cox, Edward	K	N.234
1797	Cox, Gone	K	N.177
1774	Cox, Isaac	K	L.149

1714	Cox, John	N	Misc.1.38
1782	Cox, Powell	K	M.4
1772	Cox, Thomas	K	L.112
1796	Cox, William	K	N.156
1793	Coxe, John, Jr.	K	N.59/60
1754	Crafford, James	N	Misc.1.47
1717	Craig, Edward	S	A.120/1
1787	Craig(e), Esther	S	D.133/4
----	Craig, Harmon	S	A.67-147/8
1791	Craig, Isabella	K	M.263
1770	Craig, James, Sr.	N	Misc.1.65
1735	Craig, James	K	H.87
1738	Craig, John	K	H.153
1795	Craig, John	K	N.133
1775	Craig, Robert	S	A.67-156
1788	Craig, Robert	S	A.67-157
1763	Craig, Robert	S	B.263/7
1789	Craig, Samuel	K	M.210
1739	Craig, Sarah	K	A.11-193
1789	Craig(e), Sarah	S	D.217
1790	Craig, Sophia	K	M.239
1755	Craig, William	S	B.110/1
1772	Craige, Agnes	K	A.11-146
1777	Craige, Alexander	K	L.196
1775	Craige, Analena	K	L.168
1751	Craige, Andrew	K	K.36
1741	Craige, George	K	I.58/9
1763	Craige, Hugh	K	K.322
1789	Craige, Isbel	K	M.203/4
1754	Craige, Isabella	K	K.91
1777	Craige, James	K	L.189
1771	Craige, James	K	L.94/5
1784	Craige, James	K	L.271
1787	Craige, James	K	M.130
1796	Craige, Jame	K	A.11-164
1766	Craige, John	K	L.18
1769	Criage, John	K	L.65
1774	Craige, John	S	A.67-150
1739	Craige, Moses	K	I.27
1768	Craige, Moses	K	L.43/4
1739	Craige, Sarah	K	I.64

1768	Craige, Thomas	K	L.39
1726	Cramer, William	K	F.19/20
1787	Crammer, Thomas	K	M.143/4
1783	Craner, Charles, Sr.	K	M.6
1796	Crankfield, Nancy	K	N.141
1752	Crapper (Croopoer), John	S	B.37
178	Crapper, John, Sr.	S	D.105
1794	Crapper, Joihn, Jr.	S	A.67-167/8
1775	Crapper, Levin	S	C.80/3
1777	Crapper, Moulton	S	C.114/5
1797	Crapper, Susannah	S	A.67-180/1
1775	Crapper, Zadoc	K	L.162
1799	Crapper, Zadoc	K	N.248
1797	Crathers, William	K	N.170
1769	Crawford, David	K	L.67
1766	Crawford, David	K	L.16
1748	Crawford, James	N	G.202
1790	Crawford, John	N	N.98
1747	Crawford, Margaret	N	G.103
1752	Crawford (Crafort), Mary	N	Misc.1.45
1785	Crawford, Oliver	K	M.73
1732	Crawford, Thomas	K	H.34
1757	Crawford, William	N	Misc.1.54
1739	Creagan, Hugh	N	Misc.143
1789	Credy, Martin	N	N.62
1784	Creighton, John	K	M.21
1748	Creighton, Robert	N	G.208
1795	Creighton, Robert	N	O.107
1764	Creighton, Thomas	K	K.343
1771	Creightin, William	K	L.99
1713	Crew, John	S	A.118/9
1721	Crippen, John	K	D.42/3
1791	Crippen, John	K	M.268/9
1761	Crippen, William, Sr.	K	K.256
1799	Crippin, James	K	N.230
1740	Crispin, Joseph	K	I.16/17
1786	Crocket, Margaret	K	M.95
1796	Crockett, Elizabeth	S	D.417/8
1778	Crockett, Jesse	K	L.200
1770	Crockett, John	K	L.79
1781	Crockett, John	S	C.249/50

1789 Crockett, John K A11.245/7
1795 Crockett, Jonathan K N.121
1787 Cro(c)kt(t), Richard S D.126/7
1782 Croney, John S C.307/8
1718 Crosley (Crosly), Richard K D.39
1772 Cross, William K L.110
1788 Crossan, Jean N M.345
1698 Crosse, William N B.70
1796 Crouch, John S A67.202
1797 Crouding, George N O.225
1698 Croutch, John S ——
1789 Crow, George N N.68
1796 Crow, George Wood N O.145
1773 Crozier, Matthew K L.141
1760 Crumeen, Thomas K K.245
1773 Crumey, Elizabeth N K.61
1763 Crumpton, John K K.319
1764 Crumpton, John K K.332/3
1775 Crumpton, John K L.171
1798 Crumpton, John K N.215
1786 Crumpton, Mary K M.98
1784 Cubbage, Thomas K M.18
1786 Culbertson, William N M.219
1790 Culbreath, John K M.248
1721 Cuff, Absolom K D.47
1695 Cullen, Cornelius K A.10
1787 Cullen, George S D.131
1797 Cullen, Hezekiah K N.180
1775 Cullen, John K L.161
1784 Cullen, John K M.26
1784 Cullen, John K M.30
1775 Cullen, Jonathan K L.170
1778 Cullen, William K L.208
1789 Cullipher, Benjamin K M.188
1780 Cully, Arthur K L.221
1782 Culver, George S C.319/21
1797 Culver, James S A67.219
1757 Cuming (alias Newman), Lumino K K.164/5
1746 Cuming, Robert K A12.136
1735 Cumming, Robert K H.92
1749 Cumming, Robert K I.259

1788	Cummings, Daniel	K	M.167
1775	Cummings, William	N	K.268
1794	Cummins, Alexander	N	N.400
1797	Cummins, Daniel	K	N.178
1790	Cummins, James	K	M.257
1711	Cummins, George	N	G.153
1748	Cummins, George	N	K.138
1766	Cummins, Robert	K	A12.134/5
1778	Cummins, Robert	K	L.201
1790	Cummins, Sarah	K	M.251
1746	Cummins, Timothy	K	I.122&139
1747	Cunningham, Andrew	K	I.191
1748	Cunningham, John	K	I.205
1748	Currey (Corey), John	K	I.265
1774	Curry, Abigail	N	K.138
1789	Curry, Henry	N	N.36
1764	Curry, James	K	K.349
1777	Curry, William	K	L.186
1790	Curtis, Comfort	K	M.217
1698	Curtis, John	K	B.26&32
1733	Curtis, John	N	——
1740	Curtis, John	K	I.32
1787	Curtis, John	K	M.137
1795	Curtis, John	K	N.110
1733	Curtis, Joshua	N	K.77
1695	Curtis, Richard	K	A.17
1748	Curtis, William	K	I.207
1753	Curtis, Zehu	N	Misc.1.46
1793	Curwell, Clayton	K	N.49
1788	Cutler, Thomas	K	M.173

– D –

1782	Dagworthy, John	S	D.52/4
1774	Darby, Elizabeth	S	A68.16
1762	Darby, Ephraim	S	B.245/7
——	Darbym Ephraim	S	A68.19
1788	Darby, John	S	A71.235/6
1779	Darby, Samuel	S	D.4/5

1692	DaRingh, ----	N	Misc.2.30
1769	Darling, James	K	L.51
1796	Darling, James	K	N.148
1789	Darling, Robert	K	M.194
1759	Darling, William	K	K.198
1775	Darling, William	K	L.162
1790	Darnall, William	K	M.239
1733	Darson (Dorson), Richard	K	H.86/87
1790	Darter, Thomas	S	D.273/4
1750	David, Benjamin	K	A12.209
1791	David, Daniel, Sr.	K	N.6
1798	David, Daniel	K	N.198
1748	David, Evan	K	I.252
1748	David, Evan, Sr.	N	G.207
1748	David, James	K	I.253
1773	David, James	K	L.140
1774	Davis, Jane	N	K.168
1736	David, John	K	H.134
----	David, John	K	A12.222/3 & 230
1772	David, John, Sr.	N	K.26
1783	David, John	K	L.275/6
1786	David, John	K	M.122
1791	David, Joseph, Sr.	K	M.275
1767	David, Joshua	K	L.21
1761	David, Lewis	K	A7.234/5
1776	David, Lewis	K	L.179
1768	David, Owen	K	L.43
1749	David, Sarah	K	I.268
1793	David, Thomas, Sr.	N	N.390
1761	David, William	N	H&I.545
1789	Davidge, Rachel	N	N.48
1690	Davids, George	S	AM2013.127
1775	Davidson, James	S	A.359/61
1790	Davis, Abel	N	N.122
1793	Davis, Edward	N	N339
1781	Davis, Elizabeth	K	----
1770	Davis, Jane	K	L.8
1790	Davis, John	K	M.243
1747	Davis, John	K	I.180
1722	Davis, John	S	A.158

1722	Davis, John	N	C.331
1773	Davis, John	N	K.69
1799	Davis, Mark	S	E.231/4
1788	Davis, Mary	S	D.203
1791	Davis, Mary Tilney	S	——
1792	Davis, Mary	S	D.376
1785	Davis, Matthias	K	M.119
1772	Davis, Moses	K	L.115
1787	Davis, Nehemiah	S	D.133
1788	Davis, Nehemiah, Sr.	S	D.203
1798	Davis, Nehemiah	S	E.193/4
1794	Davis, Robert	K	N.83/4
1776	Davis, Samuel	S	A.68-128
1796	Davis, Sarah	N	O.133
1795	Davis, Susannah	K	N.122
1755	Davis, Thomas	S	B.76/9
1763	Davis, Thomas	K	K.314
1698	Davis (Davies), Thomas, Sr.	S	A.26/7
1779	Davis, Thomas	K	L.213
1758	Davis, Thomas	K	K.179
1792	Davis, Thomas	K	N.14
1793	Davis, Zerobabel	S	A.68-142
1774	Dawes, Edward	N	K.142
1750	Daws, Sarah	N	G.417
1748	Daws, William	K	I.209
1768	Daws, Wiliam	K	L.418
1797	Dawson, Edward	S	A.68-143/4
1763	Dawson, Isaac	K	K.318
1777	Dawson, Isaac	K	L.188
1777	Dawson, Isaac	K	L.173
1680	Dawson, John	K	A.1
1748	Dawson, John	K	I.206/7
1771	Dawson, Joshua	K	L.98
1772	Dawson, Joshua	L	L.172
1709	Dawson, Richard	K	B.77
1759	Dawson, Richard	K	K.196
1754	Dawson, Thomas	K	K.87/8
1744	Day, George	S	A.361
1796	Day, John	K	N.212/4
1741	Day, Wiliam	S	A.326/7

1774	Day, William	S	A.68-187/9
1796	Dazey, Moses, Sr.	S	E.78/9
1777	Dazey, Thomas, Sr.	S	C.129/32
1789	Deakyne, John	N	N.81
1792	Deakyne, John	N	N.301
1798	Deal (Dale), Elias	K	N.221
1787	Dean, Charles	S	A.68-21
1720	Dean, James	K	D.301
1793	Dean, John	S	A.68-217
1721	Dean, Mary	K	D.40
1766	Dean, Thomas	K	L.17
1736	Deart, William	K	H.129
1782	Debety (Deputy), Solomon	S	A.68-214
1687	Decon, Isack	N	A.89
1708	Deffoss, Hance	N	B.145
1708	Defoss, Mathias	N	B.142
1710	Defraux (Dutrux), Jacob	N	B.209
1750	DeGon, Nases	N	G.542
1695	deHaes, Johannes	N	B.14
1716	Dehaes, Roeloff	N	C.74
1794	Dehorty, John	K	N.78
1753	Delap, Allen	K	K.89/90
1742	Delap, Robert	K	I.62/3
1753	Delap, Sarah	K	K.90
1789	Delop, Catherine	K	M.185
1799	Deloplain, Samuel	N	O.486
1720	Deming (Dunnen), James	N	C.252
1728	Denis, Frederick	K	G.20
1744	Denney, Philip	K	I.86/7
1779	Dennum (Denman), Frederick	K	L.210/11
1783	Denny, Christopher, Sr.	K	M.7
1788	Denny, Joseph	K	M.181
1757	Denny, Philip	K	K.161
1773	Denny, Philip	K	L.143
1684	Deprae, John	S	AM2013-27/8
1690	Depray, Andrew	S	A.12/3
1706	Depray, John	S	B.293/5
1790	Deputy, Joshua	S	A.68-237
1766	Derham, John, Jr.	K	L.180
1795	Derham, Thomas	K	N.126
1785	Derochbrune, Joseph	K	M.48

1787	Derrickson, Benjamin	S	A.69-23
1787	Derrickson, Cornelius	N	M.259
1791	Derrickson, John	S	A.69-29
1779	Derrickson, Mary	N	L.178
1781	Derrickson, Peter	S	A.69-69
1798	Derrickson, Peter	N	O.390
1798	Derrickson, William	N	O.368
1748	Derrickson, Zachariah	N	G.277
1776	Derrickson, Zacharias	N	K.289
1772	deVou, Benjamin	N	K.9
1796	Devou, David	N	O.153
1791	Deweese, Cornelius	K	M.266/7
1787	Deweese, Daniel	K	M.133
1799	Deweese, David	K	N.243/4
1743	Deweese, Lewis	K	I.65
1792	Deweese, Rachel	K	N.13
1754	Deweese, Samuel	K	A.14-51
1753	Deweese, Samuel	K	K.65/6
1761	Deweese, William	K	K.257
1684	DeWitt, Peter Themis	N	A.63
1795	Dickerson, Edmond	S	E.20/1
1796	Dickerson, Elisha	S	———
1787	Dickerson, Somerset	S	D.144/5
1772	Dickey, John	N	K.38
1792	Dickinson, Joseph	N	N.296
1795	Dickinson, John	K	N.134
1760	Dickinson, Samuel	K	K.230/1
1720	Dickinson, Walter	K	D.30
1768	Dickson, Richard	K	L.46
1708	Dickson, William	N	B.164
1773	Dicus, John	K	L.133/4
1796	Dicus, William	K	N.144
1793	Dier, John	S	D.398
1734	Dighton (Dithan), Richard	K	H.80
1773	Dill, Edward	K	L.142
1771	Dill, George	K	L.99
1790	Dill, James	K	M.234
1793	Dill, John	K	N.45
1792	Dill, John	K	N.13
1799	Dill, Mary	K	N.266
1799	Dill, Solomon	K	N.226

1783	Dill, William	K	M.15
1799	Dillon, John	K	N.233/4
1744	Dillon, Richard	K	I.86/7
1786	Dingee, Daniel	S	D.99
1778	Dingle, Richard	S	C.161
1683	Direckson, Gysbert	N	A.64
1795	Dirickson, Andries	S	A.69.21
1798	Dirickson, George	S	E.154/5
1791	Dirickson, Joseph	S	D.352
1746	Dishane, Charles	K	I.133
1702	Ditton, John	K	B.44
1798	Dixon, Charles	K	N.220
1775	Dixon, Sarah	K	L.161
1736	Dixon, Thomas	K	H.124/5
1776	Dixon, William	K	L.180
1777	Dixson, Hannah	N	K.340
1790	Doaney, Charles	K	M.217
1791	Doaney, Charles	K	A14-173
----	Doany (Doney), James	K	M.203
1798	Dobson, Edward	K	N.220
1752	Dobson, Eleanor	S	B.34
1791	Dodd, Hepburn	S	A69-100
1779	Dodd, Moses	S	C.334/6
1793	Dodd, William	S	D.403
1781	Dodds, John	N	L.247
1773	Doherty, Morgan	K	L.139
1784	Dolbee, Jonathan	S	D.41/3
1784	Dolbee, Peter	S	D.6/7
1793	Dolbee, Upshed	S	A61.184
1738	Donaldson, Alexander	K	I.12/13
1724	Donaldson, Charles	K	D.65
1702	Donaldson, John	N	G.416
1775	Donally, William	N	----
1724	Donavan (Dunnavan), Randall	K	D.66
1753	Doney, John	K	K.83/4
1756	Doney, Pater	K	K.146
1719	Donn, Thomas	K	D.11
1796	Donnald, John	N	O.180
1772	Donnocho, Nicklos	N	K.12
1784	Donoho, Joshua	N	M.43
1776	Donoho, Thomas	S	A69.134

1737	Donovan, Daniel	K	H.114
1793	Donovan (Dunavan), Foster	S	D.382/3
1794	Donovan, John	S	A69.150
1797	Donovan, Naomi	S	A69.150
1777	Dorman, Charles	S	C.100/2
1777	Dorman, Major	S	C.73/4
1781	Dorrell, James	K	L.229
1792	Douce (Dous), Elizabeth	S	D.376
1790	Douce, Levin, Sr.	S	D.304
1797	Dougherty, Hugh	N	O.262
1780	Dougherty, James	N	L.214
1778	Dougherty, John	N	L.103
1783	Dougherty, Neill	N	L.368
1796	Doughurty, Daniel	K	N.153
1775	Douglass, Adam	K	L.176
1727	Douglass, Archibald	K	G.7/8
1748	Dowding, Joseph	K	I.207/8
1748	Dowell, Philip	K	I.262
1744	Dowling, John	K	I.99
1771	Downey, Martha	S	B.433/5
1739	Downham, John	K	I.27
1794	Downham, Isaac	K	N.112
1797	Downham, James	K	N.169
1797	Downham, Mary	K	N.173
1773	Downham, Richard	K	L.137/8
1719	Downham, Thomas	K	D.2
1759	Downham, Thomas	K	K.199/200
1791	Downing, Ann	K	A14.238
1796	Downing, Benjamin	K	A14.239/40
1782	Downing, Joseph	K	L.231
1780	Downing, William	K	L.219
1782	Downom (Downham), John	S	A69.173
1790	Downs, Henry	S	D.283
1795	Downs, James	K	N.138
1790	Downs, William	K	M.254
1743	Draper, Alexander	K	I.70
1785	Draper, Avery	K	M.52
1737	Draper, Henry	S	A.281/2
1784	Draper, Henry	S	A69.191
1751	Draper, Isaac	S	B.18
1758	Draper, Isaac	S	A69.193

1784	Draper, James	S	A69.196
1787	Draper, John	S	A69.197/8
1790	Draper, John	S	A69.28
1752	Draper, Lawrence	K	K.51
1794	Draper, Lemuel	K	N.95
1767	Draper, Nehemiah	S	B.317/9
1784	Draper, Nehemiah	S	A69.215
1743	Draper, samuel	S	A.352/3
1785	Draper, Samuel	S	A69.219
1788	Draper, Samuel	S	A69.220/1
1743	Draper, Sarah	S	A.348/50
1785	Draper, Sarah	S	A69.224/6
1774	Draper, Sarh	K	L.154
179-	Draper, Whittington	K	N.138
1761	Draper, William	S	B.237/9
1792	Draper, William	K	N.15
1785	Draughton (Drayton), John	K	M.85
1788	Drayton, William	K	A15-83
1761	Drew, William	K	K.265
1788	Driggass, Drake	S	A69.232
1797	Driskill, Capt. Joseph	K	N.184
1754	Driskle, Dennis	K	K.99
1695	Druett, Morgan	N	B.46
1782	Drugan, Thomas	N	L.333
1743	Drummond, James	K	I.78
1785	Duhadaway, Daniel	K	M.42
1798	Duhadway, Catharine	K	N.212/14
1791	Dukes, isaac	S	D.357/8
1700	Dun, John	K	B.37
1701	Dun, John	K	B.42
1748	Dunanen, Randal	S	A.391/2
1789	Dunbar, Samuel	K	M.184
1775	Duncan, John	K	L.173
1781	Duncan, John	K	L.244
1780	Dunkin (Duncan), Elizabeth	K	L.217
1796	Dunlap, James	N	O.197
1758	Dunlap, John	K	K.184
1755	Dunn, Joseph	K	K.125
1700	Dunn, Margaret	K	B.39
1774	Dunning, Lydia	N	K.147
1773	Dunning, Martha	K	L.131

1760 Dunning, Samuel K K.240
1769 Dunning, Samuel k L.96
1786 Dunning, William K M.102
1783 Dunwiddie, Samuel K M.3
1798 Durborough, David K N.201
1797 Durborough, Hugh K N.171
1795 Durborough, Rebecca K N.97
1782 Durborow, Daniel K L.263/4
1782 Durborow, David K L.231
1762 Durborow, Elizabeth K K.274
1755 Durborow, Hugh K K.108
1752 Durborow, John K K.57
1786 Durham, Daniel K M.118
1793 Durham, George S A70.8
1788 Durham, John K M.170/1
1748 Dushane, Ann N Misc.1.71
1759 Dushane, Anthony N Misc.1.71
1792 Dushane, Elizabeth N N.234
1790 Dushane, Isaac N N.105
1775 Dushane, Jerome N K.219
1775 Dushane, John N K.213
1779 Dushane, Valentine N L.147
1785 Dushane, Valentine N M.80
1789 Duyer, Joseph K M.183
1744 Dwoolf, Edward K I.108/9
1798 Dyer, Dennish K B.66
—— Dyer, Edward K L.224
1749 Dyer, Henry N G.430
1749 Dyer, John K I.256
1790 Dyer, John K M.256
1728 Dyer, William K G.16/7

- E -

1796 Eagle, Thomas K N.148
1783 Eakin, Alexander N L.334
1796 Eakin, Robert N O.166
1783 Eakin, Samuel N L.366
1771 Ebtharp, Elizabeth K L.91/2

1796	Eckles, Ann	K	N.146
1796	Eckles, John	K	N.146
1796	Eckles, Richard	K	N.146
1783	Eckles, Richard	K	M.12/13
1799	Edenfield, Samuel	K	N.249
1791	Edenfield, William	S	D.352/3
1791	Edgen, Benjamin	S	A70.33
1791	Edger, Henry	S	A70.37
1788	Edger, James	S	A70.38
1720	Edinfield, John	K	D.32
1747	Edingfield, James	K	I.171
1759	Edingfield, John	K	K.206
1771	Edingfield, John	K	L.103
1772	Edingfield, Pearsis (Persis)	K	L.111
1756	Edingfield, William	K	K.128/9
1781	Edmonds, Alice	K	L.229
1709	Edmonds, John	K	B.75
1783	Edmondson, Francis	K	M.11/12
1781	Edmondson, John	K	M.134/5
1787	Edmondson, John	K	M.135
1796	Edmondson, John	K	N.153
1799	Edmondson, Peter	K	N.255
1796	Edmondson, Thomas	K	N.153
1770	Edmunds, James	K	L.74
1774	Edwards, James	K	L.156
1775	Edwards, John	K	L.170
1780	Edwards, John	N	L.194
1785	Edwards, John	K	M.90
1795	Edwards, Morgan	N	O.57
1780	Edwards, William	K	L.223
1749	Eghmont (Egmount, Edgmant), Cornelius	K	K.13/14
1771	Egland, John	K	L.96
1749	Elder, Benjamin	N	G.311
1762	Eldridge, Joseph	S	B.257/60
1766	Eldridge, Mary	S	B.306/8
1780	Eliason, Cornelius	N	L.210
1785	Ellars, Carty	K	M.38
1777	Ellegood, John	S	C.122/4
1773	Ellet, Thomas	K	L.144/5
1783	Elliot, Alexander	N	L.385
1784	Elliot, Isaac	K	M.27

1779	Elliot, John	N	L.154
1685	Elliott, Christopher	N	A.67
1782	Elliott, Isaac	K	L.232
1799	Elliott, Jane	N	O.453
1775	Elliott, John	N	K.237
1797	Elliott, John	S	E.129/30
1784	Elliott, Margaret	S	D.65
1788	Elliott, Mark, Jr.	N	M.343
1786	Elliott, Ruth	K	A16.100/1
1783	Elliott, William	N	L.376
1797	Elliott, William, Jr.	N	O.242
1799	Elliott, William, Jr.	N	O.467
1722	Ellis, Benjamin	K	D.58
1722	Ellis, Benjamin	K	D.54/5
1788	Ellis, Eleanor	K	M.8182
1719	Ellis, Thomas	K	D.15
1709	Ellit, Susanna	K	C.80
1720	Ellitt, John	K	D.28/9
1719	Elson, Richard	N	C.173
1747	Emerson, Emanuel	K	A11.122
1794	Emerson, George	K	N.82
1706	Emerson, Jacob	K	B.57
1784	Emerson, Jonathan	K	M.24/5
1776	Emerson, Michael	K	L.182
1787	Emerson, Michael	K	M.163
1772	Emerson, Unity	K	L.119
1721	Emerson, Vincent	K	D.43
1746	Emmett, John	K	A16.177
1789	Emory, Thomas, Sr.	K	M.200/1
1791	Emory, Thomas	K	M.274/5
1710	Empson, Cornelius	N	B.224
1734	Empson, Cornelius	K	H.89
1795	Empson, Hannah	K	N.128
1782	England, David	K	L.261
1756	England, Isaac	K	K.143&151
1791	England, Joseph, Sr.	N	N.192
1748	England, Joseph	N	G.281
1708	England, Philip	N	B.174
1774	English, David	N	K.139
1797	English, Jannat	N	O.223
1741	Enis, Jesse	S	A70.139

1782	Enloe, Rigbal	K	L.233
1758	Enloe, Thomas	K	K.178/9
1790	Ennis, William Brittingham	S	D.25
1794	Ennos, Francis	N	O.32
1782	Enos, Joseph	N	L.259
1748	Enos, Richard	N	G.183
1773	Enos, Samuel	N	K.78
1784	Entwesle, Edmund	K	M.30
1792	Entwezle, Mary	K	N.28/9
1782	Erb, Jacob	K	L.260/1
1774	Ernester, Simon	N	K.169
1787	Errickson, Mathew	K	M.163
1780	Ervy, William	K	L.216
1797	Erwin, John	N	O.245
1795	Estell, William	K	N.123
1695	Eustason, Lawrence	N	B.11
1778	Eustice, Charles	K	L.199
1775	Evan, David	K	A16.220
1741	Evan, Gwenllian	K	I.40/1
1739	Evan, Joshua	K	I.15
1786	Evans, Benjamin	N	——
1797	Evans, Catharine	S	E.135
1799	Evans, Charles	N	O.474
1748	Evans (Evens), Curtis	K	I.243/4
1736	Evans, David	K	H.136
——	Evans, David	K	K.26
1777	Evans, David	K	L.187
1797	Evans, Elisha	S	E.135/6
1799	Evans, Hannah	S	E.246/8
1797	Evans, Isaac	S	E.144/5
1717	Evans, John	N	C.100
1788	Evans, John	S	D.195/6
1794	Evans, John	S	D.419
1795	Evans, John	S	E.48/9
1797	Evans, John	N	O.251
1785	Evans, Joshua	S	D.82/5
1750	Evans, Margaret	K	K.29
1785	Evans, Mary	N	M.156
1795	Evans, Samuel	S	A71.10/12
1799	Evans, Sophia	S	E.239/40
1799	Evans, Stephen	S	E.207/8

1750	Evans, Thomas	K	A16.229
1748	Evans, Thomas	N	G.111
1777	Evans, Thomas	S	D.56/7
1796	Evans, Thomas	N	0.191
1789	Evans, Thomas	K	——
1796	Evans, Walter	S	E.74/5
1751	Evens, Edmond	K	K.31/2
1695	Everett, Mark	K	A.16
1791	Evertson, Evart	N	N.229
1783	Eves, James	N	L.343
1748	Eves, Samuel	N	G.193
1780	Ewbank, Benjamin	K	L.221/2
1748	Ewin (Ewing), James	K	I.243
1755	Ewing, James	K	K.198/9
1722	Ewins, Abraham	K	D.57
1753	Exall (Excell), Samuel	K	K.64
1793	Eymon, Stephen	K	N.60
1720	Eyre, Daniel	S	A.138/9
1721	Eyre, Elizabeth	S	A.142/3

- F -

1749	Falconer, John	K	K.3
1786	Falconer, William	K	M.110
——	Falkner, Joshua	S	A71.56
1767	Falkner, John	K	L.20
1768	Falkner, Samuel	K	A17.93
1785	Faries, Alexander	N	M.145
1792	Faries, Jona William	N	N.246
1777	Faries, Samuel	N	K.356
1787	Faries, William	N	M.228
1783	Faris, Matthew	K	L.273
1781	Farmer, John	K	M.101
1749	Farres, Robert	N	G.333
1797	Farrow, Ebenezer	K	N.169
1782	Farson, Henry	K	M.95/6
1786	Farson, William	K	M.111
1798	Farsons, Henry	K	N.199
1793	Farsons, Jane	N	N.321

1799	Farstt, Smith	K	N.230
1745	Fasset, William	S	A.370/2
1787	Fauss, Nicholas	N	M.247
1783	Feares, Mary	N	L.393
1793	Fentham, William	S	A71.58
1789	Fenwick, William	S	——
1798	Fergus, James	S	E.161/2
1754	Ferguson, Dugood	S	A.67/8
1796	Ferguson, John	K	N.152
1784	Ferris, David	N	L.424
1751	Ferris, John	N	G.493
1773	Ferriss, Deborah	N	K.64
1795	Ferriss, Mary	N	0.112
1794	Ferriss, Ziba	N	N.424
1786	Few, Abraham	N	M.218
1761	Few, Daniel	K	K.253
——	Fforat, Elizabeth	N	B.57
1729	Fields, Abraham	K	D.24
1797	Fields, Abraham, Sr.	N	0.231
1797	Fields, Allen	N	0.230
1797	Fields, Marian	K	N.161
1783	Fields, William	N	L.321
1790	Filpot, Bridget	N	N.152
1777	Finel, Onery	N	K.366
1747	Finlay, Joseph	K	I.183
1737	Finley, Nehemiah	K	H.145
1774	Finney, John	N	K.129
1794	Finney, John French	N	N.416
1766	Finney, Samuel Latham	S	B.341/2
1740	Finney, William	K	I.21
1733	Finwick, James	S	A.262/3
1766	Finwick, Sidney	S	B.304/5
1732	Finwick, Thomas	S	A.262/3
1725	Fisher, Adam	K	F.3
1791	Fisher, Edward	K	M.278/9
1777	Fisher, George Hardy	S	E.212/4
1766	Fisher, Hannah	K	L.16
1746	Fisher, Henry	S	A.380/1
1746	Fisher, Isaac	K	I.121/2
1742	Fisher, Jabez Maud	S	A.336/8
1787	Fisher, Jabez	S	D.102/3

1747	Fisher, James	S	A.384/5
1790	Fisher, James	S	A71.128
1793	Fisher, James	S	A71.129/30
1794	Fisher, John	S	E.14
1768	Fisher, John	K	L.45
1763	Fisher, John	K	K.304/5
1770	Fisher, John	S	B.279/81
1785	Fisher, Jonathan	S	A71.141/2
1729	Fisher, Joseph	K	G.13
1796	Fisher, Mary	S	A71.149
1795	Fisher, Sarah	K	M.129
1713	Fisher, Thomas	S	A.81/3
1788	Fisher, William	S	A71.160/2
1725	Fisher, William	S	A.197/9
1789	Fitz, Jarold	K	M.212
1701	Fitz, Jarrell	K	B.43
1727	FitzGarreld, James	K	G.2/3
1714	Fitzgerald, Patrick	N	C.111
1762	Fitzgerald, Robert	K	K.281
1786	Fitzgerald, Thomas	N	M.193
1786	FitzJarrell, Eleazar	K	M.111
1755	Fitzsimons, Thomas	K	K.110
1708	Flaherty, Katharine	N	———
1794	Fleetwood, John	S	D.420/1
1767	Fleming, Alexander	K	A17.166
1770	Fleming, Alexander	K	L.86
1751	Fleming, Archibald	K	K.44/5
1789	Fleming, Elizabeth	K	M.192
1759	Fleming, George (Cooper)	K	K.205
1737	Fleming, Isabella	K	H.135
1789	Fleming, John	S	D.239/40
1773	Fleming, Joseph	K	L.131
1754	Fleming, Robert	K	K.94
1795	Fleming, Robert	K	N.113/4
1748	Fleming, Samuel	K	I.210
1766	Fleming, William, Sr.	K	L.13
1784	Fleming, William	K	A17.205&208
1799	Flharty, Rachel	N	0.512
1722	Fling, Daniel	S	A.163/5
1733	Flood, William	K	H.112

1784	Flower, John	S	D.27/8
1789	Flower, Thomas	S	D.213/4
1787	Flowers, Charles McKeil	S	D.129
1704	Flowers, John	K	B.50/1
1698	Flowers, Thomas	K	B.26
1733	Flood, William	K	H.112
1777	Floyd, James, Jr.	N	K.376
1767	Floyd, Thomas	K	K.309/10
1790	Flynn, John	K	M.217
1689	Footcher, William	S	AM2013.111
1798	Footl, William	N	O.344
1696	Forat, John	N	B.55
1793	Forbes, Richard	K	A17.219
1690	Forby, James	K	AM2013.114
1791	Forcum, John	K	N.6
1793	Forcum, John	K	A17.220
1792	Forcum, Joshua	K	N.27
1774	Ford, Benjamin	N	K.107
1717	Ford, Charles	N	C.72
1742	Ford, David	K	I.105
1773	Ford, John	K	L.124/5
1794	Ford, John (Alias Benson)	N	N.414
1774	Ford, Joseph	N	K.153
1781	Ford, Mary	K	L.229
1781	Ford, Mary	K	L.235
1799	Ford, Mary	K	N.225
1785	Ford, Thomas	K	M.90
1795	Ford, Thomas	N	O.71
1769	Ford, William	N	Misc.1.71
1772	Ford, William	K	L.106/7
1790	Foreacre, Isaac	K	M.239
1791	Foreacre, Joseph	K	M.276
1799	Foreacre, Sarah	K	N.223
1784	Foreman, Henry	K	M.20
1790	Foreman, Robert	K	M.227
1773	Forkum, Renatus	K	L.136
1778	Fortner, James	K	L.203
1767	Fortner, Samuel	K	L.20
1777	Forwood, William	N	K.342
1785	Fossitt, Thomas	N	M.180
1799	Foster, Alexander	N	O.494

1742	Foster, James	K	I.71/2
1722	Foster, John	K	D.60
1689	Foster, Richard	K	AM2013.105/6
1783	Fountain, Samuel	S	A71.235/6
1788	Fountain, William	S	A71.239
1719	Fowke, Ellinor	N	C.188
1773	Fowler, Ari (Arthur), Sr.	S	A.494/5
1782	Fowler, Benjamin	K	L.232
1782	Fowler, Benjamin	K	L.266
1785	Fowler, George	K	M.85
1779	Fowler, John, Sr.	S	C.201/3
1759	Fowler, John	S	A72.160
1787	Fowler, Jonathan	S	S.233/4
1781	Fowler, William	K	L.225
1789	Fowler, William	K	M.203
1792	Fowler, William	S	A72.29
1791	Frame, Dagwood	S	A72.30
1772	Frame, Nathan	S	B.405
1765	Frame, Robert	S	A72.46/7
1786	Frame, Smith	S	D.96/7
1770	Francis, Ellis	K	L.84
1798	Fransisco, Charles	K	N.195/6
1798	Fransisco, John	K	N.221
1798	Fransisco, Lidia	K	N.221/2
1750	Fransisco, Thomas	K	A18.89
1752	Fraser, William	K	K.61
1762	Frazer, Alexander	K	K.287
1733	Frazer, James	K	H.104
1744	Frazer, Joseph	K	I.99
1762	Frazer, William	K	K.289
1782	Frazer, William	K	L.232
1767	Frazier, Elizabeth	K	L.29
1782	Frazier, John	K	L.256/7
1796	Frazier, William	K	N.151
1797	Frazor, William	K	N.182
1728	Freeland, James	K	G.13
1768	Freeman, Charles	K	L.39
1767	Freeman, Joseph	K	A18.125
1755	Freeman, Joseph	K	K.105
1771	Freeman, Joseph	K	L.91
1783	Freeman, Miriam	K	M.13

1720	Freeman, Samuel	K.	D.31
1706	Freeman, William	K	——
1703	Freeman, William	K	B.50
1773	Freeman, William	K	L.129
1775	Freeman, William	K	L.175
1796	Freeny, John	S	E.106/8
1752	French, Charles	K	K.62
1728	French, John Col.	N	Misc.1.72
1712	French, Robert	N	C.1
1726	French, Thomas	K	F.23
1694	Fretwell, Roger	S	AM2013.163/4
1716	Frogg, John	N	C.69
1748	Fullerton, Ann	K	I.242/3
1746	Fullerton, John	K	I.134
1748	Fullerton, John	K	I.242
1764	Fullerton, John	K	K.328
1765	Fullerton, William	K	L.8
1796	Fullman, Walter	N	O.140
1781	Fulton, Barbara	N	L.245
1780	Fulton, John	N	L.193
1785	Furbee, Ann	K	M.85/6
——	Furbee, Benjamin	K	L.161
1783	Furbee, Benjamin	k	A18.150
1781	Furbee, Bowers	K	L.223/4
1796	Furbee, Caleb	K	N.148
1790	Furbee, Joseph	K	M.251
1765	Furbee, Michael	K	L.6
1733	Furby, Benjamin	K	H.105/6
1783	Furchas, John	K	M.10
1784	Furniss, Robert	K	M.36
1781	Fury, Peter	K	M.107
1721	Futcher, John	S	A.141/2
1795	Futcher, John, Sr.	S	E.60/1
1754	Futcher, William	S	B.74/5

- G -

1788	Gallaher, William	N	M.317
1752	Gallaway, Peter	K	K.66

1734	Gallaway, Richard	K	H.83
1762	Galloway, Daniel	K	K.294
1775	Galloway, Joseph	K	L.174
1752	Galloway, Peter	K	K.56
1748	Galloway, Richard	K	I.264
1761	Galloway, Richard	K	K.263
1788	Galt, Thomas	K	M.171
1788	Gamble, James	N	M.323
1782	Game, Robert	K	L.267/8
1757	Gano, James	N	Misc.1.134
1790	Gano, John	K	M.231
1760	Gance, Lewis	K	K.223
1773	Gardner, James	K	L.140/1
1785	Gardner, James	K	M.39/42
1785	Gareson, Margaret	N	M.144
1793	Garland, Abraham	K	M.49
1714	Garland, John	N	C.26
1785	Garland, John	K	A18.217/8
1793	Garland, John	K	N.41
1794	Garland, John Chevins	K	N.75
1785	Garland, Rose	K	M.39
1719	Garland, Silvester	N	C.232
1723	Garne, Owen	K	D.65
1730	Garne, Owen	K	H.1/2
1792	Garnett, Elizabeth	K	N.27
1770	Garreson, John	N	Misc.1.171
1721	Garreson, Henry	N	C.315
1765	Garretson, Cornelius	N	Misc.1.155
1761	Garretson, Eliakim	N	Misc.1.151
1742	Garretson, Elizabeth	N	Misc.1.107
1755	Garretson, Garret	N	Misc.1.130
1758	Garretson, Garret	N	Misc.1.139
1734	Garretson, George	N	Misc.1.98
1722	Garretson, Henry	N	Misc.1.86
1799	Garretson, Henry	N	O.440
1694	Garretson, John	N	B.13
1748	Garretson, John	N	G.231
1766	Garretson, Judiah	N	Misc.1.162
1786	Garretson, Mary	N	M.217
1793	Garretson, Sarah	N	N.368
1757	Garrett, John	N	.2657

1788	Garrison, James	N	M.307
1726	Garritson, Casparus	N	Misc.1.90
1748	Garitson, Edmond	N	G.225
1762	Garvey, John	K	K.194
1762	Garvey, Owen	K	K.279
1720	Gascoin, John	K	D.17/8
1762	Gascoingne, Mary	K	K.290
1791	Gaskins, William	K	N.7
1794	Gaskins, William	K	N.86
1692	Gasper, Thomas	N	Misc.1.76
1758	Gathony, Peter	N	Misc.1.136
1687	Gatto, Henry	S	AM2013.78/80
1789	George, John	K	M.195
1794	George, Joseph	K	N.86
1752	Gerritson, Eliz	N	Misc.1.122
1739	Gerritson, Holliwell	N	Misc.1.102
1783	Gest, Ruth	N	L.363
1716	Gibb, Anne	S	A.91/2
1791	Gibb, Isobella	S	A72.105
1783	Gibbins, George	S	A72.114
1787	Gibbins, John	S	D.128
1686	Gibbon, Edmond	K	AM2013.70/2
1798	Gibbons, Joshua	S	E.172
1786	Gibbons, Samuel	N	M.206
1775	Gibbs, Edward	K	L.175
1784	Gibbs, Isaac	N	M.14
1783	Gibson, Robert	S	A72.136
1770	Giffen, David	K	L.76
----	Giffen, Jonathan	K	I.79
1761	Gilder, Ann	N	Misc.1.149
1789	Gilder, Henry	K	M.195
1799	Gilder, John	K	N.232
1775	Gilder, Reubin	K	L.148/9
1777	Gildersleeve, Elizabeth	K	L.191
1763	Gildersleeve, Noah	K	K.313
1756	Giles, James	K	K.150/1
1695	Gill, Benjamin	N	Misc.1.178
1792	Gill, Margaret	S	D.361/2
1786	Gill, William	S	D.104/5
1772	Gillespie, Elizabeth	N	K.14
1760	Gillespie, George	N	Misc.1.142

1758	Gillespie, James	K	K.194
1767	Gillespie, James	N	Misc.1.166
1766	Gillespie, Samuel	N	Misc.1.160
1790	Gillow, Alexander	K	M.245
1791	Gilpin, Ann	N	N.174
1777	Gilpin, George	N	K,398
1780	Gilpin, John	N	L.220
1793	Gilpin, Joseph	N	N.314
1796	Gilpin, Mary	N	O.168
1766	Gilpin, Thomas	N	Misc.1.156
1797	Glackan, Patrick	K	N.189
1774	Glann, Thomas	K	L.157
1799	Glass, Belitha	K	N.234
1744	Gleen, Merey (Glenn, Mary)	K	I.98
1781	Glenn, Mary	N	L.231
1743	Glenn, Robert	K	I.78
1747	Glenn, Robert	K	I.164
1731	Glew (Glue), Samuel	K	H.14
1684	Glover, John	K	AM2013.36
1719	Glover, Richard	K	D.11/12&17
1730	Godard, John	N	Misc.1.94
1794	Goddard, Francis Lane	S	E.10/1
1716	Godden, Michael	S	A.84/5
1707	Godin, Peter	N	B.129
1782	Godlif, John	N	L.267
1685	Godsell, Robert	S	AM2013.54/5
1694	Godwin, Caspar	S	———
1798	Godwin, Eleanor	K	N.192
1750	Godwin, Elizabeth	S	A.427/8
1789	Godwin, Ezekiel	K	M.186
1795	Godwin, Frances	K	N.136
1781	Godwin, Kimuel	K	L.249
1792	Godwin, Mary	S	A72.166
1792	Godwin, Nabor	K	N.18
1780	Godwin, Thomas	S	A72.168
1727	Godwin, William	S	A.229/30
1734	Goforth, Elizabeth	K	H.86
1734	Goforth, George	K	H.82
1794	Goforth, George	K	N.84
1750	Goforth, John	N	G.401
1798	Goforth, John	K	N.190/1

1794	Goforth, Peter	K	N.88
1785	Goforth, Sarah	K	M.84/5
1748	Goforth, William	N	G.147
1736	Goforth, Zachariah	K	H.128
1752	Goforth, Zachariah	K	K.49/50
1779	Goforth, Zachariah	K	L.190&211
1695	Goit, Peter	S	A.20/2
1767	Gold (Gould), Thomas	K	K.216
1766	Golden, Abraham	N	H&I.152
1749	Golden, Abraham, Sr.	N	G.320
1790	Goldsmith, Elizabeth	K	M.218/20
1740	Goldsmith, Thomas	S	A.309/11
1742	Goldsmith, Thomas	S	A.335/6
1799	Golt, Naomi	K	N.228
1785	Golt, Thomas	K	M.60
1760	Goodeng, John	K	K.244
1788	Goodfellow, Ann	K	M.172
1788	Goodfellow, James	K	M.172
1785	Goodfellow, Margaret	K	M.94
1793	Goodfellow, Sarah	K	N.63
——	Goodin, Samuel	K	N.134
1754	Gooding, Abraham	N	Misc.1.127
1724	Gooding, Daniel	K	D.69
1734	Gooding, Daniel	K	H.83
1715	Gooding, Isaac	N	Misc.1.83
1767	Gooding, Mary	N	Misc.1.163
1717	Gooding, Phillip	N	C.112
1763	Gooding, Sarah	K	K.313/4
1785	Goodwin, Aron	K	M.73
1773	Goodwin, Benjamin	K	L.134
1729	Goodwin, Henry	N	Misc.1.91
1787	Goodwin, James	K	M.158
1776	Gordon, Catharine	S	C.39/41
1788	Gordon, Coe	K	M.166/7
1793	Gordon, Coe	K	A19.146&8
1795	Gordon, Coe	K	N.119
1798	Gordon, Coe	K	A19.147
1783	Gordon, David	K	L.276
1762	Gordon, Griffith	K	K.296/7
1774	Gordon, James	S	A72.178

1781	Gordon, James	K	L.234
1742	Gordon, John	K	I.47
1784	Gordon, John, Jr.	K	M.27
1791	Gordon, John	K	N.8/9
1791	Gordon, John	S	A72.179/80
1795	Gordon, Joshua	K	N.3/5
1747	Gordon, Lettisha	K	I.137/8
1793	Gordon, Mary	N	N.365
1765	Gordon, Robert	K	L.3
1771	Gordon, Robert	K	L.99
1795	Gordon, Samuel	K	N.136
1763	Gordon, Seth	K	K.330
1761	Gordon, Thomas	S	D.94
1786	Gordon, Thomas	S	D.94
1761	Gordon, Thomas, Sr.	S	D.94
1721	Gordon, Thomas, Sr.	S	A.146/8
1771	Gordon, Tobert	K	A19.179
1797	Gore, Thomas	K	N.167
1796	Gore, William	K	N.156/7
1773	Gormley, James	K	H.98
1752	Gorrell, James	K	K.49
1754	Gorrell, Ruth	K	K.92
1787	Goslee, William	S	D.148/9
1798	Goslen, Waitman, Sr.	S	E.195
1778	Goslin (Gauslen), Daniel	S	C.144/6
1789	Goslin, Samuel	K	M.209
1748	Goton (Geton), Lewis	N	G.119
1708	Gouldsmith, Elline	N	B.169
1732	Gozell, Thomas	N	Misc.1.95
1784	Gozlin, Ann	N	L.418
1743	Grafton, Richard	N	Misc.1.109
1791	Graham, Andrew	K	N.4
1760	Graham, David	N	Misc.1.146
1772	Graham, Francis	N	K.5
1793	Graham, Jean	N	——
1790	Graham, John	K	A19.288/9
1730	Graham, William	N	Misc.1.93
1724	Granger, Nicholas	S	A.178/9
1726	Grant, John	N	Misc.1.89
1708	Grant, William	N	Misc.1.80
1716	Grant, William	N	N.350

1695	Grantham, Ellen (Ellinor)	N	B.9
1760	Grantham, Jacob	N	Misc.1.137
1695	Grantham, John	N	Misc.1.77
1749	Grantham, Margaret	N	L.143
1734	Gravenraet, Isaac	N	Misc.1.96
1751	Gray, Alice	N	G.466
1761	Gray, Andrew	K	L.13
1773	Gray, Ann	K	L.147
1777	Gray, Bridget	S	C.66
1793	Gray, Darcus	K	N.46
1720	Gray, David	S	A.128/9
1775	Gray, David	S	E.179
1795	Gray, David	K	N.127
1757	Gray, Jacob	K	K.161
1782	Gray, James	K	L.232
1787	Gray, James	S	A73.7
1793	Gray, James	K	N.40
1798	Gray, James	S	E.179
1797	Gray, Jesse	S	A73.10
1737	Gray, John	K	A.20/21
1748	Gray, John	N	G.227
1783	Gray, John	K	M.12
1795	Gray, Margaret	N	O.128
1744	Gray, Mary	K	I.94
1743	Gray, Robert	K	I.78
1694	Gray, Samuel	S	AM2013.159
1755	Gray, Samuel	S	B.100/2
1766	Gray, Samuel	K	L.17
1780	Gray, Thomas	S	D.5/6
1786	Gray, Thomas	S	A73.30
1767	Gray, William	K	L.25
1797	Gray, William	K	N.159/60
1774	Graydon, Alexander	K	L.148
1750	Graydon, John	K	K.9
1773	Greave, John	N	K.56
1774	Greave, Jonathan	N	K.100
1741	Greave, Samuel	N	Misc.1.107
1746	Greave, Samuel	N	Misc.1.114
1787	Green, Christopher	K	M.155
1736	Green, Edward	N	——

1779	Green, Elinor	S	A73.50
1720	Green, George	K	D.36
1752	Green, Issachar	N	Misc.1.121
1791	Green, James	K	M.278
1772	Green, James	K	L.111
1742	Green, John	K	I.63
1771	Green, John	K	L.100
1796	Green, John	K	N.141
1777	Green, John	S	A73.64
1797	Green, John	K	N.168
1796	Green, Jonathan	K	N.144
1733	Green, Mercy	K	H.110
1779	Green, Naomi	S	A73.66
1728	Green, Nicholas	S	A.186/7
1726	Green, Richard	N	Misc.1.89
1774	Green, Stephen	S	B.525/9
1780	Green, Stephen	S	C.345
1755	Green, Thomas	K	K.100/01
1766	Green, Thomas, Sr.	K	L.22
1784	Green, Thomas, Jr.	K	M.36
1686	Green, William	K	AM2013.62
1710	Green, William	K	B.76
1769	Green, William	K	L.61
1750	Green, William	K	K.29/30
1736	Green, William	K	I.55
1790	Green, William	S	A73.76
1799	Green, William	K	N.243
1766	Greenaway, John	K	L.14
1729	Greenaway, Nicholas	K	A26.1545
1755	Greenlee, John	K	K.113
1789	Greenlee, Michail	K	M.182/3
1721	Greenwater, John	N	Misc.1.185
——	Greenway, Nicholas	K	F.12
1777	Greenwood, Benjamin	K	L.192
1757	Greenwood, Fennes	K	K.155/6
1763	Greenwood, John	K	K.306
1790	Greenwood, John	K	M.221
1753	Greenwood, Jonas	K	A20.152
1744	Greenwood, Jonathan	K	I.93
1769	Greenwood, Jonathan	K	L.62
1773	Greenwood, Joseph	K	L.1326

----	Greenwood, Margaret	K	M.246
1769	Greenwood, Maryann	K	I.57
1775	Greenwood, Robert	K	L.168/9
1790	Greenwood, Thomas	K	M.237
1750	Greenwood, William	K	K.27
1743	Greer, John	K	I.75
1795	Greer, John	K	N.127
1797	Greer, John	K	N.161
1773	Greer, Susanna	K	L.131
1748	Greer (Grier), William	K	I.216/7
1701	Greeves, Mathew	K	B.43
1753	Greffin, David	N	Misc.1.126
1774	Gregg, Ann	N	K.134
1744	Gregg, George	N	Misc.1.112
1773	Gregg, Henry	N	K.90
1738	Gregg, John	N	Misc.1.99
1785	Gregg, Mark	K	M.61
1790	Gregg, Rebecca	K	M.229
1790	Gregg, Rebecc	K	M.246
1793	Gregg, Rebecca	K	A20.51
1754	Gregg, Richard	N	Misc. 1.128
1767	Gregg, Samuel	N	H&I.195
1747	Gregg, William	N	G.477
1768	Gregg, William	N	Misc.1.167
1751	Gregorie, Jeremiah	K	K.47/8
1734	Grewell (Greuwell), John	K	H.63
1764	Grewell, John	K	K.344
1796	Grewell, John, Sr.	K	N.156
1748	Grewell (Gruwell), Mary	K	I.215/6
1774	Grewell, Peter	K	L.152
1746	Grey, Robert	K	I.136
1747	Gribb, Ebenezer	N	Misc.1.120
1791	Grice, Ruth	S	D.358
1789	Grice, Thomas	S	D.217/9
1790	Grice, Thomas	S	A78.89/90
1738	Grier, Catherine	K	I.4
1736	Grier, David	K	H.119
1727	Grier, George	K	F.25
1737	Grier, John	K	H.138
1736	Grier, Mark	K	H.139
1790	Griffen, David	K	M.23

1798	Griffen, John	K	N.199
1683	Griffen, Joseph	K	AM2013.10
1790	Griffen, Oliver	S	D.232/3
1700	Griffen, William	K	B.37
1746	Griffeth, Daniel	K	I.128
1747	Griffeth, David	N	——
1781	Griffin, Ann	K	L.249
1791	Griffin, Ann	K	N.4
1789	Griffin, Lydia	K	M.210
1773	Griffin, Matthew	K	L.146/7
1797	Griffin, Matthew	N	O.240
1767	Griffin, Owen	K	L.25
1795	Griffin, Samuel	K	N.103/5
1769	Griffin, Samuel	K	L.56
1769	Griffin, Samuel	K	L.63
1774	Griffin, Samuel	K	A20.226
1769	Griffin, Timothy	K	L.68
1783	Griffin, William	K	L.274
1791	Griffin, William	K	M.4
1751	Griffing (Griffin), George	K	K.42
1729	Griffing, Samuel	N	Misc.1.92
1740	Griffis, Benj	N	Misc.1.104
1775	Griffith, Amy	N	K.242
1761	Griffith, Anne	N	Misc.1.150
1750	Griffith, Catherine	N	G.459
1793	Griffith, Charles	S	A73.95/6
1716	Griffith, David	N	C.46
1733	Griffith, Eynon	K	H.50
1790	Griffith, Griffith	N	N.147
1758	Griffith, Henry	N	Misc.1.137
1788	Griffith, Jean	K	M.170
1736	griffith, John	N	Misc.1.99
1739	Griffith, John	N	——
1749	Griffith, John		G.295
1756	Griffith, John	N	Misc.1.134
1783	Griffith, John	N	L.289
1787	Griffith, Joram (Toram)	S	D.132
1773	Griffith, Joseph	N	K.90
1735	Griffith, Margaret	K	H.90
1777	Griffith, Martha	K	.235
1752	Griffith, Richard	N	Misc.1.124

1774	Griffith, Samuel	K	L.148/9
1780	Griffith, Samuel	S	A73.136
1786	Griffith, Samuel	S	D.113
1721	Griffith, Thomas	N	——
1776	Griffith, William	S	A73.150
1762	Grimes, James	N	Misc.1.152
1777	Grimes, John	K	L.186
1758	Grimes, Philip	N	Misc.1.140
1716	Grimes (or Graham), Thomas	N	C.65
1781	Grimes, William	N	L.240
1751	Griscomb, Tobias	K	K.33
1701	Groendick, Peter	K	B.43
1686	Grover, Joseph	K	Am2013.60
1690	Groves, Thomas	K	——
1787	Groves, Thomas	S	D.137/8
1767	Grubb, Emanuel	N	Misc.2.25
1799	Grubb, Emanuel	N	O.482
1791	Grubb, George	N	N.169
1788	Grubb, Henry	N	M.319
1708	Grubb, John	N	Misc.1.82
1758	Grubb, John	N	Misc.1.138
1796	Grubb, John	N	O.202
1783	Grubb, Moses	N	L.328
1775	Grubb, William	N	K.208
1789	Gruwell, Eleazer	K	M.183
1708	Guest, John	N	Misc.1.79
1796	Gullet, George	K	N.156/7
1797	Gullett, John	K	N.177/8
1787	Gum, Jacob	S	——
1710	Gumley,, Benjamin	K	C.83/4
1721	Gumley, Benjamin	K	D.50
1769	Gunnis, Henry	N	Misc.1.170
1750	Guthery, Robert	N	G.427
1746	Guthery, Samuel	N	——
1775	Guthery (Guttery), William	N	K.205
1788	Guttery, James	N	M.346
1784	Guttery, John	S	A73.173
1767	Guy, Andrew	K	L.25
1771	Gyles, John	N	Misc.1.131
1793	Gythen, John	N	N.337

- H -

1782	Hackett, John	N	L.270
1720	Hackett, William	N	C.248
1756	Hackney, John	K	K.141
1790	Hadley, John	N	N.158
1756	Hadley, Simon	N	Misc.1.218
1777	Haines, Jacobus	N	K.389
1770	Haines, Rchael	K	A23.73
1786	Hair, Joseph	N	M.186
1732	Hairgrove, George	K	H.99
1796	Hairgrove, George	K	N.151
1790	Hairgrove, Sarah	K	M.234
1775	Haithorn, William	N	K.218
1779	Halbert, Sarah	S	A76.176
----	Halbert, Samuel, Jr.	S	A73.175
1730	Haley (Healey), James	N	Misc.1.187
1752	Hall, Absolom	K	K.61
1783	Hall, Alexander	K	L.273
1794	Hall, Alexander	N	N.445
1791	Hall, Casa	S	D.323/4
1793	Hall, Chambers	N	N.320
1769	Hall, David	K	L.53
1773	Hall, David	K	----
1789	Hall, Elijah	S	D.243
1786	Hall, James	S	A73.210
1709	Hall, John, Sr.	K	B.74
1796	Hall, John	S	A73.216
1754	Hall, John	S	B.61/3
1724	Hall, John	K	F.29/30
1746	Hall, John	K	I.161
1743	Hall, John	K	I.232/3
1764	Hall, John	K	K.337
1709	Hall, John, Jr.	K	B.78
1759	Hall, John, Sr.	K	A21.94
1795	Hall, John, Jr.	K	A21.94
1760	Hall, John	K	K.239
1763	Hall, John	S	B.270/21
1783	Hall, John	K	L.268/9

1791	Hall, John	N	N.187
1772	Hall, Jonas	K	L.119
1738	Hall, Letitia	K	I.5
1744	Hall, Mary	K	I.103/4
1794	Hall, Mary	S	D.424
1774	Hall, Mary	S	C.87/8
1784	Hall, Moses	S	A73.232
1735	Hall, Nathaniel	S	A.277/9
1772	Hall, Oliver	K	L.112
1692	Hall, Robert	K	A.4
1774	Hall, Robert	K	L.156
1796	Hall, Samuel	S	A74.1/2
1791	Hall, Shadrack	S	D.322
1769	Hall, Thomas	S	B.360/2
1772	Hall, William	K	L.112
1793	Hall, William	S	D.384/5
1795	Hall, William	N	O.105
1798	Hall, William	S	E.178/9
1741	Hallans, Jehosaphat	K	I.59/60
1746	Hallans (Hallands), Jehosaphat	K	I.147
1695	Halliday, James	N	B.27
1719	Hallowell, Richard	N	C.162
1710	Halso, Henry	N	B.198
1782	Hambilton, John	N	L.296
1797	Hambleton (Hamilton), James	K	N.172
1785	Hambleton, Joseph	S	D.75/6
1778	Hambly, Richard	N	L.41
1774	Hamer, John	K	L.156/7
1771	Hamilton, Alexander	K	L.97
1780	Hamilton, James	K	L.216
1749	Hamilton, James	N	G.312
1766	Hamilton, John	K	L.11
1792	Hamilton, John, Jr.	K	N.27
1773	Hamilton, Mary	K	L.141/2
1780	Hamilton, Mary	K	L.217
1776	Hamilton, Robert	K	L.176
1758	Hammans, Thomas	K	K.187
1755	Hammans, William	K	K.110/1
1725	Hammitt, Elizabeth	K	F.6
1740	Hammitt, John	K	I.25
1780	Hammond, Bowden	S	C.344/5

1787	Hammond, Laurance (Lawrence)	K	M.134
1773	Hammons, Mary	N	K.67
1774	Hampton, David	K	L.158
1793	Hanaway, Thomas	N	N.263
1794	Hance, John	N	N.439
1768	Hander (Hanson), William	K	L.43
1792	Handson, Rachel	N	N.258
1783	Handy, Elizabeth	S	D.11/2
1777	Handy, William	K	L.188
1777	Handzer, Aminadab	S	A.122
1784	Handzer, David, Jr.	S	A74.48
1791	Hane, Abraham	K	M.263/4
1788	Hanson, Elizabeth	N	M.313
1696	Hanson, Hans	N	——
1754	Hanson, Hans	N	——
1774	Hanson, John	N	K.135
1783	Hanson, John	N	L.320
1782	Hanson, Joseph	K	L.268
1791	Hanson, Mary	K	M.274
1785	Hanson, Nathaniel	N	M.71
1731	Hanson, Peter	N	Misc.1.189
1768	Hanson (Hance), Peter	N	Misc.1.243
1795	Hanson, Samuel	K	N.99/102
1783	Hanson, Thomas	K	M.13/15
1754	Hanson, Timothy	K	K.95/96
1798	Hanson, Timothy	N	O.393
1768	Hansor, William	K	L.39/40
1795	Hardcastle, Peter	K	N.99
1773	Hardin, John	K	L.128/9
1763	Hardin, Thomas	K	K.304
1769	Hardin, Thomas	K	L.52
1761	Harding, John	N	H&I.549
1790	Harding, John	K	M.217
1790	Harding, Nancy	K	M.231
1780	Hardy, Betty Jones	S	A74.64
1786	Hardy, Joseph	S	D.116
1786	Hardy, Margaret Fillet	S	A74.68
1797	Hardy, Phillis	S	E.121
1793	Hardyknight, John	S	D.393/4
1775	Hare, Lydia	K	L.173
1709	Harford, Thomas	S	A.3/4

1797	Hargadine, William	K	N.165
1720	Hargrove, Stephen	K	D.26
1786	Harmanson, Arman	K	M.97
1704	Harmenson, John	S	A.49/50
1730	Harminson, John	K	———
1768	Harmison, Henry	K	L.43
1774	Harmon, David	K	L.153
1776	Harmon, John	S	C.41
1794	Harmon, Thomas	K	N.86
1785	Harmonsen, John	S	D.81/2
1708	Harmonson, Christian	S	A.71/5
1785	Harper, Agnes	K	M.56/7
1768	Harper, James	S	B.334/6
1785	Harper, James	K	M.68
1749	Harper, John	K	K.10/11
1768	Harper, John	K	L.39
1796	Harper, John	K	N.154/5
1798	Harper, John	K	N.217
1796	Harper, Joseph	K	N.158
1797	Harper, Thomas, Sr.	K	N.175/6
1732	Harper, William	K	H.62
1788	Harper, William	S	D.157/8
1794	Harper, William	K	N.79
1769	Harraway, William	N	Misc.1.244
1777	Harrington, Gedion	K	L.186
1781	Harrington, Henry	K	A22.96&99
1784	Harrington, Henry	K	L.269
1762	Harrington, James	k	K.295
1787	Harrington, John	K	M.134
1794	Harrington, Samuel	K	N.95
1798	Harris, Abraham, Sr.	S	E.179/80
1787	Harris, George	K	M.137
1754	Harris, Jacob	N	Misc.1.204
1786	Harris, James	N	M.184
1730	Harris, John	N	Misc.1.188
1736	Harris, John	N	Misc.1.199
1777	Harris, Joseph	N	L.89
1750	Harris, Sapiens	N	G.442
1771	Harris, William	K	L.98
1798	Harris, Zachariah	S	E.191/2
1765	Harriss, James	N	L.215

1690	Harriss, Thomas	N	Misc.1.177
1755	Harrow, James	N	Misc.1.206
1746	Harrow, Jared	N	Misc.1.202
1784	Hart, Aron	K	M.30
1702	Hart, George	K	B.45/6
1747	Hart, George	K	I.198
1779	Hart, Govey	K	L.209
1779	Hart, Hannah	K	L.210
1732	Hart, Henry	K	H.93/4
1768	Hart, Henry	K	L.48
1771	Hart, James	K	L.98
1748	Hart, John, Jr.	K	I.258
1753	Hart, John	S	A.50/2
1784	Hart, John	S	D.65/6
1774	Hart, Mary	N	K.165
1779	Hart, Robert	S	C.213
1685	Hart, Robert	S	AM2013.56
1685	Hart, Robert	S	AM2013.157
1687	Harte, Jacob	S	AM2013.83
1798	Hartley, Jane	N	O.406
1778	Hartley, William	N	L.109
1694	Hartnell, Nicholas	K	A.8
1795	Hartshorne, John	K	N.124/5
1710	Hartup, Ann	N	B.190
1700	Hartup, Robert	B	B.188
1785	Harvey, Elizabeth	N	M.73
1784	Harvey, Ginnethon	S	D.41
1766	Harvey, Job	N	H&I.154
1722	Harvey, John	N	Misc.1.182
1796	Harvey, Thomas, Sr.	S	E.89/90
1795	Harwood, Jasper	K	N.183
1790	Harwood, John	K	M.241/2
1790	Harwood, John	K	M.253
1797	Harwood, Mary	K	N.164
1799	Harwood, Robert	S	A784.161
1792	Harwood, Thomas	K	N.19
1786	Harwood, Samuel	K	M.95
1797	Harwood, Samuel	K	N.164
1777	Haslet, Jemima	K	L.188
1777	Haslet, John	K	L.186/7
1783	Hastings, Isaac	K	A22.231

1791	Hastings, John	S	D.354/5
1799	Hastings, Joshua	S	E.218/9
1750	Hastings, Peter	N	G.440
1783	Hatfield, Cottingham	S	A74.231
1788	Hatfield, Elizabeth	S	A74.232
1773	Hatfield, John, Sr.	K	L.143
1788	Hatfield, John	K	M.178
----	Hatfield, William	S	D.371
1797	Hatfield, William	K	N.174/5
1784	Hathaway, Agnes	S	O.37/8
1752	Hathorne, Ebenezer	K	K.59
1687	Hatten, William	N	Misc.1.174
1794	Haughey, Robert	N	N.394
1787	Haughey, Sarah	N	M.265
1790	Havoloe, Luke	K	A23.178
1693	Haward (Howard), (no first name)	S	AM2013.151
1774	Hawkens, John	K	L.1250
1703	Hawkey, Ursilla	K	B.47
1726	Hawkey, William	K	F.18/19
1743	Hawkins, Allen	K	I.64
1772	Hawkins, Dohority	K	L.107/8
1758	Hawkins, Jacob	K	K.194
1790	Hawkins, Jacob	K	M.221
1748	Hawkins, John	K	I.246
1789	Hawkins, John	K	M.205
1796	Hawkins, Simon	K	N.141
1762	Hawkins, Thomas	K	K.294
1769	Hawkins, Thomas	K	L.59
1746	Hawkins, William	K	I.147
1777	Hawkins, William	K	L.189
1787	Hawkins, William	K	M.131
1763	Hay, William	N	Misc.1.217
1770	Hayes, David	K	L.85
1720	Hayes, Elizabeth	K	D.18
1708	Hayes, James	N	B.157
1713	Hayes, Robert	N	C.13
1778	Hayes, Thomas	S	A75.30
1732	Haylor (Haytor), William	K	H.33
1708	Haynes, Charles, Sr.	S	A.61/3
1764	Haynes (Hanes), Daniel	K	K.345
1794	Hays, Benjamin	N	N.402

1771	Hays, Darby	K	L.100
1779	Hays, Richard	S	C.102/4
1748	Hays, Thomas	N	G.164
1795	Hays, Thomas	S	E.59/60
1787	Hazel, Barthia	K	M.148/9
1783	Hazell, Benjamin	K	M.2/3
1788	Hazell, Benjamin	K	M.168
1768	Hazell, Isaac	K	L.43
1789	Hazle, Martha	K	M.194
1778	Hazlet, William	N	L.46
1771	Hazzard, Cord	S	B.411
1790	Hazzard, Elon	S	D.387
1778	Hazzard, David	S	C.156/7
1790	Hazzard, David	S	D.308/9
1795	Hazzard, Hap.	S	E.52/3
1794	Hazzard, Joseph	S	E.3/5
1786	Hazzard, Mary	S	D.117/8
1789	Hazzard, Rachel	S	D.219
1780	Hazzard, Sarah	S	C.235/6
1788	Hazzard, William	S	A75.138
1796	Hazzard, William	S	----
1782	Hazzard, William	S	D.72/3
1701	Heaberky, Anthony	S	A.32/3
1798	Headen, Edward	K	A23.112
1791	Headon, Edward	K	M.274
1786	Hearn, Ebenezer	S	A75.146
1794	Hearn, Jonathan	S	D.409/11
1796	Hearn, Priscilla	S	E.84/5
1748	Heath, John	N	G.69
1795	Heath, Margaret	N	O.69
1785	Heath, Mary	K	M.73
1731	Heath, Thomas	K	H.25
1786	Heavabo, Andrew	S	D.97/8
1789	Heavebo, Daniel	S	D.229/30
1796	Heavelo, Hannah	A	E.63
1798	Heavelo, John	S	E.150/7
1784	Heavelo, John	S	A75.224
1790	Heavelo, Sarah	S	A76.14
1799	Heavelow, James	S	E.237/9
1750	Heaverbo, Anthony	S	A.405/7

1798	Heazel, James	K	N.201/2
1785	Hecket, Fanny	N	M.77
1732	Heddger (Hidgar), William	K	HD.101/2
1772	Hedges, Mary	N	K.63
1765	Hedges, William	N	Misc.1.238
1785	Heffernan, William	K	M.61
1722	Hemmons, John	S	A.151/2
1789	Hemmons (Hemens), John	S	D.247/8
1791	Hemmons, Jonathan	S	A76.34
1716	Hemmons, Thomas	S	A76.40
1778	Hemmons, Thomas	S	A76.141
1745	Henderson, Alexander	K	I.115
1760	Henderson, Andrew	K	K.232
1777	Henderson, John	N	K.363
1798	Henderson, John	K	N.214
1777	Henderson, Mary	N	K.361
1748	Hendricham (Hendrickson), Moses	K	I.222/3
1771	Hendricks, Sarah	K	L.97
1756	Hendrickson, Andrew	N	Misc.1.207
1758	Hendrickson, Andrew	N	Misc.1.211
1759	Hendrickson, Hendrick	K	K.215
1798	Hendrickson, Jecobus	K	N.199
1689	Hendrickson, John	N	Misc.1.175
1745	Hendrickson, John	N	Misc.1.199
1758	Hendrickson, John	K	K.174
1768	Hendrickson, John	N	Misc.1.241
1761	Hendrickson, Peter	N	Misc.1.215
1718	Hendry, David	K	A23.128
1758	Henry, Edward	K	K.185/6
1726	Henry, Gabriel	S	A.192/3
1753	Henry, John	K	K.63
1786	Henry, Matthew	K	M.104
1799	Henry, Matthew	K	N.229
1786	Henry, Robert	K	M.95
1779	Hepburn, Abigail	S	A76.57
1784	Herbert, Elizabeth Ann	N	L.444
1748	Hering, James	K	I.251
1796	Herington, John	K	N.45
1788	Heritage, John	K	M.180
1780	Herren, George	K	L.221
1738	Herresle, William	K	H.155

1737	Herring, Alexander	S	A.288/90
1784	Herring, George	K	A23.165/6
1796	Herrington, Martha	K	N.152
1798	Herrington, Nathan	K	N.195
1763	Hewes, Isabel	K	K.302/3
1695	Hewthat, Thomas	K	A.20
1744	Heyburn, Henry	K	I.107
1768	Heyse, John	K	L.45/6
1795	Hickey, Thomas	K	N.128
1789	Hickey, Thomas	K	A25.72
1772	Hickland (Kirkland), William	N	K.27
1791	Hickman, Jacob	S	D.340/2
1735	Hickman, Joshua	S	A.271/3
1785	Hickman, Joshua	S	D.71/2
1789	Hickman, Joshua	S	A76.75
1794	Hickman, Levin	S	D.418/9
1793	Hickman, Rachel	S	D.402/3
1790	Hickman, William	S	A76.96/7
1697	Higgins, Francis	K	A.19
1789	Higgins, Lawrence	N	N.78
----	Hignet, James	S	----
1771	Hiles, George, Sr.	N	N.427
1764	Hilford, Matthew	K	K.351
1796	Hilford, Matthew	K	N.152
1790	Hilford, Thomas	K	M.257
1726	Hill, Clay	K	F.17
1745	Hill, Elizabeth	K	I.113
1770	Hill, Elizabeth	K	L.80
1760	Hill, George	N	Misc.1.213
1786	Hill, George	S	D.124/5
1725	Hill, John	S	A.204/6
1748	Hill, John	N	G.187
1772	Hill, John	K	L.114
1776	Hill, John	N	K.295
----	Hill, John	S	C.119/20
1781	Hill, John	S	A76.132
1762	Hill, Joseph	N	H&I.31
1797	Hill, Joseph	K	N.168
1776	Hill, Mary	N	K.319
1783	Hill, Penelope	S	D.17/8
1787	Hill, Rachel	K	M.147

1789	Hill, Rachel	K	M.196/200
1719	Hill, Richard	A	A.113/4
1770	Hill, Robert	K	L.86
1773	Hill, Robert	K	L.130
1697	Hill, Samuel	K	A.18
1778	Hill, Solomon	S	C.328/9
1766	Hill, Susannah	K	L.14
1746	Hill, Thomas	K	I.146
1767	Hill, Thomas	K	L.130
1773	Hill, Thomas	K	L.130
1775	Hill, Thomas	N	K.215
1778	Hill, William	S	C.138/40
1796	Hill, William	K	N.141/2
1710	Hillford, Ann	K	L.85
1774	Hillford, David	K	L.159
1781	Hilliard, Philip	K	L.250
1778	Hilliard, Rebecca	K	L.197/8
1749	Hilliard, Thomas	K	K.4/5
1730	Hillyard, Charles, Jr.	K	H.9
1757	Hillyard, Charles	K	K.166
1758	Hillyard, Charles	K	A6.51/2
1761	Hillyard, Charles	K	K.252
1799	Hillyard, Christopher	K	N.235/6
1684	Hillyard, John	K	G.25/6
1720	Hillyard, John	K	D.27
1732	Hillyard, John	K	H.37
1773	Hillyard, Joseph	K	L.126
1755	Hillyard, Martha	K	K.112
1744	Hillyard, Oliver	K	I.95/6
1757	Hillyard, Steel	K	K.170
1759	Hillyard, Steel	K	K.223/4
1799	Hillyard, Thomas	K	N.239
1727	Hillyard, William	K	F.21
1789	Hilyard, Charles	K	M.202
1790	Hilyard, Elizabeth	K	M.237
1794	Hilyard, John	K	N.89
1783	Hinds, Benjamin	S	A76.169
1783	Hinds, Charles	S	A76.176
1795	Hinds, Daniel	S	E.44
1786	Hinds, Jacobus	N	M.183
1783	Hinds, John Tilton	S	A76.172

1757	Hinds, Mary	K	K.157
1783	Hinds, Sarah	S	A76.174
1768	Hinds, Thomas	S	B.336/8
1757	Hinds, William	K	K.157
1793	Hindsley, Ambrose	K	N.38
1799	Hindsley, Patience	K	N.232
1769	Hines, John	K	L.58
1724	Hinman, John	S	A.217/9
1742	Hinman, Richard	S	A.342/3
1796	Hinsley, Amos, Sr.	K	N.141
1752	Hirons, Charles	K	K.58
1772	Hirons, Charles	K	L.111
1790	Hirons, JOseph	K	M.237
1769	Hirons, Luke	K	L.50
1769	Hirons, Mark	K	L.57
1793	Hirons, Mary	K	N.38
1752	Hirons, Mary Ann	K	K.81
1724	Hirons, Robert	K	D.69
1789	Hirons, Robert	K	M.194
1746	Hirons, Simon	K	I.144
1706	Hirons, Simon, Sr.	K	B.56
1742	Hirons, Simon	K	I.49/50
1780	Hirons, Simon, Jr.	K	A24.102
----	Hirons, William	K	K.223/4
1798	Hitch, Isaac	S	E.176/7
1797	Hitch, Spencer	S	E.119
1796	Hitch, William	S	E.73
1790	Hitchcock, Elinor	S	D.320
1783	Hitchens, Ezekiel	S	D.23/4
1794	Hitchens, Levin Smith	S	A77.28/9
1791	Hitchens, Tamer	S	D.329/30
1750	Hoalston, Thomas	K	K.27
1790	Hobbs, Stephen	K	M.217
1784	Hockley, Thomas	N	M.37
1794	Hodgson, Gammage	S	A77.44
1784	Hodgson, Jacob	S	A77.45
1791	Hodgson, Robert	K	M.274
1784	Hodgson, Train (Traney)	K	A24.135/6
1794	Hodgson, Train	K	N.84
1692	Hodkins, Jane	S	AM2013.148
1748	Hogg, George	N	G.134

1721	Hogg, George, Sr.	N	Misc.1.179
1797	Hogg, Samuel	N	O.282
1784	Holden, Frederick	K	M.23/4
1792	Holder, John	S	D.359
1761	Holegeros, Mary	K	K.268/9
1778	Holegor (Holleger), Ephraim	S	C.175/7
1788	Hollahan, Con.	N	M.355
1798	Holland, Israel	S	A77.82
1735	Holland, James	S	A.270/1
1782	Holland, James	S	A77.87
1780	Holleger (Holeagor), Nathaniel	S	A77.51
1749	Hollet, Mary	K	A24.190
1746	Holliday, John	K	I.133/4
1773	Holliday, John	K	L.131
1787	Holliday, John	K	M.155
1778	Holliday, Joseph	N	L.82
1787	Holliday, Joseph	K	M.132
1774	Holliday, Richard	K	L.153
1785	Holliday, Richard	K	M.55
1795	Holliday, Amuel	K	N.117/8
1771	Holliday, Thomas	K	L.99
1755	Holliday, William	N	Misc.1.205
1776	Holliday, William	K	L.180
1767	Holling, Abraham	K	L.21
1795	Hollingsworth, Isaac	N	O.124
1782	Hollingsworth, Margaret	K	L.231
1727	Hollingsworth, Thomas	N	Misc.1.186
1753	Hollingsworth, Thomas	N	Misc.1.202
1799	Hollingsworth, Thomas	N	O.455
1779	Holms, John	K	A24.332
1754	Holms (Holmes), Robert	S	B.80/1
1765	Holston, Benjamin	K	L.5/6
1779	Holt, Catherine	S	C.219/20
1700	Holt, John	N	B.86
1725	Holt, Obadiah	N	Misc.1.183
1797	Homes, David	K	N.172
1769	Homes (Holmes), Jannet	S	A77.154/5
1792	Hood, John	N	N.239
1794	Hood, Mary	S	E.11/12
1792	Hood, Robert	N	N.273
1784	Hook, John	N	L.414

1753	Hooker, Samuel	K	H.95/6
1790	Hooten, Elijah	N	N.145
1789	Hoover, Henry	S	C.252
1797	Hoover, Sarah	S	E.122/3
1794	Hopkins, Archibald	S	A77.176/7
1797	Hopkins, George	S	E.117/8
1799	Hopkins, Hampton	K	N.277
1799	Hopkins, James. Jr.	K	N.246
1786	Hopkins, John	K	M.113/5
1792	Hopkins, John	K	N.20
1799	Hopkins, Robert	K	N.236/7
1779	Hopkins, Robert, Sr.	S	C.332/4
1741	Hopkins, Samuel, Sr.	S	A.328/9
1764	Horn, Robert	K	K.348
1754	Horseman, Samuel	K	A25.37
1790	Horsey, Isaac	S	D.268
1787	Horsey, Nathaniel	S	D.159/60
1793	Horsey, Nathaniel	A	D.381/2
1729	Horsman, Thomas	K	H.4
1786	Hosea, Daniel	S	D.109/10
1796	Hosea, John	S	E.88/9
1776	Hosman, James	S	C.19/21
1788	Hosman, Stokely	S	D.181/8
1720	Houghten, John	N	C.221
1780	Houldson, John	K	L.222/3
1754	Housman, John	K	K.98
1773	Houston, Benjamin	K	A25.42
1774	Houston, Elijah	K	A25.42
1789	Houston, Elijah	K	M.192/3
1761	Houston, George	N	Misc.1.213
1766	Houston, John	N	H&I.141
1777	Houston, JOhn	S	C.91/3
1785	Houston, Littleton	S	D.84/5
1794	Houston, Magdelen	S	A78.107
1773	Houston, Margaret	N	K.86
1784	Houston, Micajah	S	A78.112/3
1788	Houston, Robert	S	D.168/9
1711	Houston, William	N	Misc.1.178
1760	Houstown, James	K	K.246
1712	Hovie, John	N	B.180
1784	Howard, Ann	K	M.21

1792	Howard, George	S	D.377/8
1789	Howard, Joseph	K	M.203
1789	Howard, Mary	K	M.203
1787	Howard, Stephen	K	M.138/9
1748	Howell, David	N	G.167
1770	Howell, David	N	Misc.1.245
1792	Howell, David	N	N.277
1785	Howell, Elizabeth, Jr.	K	M.57
1785	Howell, Henry	N	M.89
1706	Howell, James	K	B.55
1753	Howell, James	K	K.85/6
1772	Howell, James	K	L.109
1776	Howell, James	K	L.183
1748	Howell, Jenkin	K	I.203/4
1698	Howell, John	K	A.24
1742	Howell, John	K	I.76
1756	Howell, Joseph	K	K.145
1778	Howell, Lewis	N	L.60
1789	Howell, Mary	K	A25.72
1799	Howell, Mary	K	N.245
1747	Howell, Morris	K	I.181/2
1762	Howell, Priscilla	K	K.283
1785	Howell, Ruhanna	K	M.58
1760	Howell, Sabrit	K	K.236
1722	Howell, Samuel	K	D.60
1785	Howell, Sarah	K	M.57
1777	Howell, William	K	L.190
1785	Howell, William	K	M.58
1773	Howren, Benjamin	K	L.130
1758	Hoy, Phebe	K	K.179
1762	Hoy, Pheebe	K	K.277/8
1744	Hoy, Rachel	K	I.207
1727	Hoy, Richard	K	F.31
1782	Hubbard, Charles	K	L.232
1719	Hubbert, Robert	K	D.17
1695	Huddon, Richard	N	B.8
1749	Hudson, Alexander	K	K.4
1789	Hudson, Alexander	K	M.263/4
1775	Hudson, Amy Parker	S	A78.170
1780	Hudson, Arnold	K	L.218
1798	Hudson, Benjamin	S	A78.171

——	Hudson, Daniel	K	K.123
1773	Hudson, Daniel	K	A25.104
1787	Hudson, Daniel	K	M.133
1773	Hudson, Enoch	K	L.143
——	Hudson, John	K	L.84
1773	Hudson, John	S	B.485/7
1777	Hudson, John	S	C.71/3
1791	Hudson, John	S	D.335/6
——	Hudson, John	K	N.238
1796	Hudson, John	K	N.139
1782	Hudson, Joshua	S	A72.82
1799	Hudson, Joshua	S	A79.30
1777	Hudson, Major	S	A79.36
1798	Hudson, Margaret	K	N.210
1784	Hudson, Moses	K	M.23
1789	Hudson, Parker	S	D.206/7
1722	Hudson, Richard	K	D.54
1748	Hudson, Robert	K	I.181/2
1732	Hudson, Samuel	K	M.133
1798	Hudson, Samuel	S	A79.45/7
1732	Hudson, Thomas	K	H.34&114
1780	Hudson, William	N	L.195
1791	Hudson, William	S	D.342
1731	Huestead, Damuel	K	H.108
1734	Huff, Thoms	N	Misc.1.192
1791	Huffington, Luke	S	A79.68/70
1772	Hugg, Elias	S	B.467/8
1773	Hugg, Mary	S	B.522/3
1740	Hughes, David	S	I.27/8
1789	Hughes, David	N	N.13
1705	Huling, Walton	S	A.54/5
1766	Hull, David	K	L.18
1783	Hull, James	K	L.276
1772	Humphres, Susannah	K	L.108
1762	Humphrey, Mary	S	B.340/1
1745	Humphreys, Alexander	K	I.115
1773	Humphries, Alexander	K	L.131
1763	Humphries, Elias	N	Misc.1.236
1726	Humphries, Ellis	N	Misc.1.185
1777	Humphries, Leonard	N	K.353
1770	Humphris, John	K	L.79

1775	Hunn, Caleb	K	L.170
1774	Hunn, David	K	L.155
1750	Hunn, John	K	K.23
1792	Hunn, Jonathan	K	N.34/35
1718	Hunn, Nathaniel	K	D.5
1776	Hunn, Nathaniel	K	L.193
1796	Hunn, Mathaniel	K	H.141
1762	Hunn, Reynear	K	K.288
1777	Hunt, Robert	N	L.3
1747	Hunter, Agnes	N	G.92
1757	Hunter, James	K	K.173/4
1723	Hunter, John	N	Misc.1.182
1751	Hunter, John	K	A25.175
1772	Hunter, Mary	K	L.110
1786	Hurley, Joshua	S	D.106
1790	Hurlick, William	K	M.23
1796	Hurlock, Jacob	K	N.155
1769	Hussey, James	K	L.69
1734	Hussey, Jedediah	N	Misc.1.193
1733	Hussey, John	N	Misc.1.192
1707	Hussy, John	N	B.137
1767	Huston, Agnus	N	H&I.190
1787	Huston, Charles	K	M.133
1726	Huston, Christopher	N	Misc.1.184
1789	Huston, Hugh	N	N.77
1742	Hutchenson, Ann	K	I.49
1787	Hutchenson, John	K	M.162
1789	Hutchenson, John	K	M.207
1790	Hutchenson, Margaret	K	M.253
1790	Hutchenson, Mary	K	M.253
1797	Hutchenson, Mary	K	N.185
1687	Hutchinson, Francis	N	A.85
1782	Hutchinson, Hugh	N	L.281
1783	Hutchinson, Isabella	N	L.310
1787	Hutchinson, John	K	M.162
1789	Hutchinson, John	K	M.207
1797	Hutchinson, Mary	K	N.185
1683	Hutchinson, Ralph	N	A.61
1717	Hutchinson, Robert	N	C.88
1780	Hutchinson, William	K	L.218
1790	Hutchinson, Willikam	N	N.156

1784	Hutchison, Ann	K	M.23
1777	Hutchison, James	K	L.189
1779	Hutchison, Martha	K	L.197/8
1779	Hutchison, Matthew	K	L.210
1784	Hutson, Thomas	S	D.174
1753	Hutton, Elliner	K	K.83
1746	Hutton, Robert	K	I.126/7
1748	Hyatt, Abraham	N	G.283
1748	Hyatt, Alvan	N	G.195
1799	Hyatt, Catherine	N	O.465
1792	Hyatt, Isabella	N	N.294
1788	Hyatt, John, Jr.	N	M.360
1798	Hyatt, Mary	N	O.377
1749	Hyatt, Rachel	N	Misc.1.201
1744	Hyatt, Thomas	N	Misc.1.195
1756	Hyatt, Thomas	N	Misc.1.208
1710	Hyke, Adam	N	B.215
1774	Hylands, Merian	K	L.153

- I -

1798	Ingram, Abigail	S	E.163
1776	Ingram, Isaac, Sr.	S	C.53/4
1791	Ingram, Isaac	S	A79.142
1752	Ingram, Jacob, Sr.	S	B.28/31
1799	Ingram, Jerome	S	E.201/3
1790	Ingram, Robert	S	D.275/6
1770	Inkins, Comfort	S	B.426/8
1752	Inkins, Thomas	S	B.36/7
1703	Inloes, Anthony	S	A.43/4
1764	Inloes, Thomas	K	K.344
1792	Iron, Henry	K	N.19
1782	Irons, Aaron	S	C.312/3
1794	Irons, David	S	A79.193/4
1765	Irons, Elizabeth	K	L.4
1789	Irons, Jacob	S	A79.195/6
1790	Irons, Jane	S	A79.197/8
1793	Irons, Jane	S	A79.197
1780	Irons, John, Sr.	K	L.217/8
1791	Irons, John	K	M.264

1791	Irons, Mark	K	M.276
1790	Irons, Mary	K	M.221
1795	Irons, Mary	K	N.117
1799	Irons, Mary	K	A25.222
1784	Irons, Mary	K	M.26
1790	Irons, Sarh	K	M.253
1773	Irons, Simon (Hirons)	K	L.128
1785	Irons, Thomas	K	M.43/4
1740	Irons, Timothy	K	I.18
1761	Irons, Timothy	K	K.261
1773	Irons, Timothy	K	L.124
1774	Irons, Titus	K	L.153
1787	Ironside, John	K	M.145
1768	Ironside, John	N	H&I.240
1777	Ironside, Rachel	N	K.399
1757	Isgate, Philip	K	K.172/3

- J -

1748	Jack, William	N	G.119
1798	Jackson, Augustus	S	A80.6/7
1798	Jackson, Eben	K	N.202/3
1769	Jackson, Elizabeth	K	L.67
1785	Jackson, Elizabeth	K	M.52
1795	Jackson, Ezekiel	K	N.133/4
1779	Jackson, David	K	L.211
1794	Jackson, Henry	K	N.79
1748	Jackson, James	K	I.228
1742	Jackson, John	K	I.74
1771	Jackson, John	K	L.93
1779	Jackson, John	K	L.208
1789	Jackson, Joseph	K	M.159/60
1790	Jackson, Joseph	N	N.134
1785	Jackson, Levi	K	M.50
1758	Jackson, Moses	K	K.183
1789	Jackson, Nimrod	K	M.186
1757	Jackson, Richard	K	K.158
1774	Jackson, Richard	K	L.157

1790	Jackson, Thomas	K	N.5
1799	Jackson, Thomas	K	N.269
1748	Jackson, William	K	I.218/9
1768	Jackson, William	K	L.39/42
1748	Jackson, William	K	I.227
1798	Jacobs, Albertis	S	A80.44/5
1796	Jacobs, Bozman	K	N.157
1767	Jacobs, Hannah	S	B.314/7
1782	Jacobs, Hannah	S	A80.55
1777	Jacobs, John	S	C.68/9
1776	Jacobs, Mary	N	K.279
----	Jacobs, Nathaniel	S	A80.70
1779	Jacobs, Patience	S	A80.72
1734	Jacobs, Richard	S	A.267/70
1792	Jacobs, Speakman	K	N.19
1750	Jacobs, William	K	K.67
1766	Jacobs, William	K	L.16
1770	Jacobs, William	K	L.171
1781	Jacobs, William	K	L.222
1787	Jacquett, Ann	N	M.283
1752	Jaffray, Henry	K	K.59/60
1767	James, Ann	N	H&I.194
1732	James, Daniel	K	H.34
1799	James, Daniel	K	N.241/3
1753	James, David	N	I.247
1777	James, Dinah	N	K.391
1727	James, George	K	F.30
1748	James, Howell	N	G.154
1717	James, Howell, Sr.	N	C.96
1799	James, Isaiah	K	N.229
1756	James, James	K	K.130
1781	James, James	K	L.225
1781	James, James	N	L.255
1786	James, John	K	M.107
1794	James, Joshua	S	E.5
1799	James, Joshua	S	A80.99
1751	James, Nathaniel	K	K.126
1790	James, Reuben	S	D.289/91
1799	James, Tamar	N	O.471
1780	James, Thomas	N	L.180
1786	Jamison, Alexander	K	M.94

——	Janney, Jacob	K	A26.103
1686	Janson, Herman	N	A.74
1798	Janvier, Francis	N	O.386
1772	Janvier, Isaac	N	K.2
1776	Janvier, Sarah	N	K.285
1799	Janvier, Sarah	N	——
1753	Jaquet, John	N	M.337
1794	Jaquet, Peter, Sr.	N	N.448
1774	Jaquett, Mary	N	K.172
1796	Jarman (Jarmon), William	S	E.58/9
1790	Jarold, James	K	M.231
1790	Jarold, Stephen	K	M.217
1794	Jarrad, Matthew	K	N.76
1796	Jarral, John	K	N.150
1787	Jarrald, Stephen, Sr.	K	M.143
1789	Jarrald, Stephen, Jr.	K	M.196
1778	Jarrard, James	K	L.198
1778	Jarrard, Wilson	K	L.197
1799	Jarrel, Robert	K	N.223
1798	Jarrel, Robert	K	N.218
——	Jarrold, Stephen	K	A26.168/9
1791	Jefferson, Mar(ia)	S	A80.156
1780	Jefferson, Richard	S	C.237/40
1761	Jemison, Jenett	K	K.252
1784	Jemison, Joseph	N	M.29
1761	Jemison, Marmiduck	N	H&I.544
1786	Jenkins, Andrew	K	M.94
1790	Jenkins, Dorothy	K	M.232
1732	Jenkins, Jabey	K	H.101
1790	Jenkins, Joseph	K	M.222
1796	Jenkins, Samuel	K	N.146
1745	Jenkins, Sarah	K	——
1790	Jenkins, Sarah	K	M.209
1778	Jenkins, Timothy	K	N.35/6
1797	Jennings, John	K	N.169
1712	Jeoffrey, Edward	N	B.249
1768	Jerrard, Matthew	K	L.49
1790	Jervis, Caleb	K	M.233
1694	Jesop, Jesop	K	A.9
1796	Jesson, William	K	N.151
1771	Jessons, Mary	K	L.97/8

1789	Jessop, John	S	A80.187
1785	Jessup, Aaron	S	A80.186
1789	Jessups, Patience	S	D.249/50
1776	Jester, Charles	K	L.179
1795	Jester, Isaac	K	N.128
1798	Jester, James	K	N.220
1764	Jester, Jonathan	K	K.338/9
1781	Jester, Joseph	K	L.230
1782	Jester, Joshua	K	L.232
1784	Jester, Richard	K	M.26
1796	Jester, Sarah	K	N.146
1753	Jester, Thomas	K	A27.49
1758	Jester, Thomas	K	K.191/2
1773	Jester, William	K	L.123/4
1785	Jester, William	K	M.67/8
1774	Jeton, Peter	N	K.150
1783	Jewett, William	S	A81.6/7
1780	John, David	N	L.183
1773	John, Griffith	N	K.100
1727	John, John Little	N	Misc.1.291
1720	John, Thomas	N	C.253
1758	Johns, Samuel	K	K.177/8
1707	Johnson, Aaron	N	B.131
1713	Johnson, Adam	S	A.77/9
1791	Johnson, Bacon (Baker)	S	D.339/40
1721	Johnson, Baldwin	N	C.283
1787	Johnson, Bartholemew	S	D.151/2
1683	Johnson, Cornelius	N	A.61
1789	Johnson, Elias	S	D.250/1
1748	Johnson, Francis	N	G.148
1786	Johnson, Hannah	S	A81.38/9
1799	Johnson, Isaac	S	E.199
1786	Johnson, James	N	M.178
1774	Johnson, Jean	K	L.154
1788	Johnson, Job	S	A81.52
1706	Johnson, John	N	B.102
1754	Johnson, John	K	K.92
1774	Johnson, John	K	L.154
1780	Johnson, John	K	L.219
1782	Johnson, John	S	D.11
1797	Johnson, John	S	E.115

1778 Johnson, Josephia S C.133/4
1780 Johnson, Major S C.236/7
1799 Johnson, Mary K N.299
1778 Johnson, Peter S C.337/9
1794 Johnson, Peter S D.411/2
1786 Johnson, Purnal, Jr. S A81.88
1788 Johnson, Purnal, Sr. S D.1/2
1769 Johnson, Robert N M.288
1757 Johnson, Samuel K A27.103/4
1775 Johnson, Samuel N K.265
1786 Johnson, Samuel S A81.99
1776 Johnson, Thomas N K.301
1778 Johnson, William S A81.121
1791 Johnson, William N N.194
1793 Johnson, William K N.55
1796 Johnson, William K N.171
1797 Johnston, Jonathan K N.174
1784 Johnston, William K M.57
1773 Joice, Samuel S B.482/3
1787 Jolley, Esther N M.248
1794 James, Ann K N.86
1763 Jones, Barbary K K.321/2
1756 Jones, Benjamin K K.135
1762 Jones, Benjamin K K.295/6
1773 Jones, Benjamin, Jr. K L.131
1787 Jones, Benjamin K M.159/60
1792 Jones, Benjamin K N.19
1785 Jones, Burrell S D.73/4
1741 Jones, Catherine K I.33/4
1719 Jones, Charles K D.9
1718 Jones, Charles K D.39
1694 Jones, Daniel K A.11
1748 Jones, David N G.179
1752 Jones, David K K.57
1753 Jones, David K K.103/4
1788 Jones, David S A81.139
1794 Jones, Edith N N.436
1790 Jones, Eleanor K M.271
1732 Jones, Enoch K H.113
1789 Jones, Enoch K M.216

1733	Jones, Evan	K	H.41
1720	Jones, Griffith	K	D.37
1703	Jones, Griffith	K	B.48
1754	Jones, Griffith	K	K.104
1773	Jones, Isaac	S	A81.152
1788	Jones, Isaac	S	A.178/9
1785	Jones, Isaac, Sr.	K	M.52
1790	Jones, Isaac Handy	S	D.296
1777	Jones, Jacob	K	L.189
1773	Jones, Jacob	K	L.141
1758	Jones, James	K	K.183
1769	Jones, James	S	B.62/4
1786	Jones, James	N	M.203
1798	Jones, James	K	A27.202/3
1695	Jones, John	S	AM2013.175
1729	Jones, John	K	G.31
1733	Jones, John	K	H.44/5
1757	Jones, John	K	K.171
1780	Jones, John	N	L.201
1798	Jones, John	S	E.182/3
1791	Jones, John	S	D.354
1780	Jones, Jonas	S	C.236/7
1682	Jones, Joseph	K	A.1
1789	Jones, Layton	K	M.213
1792	Jones, Layton	K	A27.237
1732	Jones, Lewis	K	H.102/3
1793	Jones, Martha	S	D.401/2
1749	Jones, Mary	N	G.388
1777	Jones, Mary	N	K.347
1789	Jones, Mary	K	M.213
1798	Jones, Mary	K	N.221
1791	Jones, Morgan	N	N.164
1790	Jones, Penelope Holt	S	D.307/8
1760	Jones, Philip	K	K.247/8
1788	Jones, Philip	N	M.327
1772	Jones, Priscilla	K	L.109
1777	Jones, Rebecca	N	K.394
1797	Jones, Robert	S	E.136/8
1744	Jones, Samuel	K	I.79
1785	Jones, Sarah	K	A28.19/20
1788	Jones, Standford	K	N.21

1790	Jones, Standford, Jr.	K	N.21
1737	Jones, Thomas	K	H.144
1791	Jones, Thomas	S	A81.188
1798	Jones, Thomas	S	E.150/1
1698	Jones, Walter	K	A.24
1741	Jones, William	K	I.33/4
1774	Jones, William	S	B.520/1
1793	Jones, William	N	N.334
1780	Jones, Zachariah	S	C.240/4
1789	Jones, Zachariah	K	M.205/6
1745	Jordan, Andrew	K	I.121
1793	Jordan, Isabell	K	A28.43/4
1756	Jordan, John	K	K.153
1796	Jordan, Joseph Jacob	S	A83.9
1784	Jordan, Joseph Jeremiah	S	A82.10
1793	Jordan, William	K	N.55/6
1748	Joy, Edward	K	I.199/200
1798	Joy, William	K	N.222
1728	Joyce, Henry	K	G.14
1788	Joyce, Samuel	S	A81.131
1721	Jubart, Peter	N	C.295
1794	Juley, Eleanor	S	D.412/3
1779	Jump, Benjamin	K	L.209
1795	Jump, Solomon	K	N.121
1792	Justis, James	N	N.242
1774	Justis, Mouns.	N	K.122
1774	Justisc, Niels	N	K.175

– K –

1700	Kairone, Timothy	K	B.37&41
1791	Kearney, Dyer	K	M.262
1722	Kearney, Philip	K	D.57
1742	Kearny, Michael	K	K.19/20
1795	Kearny, Rebecca	N	O.178
1752	Keith, Francis	K	K.82
176	Keith, Jane	K	L.3
1764	Keith, John	K	K.237
1795	Keith, Thomas	K	N.110
1775	Kellam, Benjamin	N	K.203

1772	Kellam, John	N	K.29
1793	Kellam, Richard	N	N.356
1786	Kellam, Samuel	S	A82.41
1758	Kelly, Ezemy	N	Misc.1.266
1766	Kelly, Hugh	N	Misc.1.271
1764	Kelly, John	K	K.342
1766	Kelly, Margaret	N	Misc.1.272
1777	Kelly, Michael	N	K.401
1796	Kelly, Samuel	N	O.159
1752	Kelly, Will.	N	Misc.1.260
1720	Kelly, William	K	D.24
1762	Kelly, William	K	K.297
1793	Kelly, William	K	N.64
1785	Kelso, John	N	M.171
1788	Kelson, George	K	M.171/2
1795	Kendall, John	N	O.85
1749	Kenner, Jane	N	G.383
1744	Kenney, Matthew	N	Misc.1.257
1757	Kenney, Rebecca	N	Misc.1.266
1732	Kenney, Moses	N	Misc.1.251
1778	Kenney, Robert	N	L.69
1770	Kent, Magdalen	K	L.85
1764	Keran, Oatrick	N	Misc.1.270
1789	Kerney, Morris	K	M.196
1774	Kerr, Robert	N	K.157
1773	Kerr, Samuel	N	K.74
1772	Kershey (Hershey), Elizabeth	N	K.20
1749	Kersie, James	K	I.253
1748	Ketch, James	K	I.247
1736	Kettle, Cornelius	N	Misc.1.252
1743	Kettle, John	N	Misc.1.256
1775	Kettle, John	N	K.276
1753	Kettle, Zachariah	N	Misc.1.261
1769	Killam, Isaac	K	L.61
1797	Killen, Abel	K	N.176
1771	Killen, Adam	K	L.97
1786	Killen, Henry	K	M.120/1
1787	Killen, Henry	K	M.135
1794	Killen, Mark	K	N.89
1771	Killen, Mary	K	L.89
1783	Killen, Mary	K	A28.192

1787	Killen, Susannah	K	M.134
1795	Killingsworth, John, Sr.	S	E.51/2
1729	Killingsworth, John	K	G.29/30
1749	Killingworth, George	K	I.255/6
1767	Killingworth, Josiah	K	L.21
1789	Killingworth, Rebecca	K	M.208
1774	Kimmey, Charles	K	L.154
1781	Kimmey, Jean	S	A82.79
1733	Kimmey, William	K	L.147
1790	Kimmy, Sanders	S	D.306/7
1795	Kimmy, Solomon	K	N.134
1778	King, Christian	N	L.120
1799	King, David	A	E.223/4
1773	King, Elianer	K	L.131
1746	King, Elias	N	Misc.1.259
1753	King, Francis	N	Misc.1.263
1794	King, Francis	N	O.34
1781	King, Hugh	S	C.223/4
1749	King, Isaac	K	K.10
1769	King, Isaac	K	L.68
1730	King, Jacob	N	Misc.1.248
1741	King, Jacob	N	Misc.1.254
1733	King, James	K	L.128
1749	King, James	N	G.370
1796	King, John	K	N.150
1791	King, John	S	D.338
1777	King, John	N	K.381
1797	King, John	N	O.212
1755	King, Mary	N	Misc.1.265
1778	King, Mary	N	L.26
1784	King, Michael	N	L.422
1780	King, Richard	K	C.86
1783	King, Robert	K	M.142/3
1785	Kingham, Joshua	K	M.52
1760	Kinkead, John	N	Misc.1.269
1773	Kinkead, Sarah	N	K.70
1798	Kinnamon (Keneam), Ambros	K	N.208
1790	Kinney, Joshua	S	D.313/4
1700	Kipshaven, John	S	A.130/4
1774	Kirk, Adam	N	K.178
1732	Kirk, Alice	N	Misc.1.294

1788	Kirk, Jonathan	N	N.7
1751	Kirk, Patrick	K	K.37/8
1759	Kirkpatrick, David	N	Misc.1.268
1785	Kirkpatrick, Elizabeth	N	M.109
1792	Kirkpatrick, Jane	N	N.289
1779	Kirkpatrick, Margaret	N	L.137
1768	Kirkpatrick, Samuel	N	Misc.1.276
1796	Kirkpatrick, William	S	E.130
1774	Kittle, Catherine	N	K.149
1792	Kneasborough, Mary	N	N.237
1776	Knight, John	K	L.181
1736	Knight, William	K	H.44
1787	Knight, William	K	M.163
1790	Knock, Joseph	S	A82.167
1771	Knott, Edward	N	Misc.1.278
1785	Knott, William	K	A29.83
———	Knotts, Robert	N	Misc.1.272
1799	Knowles, Betty	S	E.216/7
1791	Knowles, Richard, Sr.	S	D.331/2
1785	Knox, John	S	A82.197
1791	Knox (Knock), Mary	S	A82.168
1776	Kollock, George	S	C.45/6
1720	Kollock, Jacob	S	A.130/4
1790	Kollock, Margaret	S	D.281/2
1758	Kollock, Shepard	S	B.171
1788	Kollock, William	S	A83.19
1767	Kreig, Jacob	N	H&I.193
1777	Kruson, Jacob	N	K.396

– L –

1753	Lacey, Robert	S	B.59/61
1783	Lacey, Robert	S	A82.22
1783	Lacey, William	S	A83.29
1788	Lackey, Andrew	K	M.169/70
1729	Lackey, Gustavus	K	H.110/1
1729	Lackey, Mary	K	H.3
1767	Lacy, James	K	A29.94
1730	Lafarty, James	N	Misc.1.291

1781	Laferty, Margaret	N	L.232
1758	Lakerman, Abraham	N	Misc. 1.319
1777	Lambert, John	K	L.193
1785	Lamden, George	K	M-54
1720	LaMott, Charles	K	D-38
1797	Lampden, John	K	N-163
1758	Lamply, William	N	Misc.1.322
1747	Land, Christian	N	G-37
1736	Land, Francis	N	Misc.1.299
1730	Land, John	N	Misc.1.293
1732	Land, Rebecca	N	Misc.1.296
1749	Land, Thomas	N	G-382
1797	Lane, Anthony	K	N-165
1782	Lane, Gallant	K	L-268
1777	Lane, James	K	L-188
1785	Lane, John	K	M-54
1750	Lang, James	K	K-9/10
1786	Langrall, Asa.	S	D-104
1759	Langrell, George	K	K-195
1789	Lank, Naomi	S	D-244/5
1785	Lank, Lenin	S	A71.141/2
1796	Lank, Nathaniel	S	A83.92
1762	Larkins, John	K	K-300
1766	Larnder, Benjamin	N	Misc.1.338
1797	Laroux, JOhn	N	0.302
1782	Latcham, Joshua	K	L.232
1796	Latham, Robert	K	N.150
1777	Lattamus, James	N	K.392
1760	Lattimer, John	N	Misc.1.327
1754	Lattimer, James	N	Misc.1.318
1789	Laughinghoe, William	S	E.236/7
1783	Laughran, Joseph	N	L.330
1694	Launcelot, James	K	A.10
1719	Lautman, Jeremiah	N	C.151
1799	Laverty, Mary	S	E.196/8
1798	Laverty, Thomas	S	A63.103
1694	Lawrence, Hilburd	N	Misc.1.283
1789	Laws, Alexander	S	D.254/5
1799	Laws, Belitha	K	N.240
1781	Laws, Bolitha	K	M.8/10
1717	Laws, John	N	C.82

1788 Laws, John, Jr. S D.185/6
1788 Laws, John K M.173
1790 Laws, John S D.264/5
1796 Laws, John K N.141
1799 Laws, John K N.239
1796 Laws, Major K N.159
1797 Laws, Saxagotha S A83.152
1687 Laws, Thomas N Misc.1.282
1775 Laws, William S A83.153
1791 Laws, William S A83.156
1787 Laws, William S D.161/2
1796 Laws, William K N.149/50
1796 Lay, Baptist S A83.165
1797 Lay, Edward S A83.134
1797 Lay, Philena S E.123
1773 Lay, Thomas S A83.168
1789 Layfield, Thomas S A83.169/70
1792 Layton, Burton S D.359/60
1799 Layton, John S D.204/5
1795 Layton, Lowder S E.32/3
1796 Layton, Nehemiah S E.66
1784 Layton, Nicholas K M.21
1786 Layton, Robert S D.199/200
1775 Layton, Thomas S C.27/8
1798 Lea, James N O.400
1733 Leach, David K H.95
1774 Leadley, Moses N K.106
1766 League, John N Misc.1.337
1771 League, Samuel N Misc.1.346
1748 Leanord, James N G.145
1770 Leatherberry, William S B.383/5
1773 Leatherberry, William K L.144
1779 Leatherbury, Arthur S A84.17
1774 Leatherbury, Diana S B.505/9
1779 Leatherbury, Mary K A29.218
1774 Leatherbury, Thomas S A84.21
1745 Leatherbury, Thomas K I.104/5
1778 Leatherbury, Thomas K L.202
1779 Leatherbury, Thomas K A29.217
1754 Leatherbury, Thomas S B.67
1791 Leathum, Mary K N.4

1685	Leavith, Richard	K	AM2013.158
1776	Leby, Cadrup	K	L.180
1799	Lecat, Levin	S	E.224/5
1744	Leckey, Andrew	K	I.111/2
1790	Leckey, Andrew	K	M.223/4
1732	Leckey (Lakey), Henry	K	H.46
1732	Leckey, Hugh	K	H.79
1793	Lecky, Andrew	K	A29.223/5
1790	Lecompt, Ann	S	D.362/3
1799	Lecompt, Charles	K	A29.227
1797	Lecompte, Nathan	K	N.179/80
1796	LeCount, Thomas	K	N.138
1785	Lecourt, Philemon	S	D.75
1797	Lee, Jeremiah	K	N.172
1741	Lee, Richard	K	I.56
1798	Lee, Richard	K	N.192
1782	Lee, Richard	K	L.206
1793	Lee, Thomas	K	N.62
1774	Lee, William	N	K.104
1783	Lee, Wilson, Sr.	S	D.34/5
1760	Leich (Leach), David	K	----
1748	Legg, James	K	I.205/6
1795	Lemar, Henry	K	N.124
1687	Lemmons, Henry	N	A.94
1730	Lenick, John	K	H.10
1782	Lenick, William	K	L.265/6
1761	Lennard, Grace	K	K.265
1727	Lenton, Mary	K	F.24
1718	Lenton, Nathaniel	K	D.6
1742	Leolin, Catherin	N	Misc.1.305
1761	Leonard, John	K	K.263
1778	Leonard, Peter	N	L.11
1748	Lester, George	K	I.221
1720	Letort, Ann	K	D.29
1767	Levick, Clayton	K	L.38
1734	Levick, Richard	K	H.110
1735	Levick, Richard, Jr.	K	----
1733	Levick, Richard	K	H.94
1745	Lewden, John	N	Misc. 1.305
1754	Lewden, John	N	Misc. 1.316
1683	Lewdritt, Elizabeth	S	AM2013.7/8

1779	Lewelin, David	N	L.134
1795	Lewellen, Jane	N	O.80
1747	Lewis, Catherine	M	Misc.1.309
1761	Lewis, Daniel	K	K.265
1757	Lewis, David	K	K.155
1758	Lewis, David	N	Misc.1.323
1777	Lewis, David	N	K.380
1782	Lewis, David	K	L.268
1795	Lewis, David	K	N.113/4
1788	Lewis, Deborah	K	----
1790	Lewis, Elizabeth	K	M.233
1750	Lewis, Ellis	K	G.430
1731	Lewis, Evan	N	Misc.1.296
1753	Lewis, Evan	N	Misc.1.313
1783	Lewis, Evan, Sr.	K	M.104
1730	Lewis, Griffith	N	Misc.1.292
1799	Lewis, James	K	L.216
1778	Lewis, Joel	K	L.203
1713	Lewis, John	N	B.185
1769	Lewis, John	K	L.68
1787	Lewis, John	S	D.131/2
1795	Lewis, Jonathan	S	A84.61
1773	Lewis, Joseph	K	L.130
1761	Lewis, Josiah	N	Misc.1.328
1739	Lewis, Mary	N	Misc.1.301
1769	Lewis, Mary	K	L.65
1769	Lewis, Mary	K	L.67
1769	Lewis, Philip	K	L.65/6
1744	Lewis, Rees	K	I.88/9
1727	Lewis, Richard	N	Misc.1.287
1777	Lewis, Richard	K	L.188
1791	Lewis, Robert	K	M.272
1782	Lewis, Samuel	N	L.292
1786	Lewis, Sarah	K	M.120
1786	Lewis, Sarah	K	M.125
1788	Lewis, Sarah	K	M.168
1795	Lewis, Sarah	K	N.122
1794	Lewis, Simeon	S	E.1
1775	Lewis, Stephen	K	L.170
1763	Lewis, Susannah	K	K.312
1749	Lewis, Thomas	N	G.323

1778	Lewis, Thomas	N	L.32
1789	Lewis, Thomas	K	M.199/200
1792	Lewis, Thomas, Sr.	S	D.379/80
1799	Lewis, Thomas, Jr.	K	N.227
1796	Lewis, Thomas	K	N.146
1785	Lewis, William	K	M.59
1795	Lewis, William	K	N.97
1732	Lewis, Wrixam	S	A.258/60
1777	Lewis, Wrixam	S	A84.72/4
1700	Lewkins, Nathaniel	K	B.40
1773	Leyvick, John	K	L.138
——	Leyvick, William	K	L.99
1705	Lillingston, Elizabeth	S	A.439/40
1776	Lilly, Timothy	K	L.185
1790	Lily, John	K	M.237
1790	Linch, Jacob	S	A84.85
1798	Linch, John	S	E.181
1791	Lindale, Robert	S	A84.110
1778	Lindell, Peter	S	A84.109
1779	Lindell, Thomas	S	B.392/4
1796	Lindsey, John	N	O.157
1757	Lingo, John	S	B.153/5
1777	Lingo, Leven	S	A84.137
1796	Lingo, Samuel, Jr.	S	A84.142
1770	Lingo, William	S	B.426/8
1798	Linn, John	N	O.322
1760	Linnon (Linnin), John	K	K.240/1
1793	Lister, William	K	N.46
1794	Lister, William	K	N.110/11
1769	Liston, Edmund	N	Misc.1.342
1711	Liston, Jane	N	Misc.1.286
1708	Liston, Morris	N	Misc.1.284
1789	Liston, William	N	N.20
1788	Litman, John	N	M.335
1752	Little, Amos	S	B.27/8
1781	Little, Archibald	N	L.223
1756	Little, Jean	S	B.116/7
1778	Little, John	S	C.164/9
1748	Little, Mary	K	I.221
1798	Little, Richard	S	E.164
1799	Little, Sarah	S	E.221/6

1772	Little (Littel), William	S	B.440/1
1774	Littler, Joshua	N	K.196
1764	Littler, Mary	N	Misc.1.335
1740	Littler, Minshall	N	Misc.1.303
1757	lloyd, Samuel	K	K.165
1799	Lloyd, Thomas	S	A85.163
1712	Lloyd, Thomas	N	B.230
1768	Loatman, Benjamin	K	L.48
1761	Loatman, Jeremiah	K	K.264
1770	Lober (Lowber), Peter, Jr.	K	L.74/5
1790	Lockerman, Vincent	K	M.240
1790	Lockerman, Vincent	K	M.241
1764	Lockhart, John	N	Misc.1.332
1787	Lockwood, Armwell, Jr.	K	M.162/3
1795	Lockwood, Armwell, Jr.	K	N.126
1799	Lockwood, Armwell, Jr.	S	A84.182
1781	Lockwood, Elisha	S	A.493/4
1785	Lockwood, Mary	S	D.69
1760	Loffly, Gabriel	S	B.201/3
1755	Lofland, Cornelius	S	B.89/90
1750	Lofland, Dorman	S	A.407/8
1788	Lofland, Dorman, Jr.	S	D.202
1785	Lofland, Ebenezer	S	A85.19/20
1795	Lofland, Elizabeth	S	E.60
1773	Lofland (Loughland), John, Sr.	S	B.478/81
1793	Lofland, Joshua	S	A85.61
1799	Lofland, Littleton	S	E.202/4
1774	Lofland, Mary	S	B.474/6
1786	Lofland, William, Sr.	S	D.122/3
1791	Lofland, Zadoc	S	A85.93
1775	Loftis, John, Sr.	K	L.173/4
1797	Loftis, John	K	N.169
1787	Loftis, Sarah	K	M.136/7
1751	Logue, Ephraim	N	G.474
1721	London, Ambrose	N	C.350
1791	Long, David, Sr.	S	D.349/50
1736	Long, Edward	K	H.131
1788	Long, Elisha	S	D.185/6
1798	Long, Elisha	S	A85.111/2
1772	Long, Jane	K	L.109/10
1787	Long, John	S	A85.128

1784	Long, Samuel	K	M.20
1797	Long, Solomon	S	A85.136
1772	Long, William	K	L.109
1794	Longfellow, John	K	N.81
1799	Longfellow, Thomas	K	N.223
1690	Longpre, Cloude	K	AM2013.129
1771	Loockerman, Nicholas	K	L.92/3
1785	Loockerman, Vincent, Sr.	K	M.62/67
1698	Loper, Peter	K	B.27
1780	Lord, John	S	C.233/4
1793	Lord, Henry	K	N.45
1713	Lossan, Mathias	N	A.251
1746	Lott, Bartholomew	K	I.140
1683	Lotton, James	S	AM2013.2
1762	Louchran, Joseph	N	Misc.1.329
1695	Louder, Edward	K	A.15
1764	Loughran, Martha	N	Misc.1.331
1733	Loughten, John	S	A.265/7
1693	Love, Andrew	K	A.6
1759	Love, James	S	B.197/8
1797	Lovegrove, James	K	N.168
1707	Low, Samuel	K	B.58
1795	Low, William	S	E.31/2
1791	Lowber, Catharine	K	M.274
1796	Lowber, Daniel	K	N.142
1772	Lowber, Matthew	K	L.117
1795	Lowber, Matthew	K	M.126
1746	Lowber, Michael	K	I.122/3
1796	Lowber, Peter	K	N.148
1796	Lowber, William	K	N.154
1787	Lowden, Hannah	N	M.231
1747	Lowder, Edward	N	I.312
1793	Lowe, Ralph	S	D.294/5
1765	Lowe, Vincent	N	N.55
1793	Lowry, James	S	D.400/1
1746	Lucas, Mason	K	I.142
1721	Lucas, Peter	S	A.148
1746	Lucas, Robert	N	Misc.1.308
1760	Lucas, Thomas	K	K.246
1790	Ludrum (Lednum), John	S	D.284/5
1733	Lues, John	K	H.44

1782	Luff, Caleb	K	L.233
1783	Luff, Caleb	K	L.271
1709	Luff, Hugh	K	B.79
1760	Luff, Nathaniel	K	K.225
1786	Lukens, Joseph	N	M.191
1793	Luker, William	S	A85.177
1778	Luker, William	S	A85.178
1769	Luman, Samuel	K	L.69
1747	Lurkingsiler, John William	N	Misc.1.311
1791	Lyle, John	K	M.266
1771	Lynam, Andrew	N	Misc.1.344
1782	Lynch, Sarah	K	L.232
1782	Lynch, William	K	L.231
1782	Lynch, William	K	L.232
1749	Lyndsey, David	K	I.253/5
1768	Lynn, John	N	I.340
1783	Lynn, Moses	S	D.10/11
1764	Lyons, Patrick	N	Misc.1.333
1766	Lyson, Theophilus	K	L.20

- MC -

1742	McAlexander, John	K	I.62
1748	McAlister, Daniel	N	G.152
1794	McAntier, Ann	N	N.133
1785	McAntier, Samuel	N	M.133
1772	McAntire, Alexander	N	K.44
1763	McBride, William	K	K.309
1754	McCabe, James	K	A32.87
1732	McCahan, Daniel	K	H.58/9
1774	McCall, Alexander	K	I.82
1781	McCall, Samuel	K	L.230
1774	McCalley, Robert	N	K.186
1777	McCallmont, John	N	K.372
1792	McCallmont, Sarah	N	N.283
1748	McCarady (McCardell), James	K	I.212
1744	McCarroll, Robert	S	A.357/9
1694	McCart (MacKarta), John	N	Misc.1.348
1761	McCausland, William	N	——
1784	McCay, Alexander	S	D.36/7

1740	McCellen, Thomas	K	I.19
1774	McClay, John	N	K.115
1794	McClay, William	N	O.1
1747	McClearn, William	N	G.93
1761	McClement, Andrew	K	K.258
1787	McClintock, James	N	M.293
1741	McCludy, James	K	A32.107
1793	McClure, William	N	N..310
1789	McClyment, Robert	K	M.210
1798	McComb, Eleazer	N	———
1776	McCombs, Esther	K	L.185
1760	McCombs, Grace	K	K.242/3
1774	McCombs, Malcomb	N	K.102
1772	McComsey, Alexander	N	K.40
1729	McCook, Archibald	K	G.29&H.111
1729	McCool, Gabriel	K	H.99
1762	McCool, John	N	H&I.199
1779	McCoole, Benjamin	N	L.140
1796	McCoomb, Jonathan	K	N.153
1791	McCormick, John	S	A87.132
1793	McCoy, Andrew	K	N.44
1775	McCracken, David	S	C.12/3
1745	McCrea, Thomas	N	Misc.1.359
1773	McCreary, Robert	N	K.96
1792	McCreery, Robert	N	N.247
1781	McCukkah, John	S	C.317/8
1724	McCulley, Alexander	S	A.182/4
1793	McDaniel, Elisabeth	S	A87.146
1760	McDaniel, James	K	K.238
1788	McDaniel, Moss	S	D.194/5
1759	McDavett, Daniel	K	K.212
1758	McDevett, James	K	K.191
1749	McDonald, Archibald	N	G.302
1798	McDonald, James	N	O.391
1775	McDonnally, Margaret	N	K.235
1707	McDonnel, Bryon	N	B.153
1762	McDonnel (McDonald), James	K	A32.163
1796	McDonough, Jesse	N	O.476
1745	McDonough, Patrick	K	I.109
1736	McDowell, Hugh	K	H.133
1787	McDowell, Hugh	K	M.141

1735	McDowell, John	K	H.212/122
1787	McDowell, John	N	M.284
1797	McDowell, Joshua	S	E.134
1749	McDowell, William	N	G.367
1753	McDugall, John	N	Misc.1.362
1793	McElroy, Allen	K	----
1790	McElvain, Andrew, Jr.	S	A87.174/5
1780	McElvain, James	S	A87.191
1796	McEntire, Rachel	N	O.144
1739	McFarlan, Edward	N	Misc.1.357
1760	McFarland, Alexander	K	K.226
1769	McFarlen, John	K	L.67
1791	McFarley, William	S	A87.164
1798	McFerson, Robert	N	O.365
1799	McGarvey, William	N	O.514
1768	McGeah, Hugh	K	L.47
1783	McGear, Mary	K	L.272
1765	McGear, Michael	K	L.3
1791	McGee, Mary	S	A87.167
1787	McGloughlin, Henry	K	M.165
1796	McGonigal, Robert	K	N.128/9
1729	McGoon, James	K	G.32/3
1765	McGuire, Elizabeth	K	L.2
1763	McIlhenney, Alexander	K	K.321
1789	McIlvain, Andrew	S	D.235/7
1754	McIlvain, James	S	B.82/6
1784	McIlvain, James	S	D.38
1793	McIlvain, James	S	A87.193
1891	McIlvain, James Mills	S	A87.196
1784	McIlvain, Mills	S	A88.1/2
1789	McIlvain, Shepherd	S	A85.5
1785	McIlvain, William	S	A88.6
1726	McIlvaine (Muckelvane, McCalvane), Andrew	S	A.206/7
1748	McInteer, Samuel	N	G.191
1789	McIntier, Robert	N	N.37
1788	McKean, Thomas	N	N.161
1782	McKean, William	N	L.258
1793	McKee, Andrew	N	N.358
1789	McKee, Leonard	N	N.25
1734	McKee, Thomas	K	H.85

1747	McKell, Elizabeth	K	I.180
1738	McKemmy, Alexander	K	H.154
1703	McKenny, Edmund	K	B.49
1744	McKenny, Edward	K	I.94
1756	McKenny, Eleazer	K	K.138
1759	McKenny, Eleazer	K	A32.215
1755	McKenny, John	K	K.115
1784	McKim, Thomas	N	M.20
1740	McKinley (McGinnely), Daniel	K	I.30/31
1796	McKInley, John	N	O.185
1784	McKinney, William	N	H&I.252
1765	McKlehatan, Patrick	K	L.8
1766	McKleway (McElvain), Francis	K	L.17
1741	McKlue, James	K	I.60
1769	McKnight, Robert	N	H&I.252
1770	McKnown (McKaine), John	K	L.75
1734	McKracken, Daniel	K	A33.59
1792	McLane, Moses	K	N.284
1749	McLane (McCleane), Selena	K	I.267
1775	McLaughlin, Elizabeth	N	K.253
1788	McLonen, Agnes	N	N.10
1778	McLonen, Jannet	N	L.75
1794	McMechen, David	N	O.18
1734	McMillan, James	K	H.79
1741	McMillan, William	K	I.37
1785	McMorris, John	N	M.146
1751	McMullan, Margaret	N	Misc.1.360
1784	McMullen, James	K	M.30/2
1792	McMurphy, Alexander	N	N.249
1798	McMurphy, Archibald	N	O.327
1785	McMurphy, Robert	N	M.102
1759	McMurry, William	K	A32.215
1742	McNatt, John	K	I.71
1788	McNeill, James	S	A88.13
1754	McNeill (McNaill), James	S	B.69/71
1783	McNeill, William	S	A88.15
1771	McNitt, Jane	K	L.104
1789	McSparon, Archibald	K	M.205
1792	McSparron, Archibald	K	N.27&33
1793	McSparron, Meriam	K	N.49/50
1760	McSparrow, John	K	K.239

1772	McVay, Davis	K	L.113
1786	McVay, Denis	K	M.122
1786	McVay, John	N	M.226
1749	McWhirtor, Hugh	N	G.372
1748	McWhorty, Andrew	K	I.204
1786	McWilliam, Richard	N	M.197
1784	McWilliam, Stephen	N	M.25

- M -

1748	Maccay, Robert	N	G.142
1725	Macedo, James	K	F.5
1799	Macey, Daniel	K	N.245
1796	Macey (Massy), John	K	N.149
1783	Macey, Mary	K	L.273
1753	Macey, Thomas	K	K.65
1790	Mack, Esther	N	N.150
1732	Mackadow (McAdow), William	K	H-26
1785	Macklen, Thomas	S	D.93/4
1786	Macklin, Rachel	S	D.109
1708	Macknab, Joseph	S	A.63/4
1776	Macknath, William	K	L.183
1691	Mackony (McAnthony), John	N	Misc.1.348
1748	Macky, John	N	G.237
1796	Macy, Thomas	K	N.151
1756	Maddin, Patrick	K	K.127
1773	Maddox, Alexander	K	L.132
1789	Maddox, Lazarus	S	A86.20
1784	Maeslander, Peter	N	A.62
1757	Maffett, John	K	K.169
1787	Maffett, John	K	M.1354
1787	Maffett, Robert	K	M.135
1794	Magair, Mary	K	A33.67
1797	Magee, Benjamin	S	A86.21
1756	Mahanna, John	K	K.142
1727	Mahon, John	K	F.29
1790	Mair, Janet	K	M.228/9
1747	Makkary, Daniel	N	G.58
1784	Manering, William	K	M.28
1748	Manin, John	K	I.206

1741	Maning, John	K	I.42/3
1708	Mankin, Richard	N	B.166
1715	Mankin, Richard	N	C.27
1769	Manlove, Absalom	K	L.67/8
1782	Manlove, Ann	K	L.230
1797	Manlove, Asa	K	N.182
1772	Manlove, Ebenezer	K	L.120
1760	Manlove, Emanuel (Amanuel)	K	K.236
1732	Manlove, Ephraim	K	H.57/8
1695	Manlove, George	K	A.14
1765	Manlove, George	K	L.6
1766	Manlove, George	K	L.11/12
1787	Manlove, George	S	A86.33
1799	Manlove, George	K	N.237/8
1770	Manlove, John	K	L.76
1721	Manlove, Jonathan	K	D.41
1777	Manlove, Jonathan	K	L.195/6
1727	Manlove, Joseph	K	F.32,33&36
1708	Manlove, Luke	K	C.84/5
1755	Manlove, Luke	K	K.118
1770	Manlove, Magdalene	S	B.406/7
1743	Manlove, Manuel	S	A.345/7
1772	Manlove, Manuel	S	A86.40
1718	Manlove, Mark	S	A86.41
1720	Manlove, Mark	K	D.20
1749	Manlove, Mark	K	K.18/19
1735	Manlove, Matthew	K	H.115/7
1743	Manlove, Matthew	K	I.53
1773	Manlove, Matthew	K	L.147/8
1734	Manlove, Samuel	K	H.53
1775	Manlove, Sarah	K	L.161
1740	Manlove, Susannah	K	I.34
1797	Manlove, Tredwell	K	N.188
1694	Manlove, William	K	A.8
1730	Manlove, William	K	H.6
1761	Manlove, William	K	K.260
1748	Manlove, William	K	I.226
1760	Mann, William, Sr.	K	K.219
1792	Mannering, William	K	N.27/8
1779	Manning, James	K	L.209
1794	Mansfield, Edward	K	N.95

1790	Mansfield, Thomas	K	M.247
1773	Manship, George	K	L.127
1773	Manship, George	K	L.148
1777	Manson, James	N	K.336
1769	Manson, William	K	L.51
1769	Manson, William	K	L.65
1685	Mansur, John	K	AM2013.59
1793	Manwaring, Elizabeth	K	N.56
1760	Manwaring, Richard	K	K.243
1794	Manwaring, Richard	K	M.89/90
1795	Many, Francis	K	N.108
1779	Mardock, Michael	N	L.129
1793	Maree, John	K	N.47
1720	Marim, Charles	K	D.33
1781	Marim, Charles	K	L.245
1755	Marim, John	K	K.113/4
1752	Marin, Thomas	K	K.56
1795	Mariner, Gilbert	S	E.37/8
1768	Mariner, Richard	S	B.352/4
1773	Mariner, Sarah	S	A86.76/7
1748	Mariner, Thomas, Jr.	S	A.398/9
1749	Mariner, Thomas	S	A.410/1
1752	Mariner, William	S	A.410/1
1772	Mariner, William	S	A66.88/9
1777	Marker, Philip	K	L.189
1794	Marley, Abraham	K	N.80
1793	Marra, Catharine	N	N.373
1717	Marrarty, Mary	N	C.91
1747	Marret, Mark	K	I.179
1740	Marrett, Zachariah	K	I.29
1784	Marriner, Nathaniel	S	A86.63
1784	Marriner, Richard	S	A86.71
1777	Marriner, Thomas	S	C.112/14
1786	Marriner, William	S	D.114
1773	Marsatt, Isaac	K	L.140
1795	Marsatt, Joseph	K	N.129/30
1708	Marsh, Hugh	N	Misc.1.349
1684	Marsh, Paul	S	AM2013.37
1725	Marsh, Peter	S	A.199/200
1769	Marsh, Peter	S	B.375/9
1746	Marsh, Robert	N	G.149

1757	Marshall, David	K	A33.202/3
1759	Marshall, Edward	K	K.300
1778	Marshall, Eleanor	N	L.65
1734	Marshall, George	K	H.84
1777	Marshall, William	N	L.86
1739	Martain, James	K	H.157
1725	Marten, Charles	K	F.4
1743	Martin, James	S	A.388/9
1729	Martin, George	K	G.27/8
1794	Martin, James	S	A86.146
1774	Martin, John	N	K.159
1775	Martin, Josias	S	C.6-8
1758	Martin, Mary	K	K.182
1782	Martin, Mary	N	L.269
1761	Martin, Patrick	K	K.259
1750	Martin, William	K	K.43/4
1796	Marvel, David	S	E.69/70
1786	Marvel, Joseph	S	D.123/4
1795	Marvel, Philip, Sr.	S	E.36/7
1791	Marvel, Rachel	S	D.318/9
1794	Marvel, Thomas	S	E.79
1767	Marydith, Robert	K	L.37
1791	Mason, Carman	K	M.260
1791	Mason, Catharine	K	M.276
——	Mason, Elias	S	A87.37/9
1792	Mason, Jacob	K	N.16
1786	Mason, Joseph, Sr.	K	M.90/1
1743	Mason, Isaac	K	A33.230/1
1779	Mason, Isaac	K	L.208/9
1737	Mason, Mary	K	H.145
1769	Mason, Mary	K	L.65
1732	Mason, Michael	K	H.57/8
1794	Mason, Richard	K	N.74
1708	Mason, William	S	A.66/7
1750	Mason, William	K	K.27
1797	Mason, William	K	N.279
1798	Massey, Absolam	S	A87.45
1779	Massey, Daniel	S	C.211/3
1795	Massey, Hannah	K	N.134
——	Massey, Joseph, Sr.	S	C.314/5
1794	Massey, Joshua	K	N.96

1787	Massey, Levin	S	D.140
1767	Massey, Nathan	K	L.38
1755	Massey, Thomas	S	B.96/7
1794	Masten, Gilbert	K	N.85
1778	Masten, John	S	C.179/80
1797	Masten, John	K	N.183
1772	Mastin, William	K	L.106
1776	Mastin, William	K	L.179
1719	Mathews, Hugh	K	D.16
1786	Mathews, John	K	M.104
1701	Mathews, Samuel	K	B.43
1708	Mathewson, Anrew	K	B.71
1683	Mathysen, Pelle	N	A.62
1777	Matthews, John	N	K.382
1777	Matthews, James	N	K.360
1792	Matthews, James	N	N.242
1775	Mawah, Robert	S	C.3/4
1787	Mawhorter, Hughey	N	L.420
1773	Maxfield, William	K	L.127/8
1798	Maxwell, Bedwell	K	N.215
1758	Maxwell, Elinor	K	K.178
1695	Maxwell, James	K	B.37
1755	Maxwell, James	K	K.121
1771	Maxwell, James	K	A34.85
1769	Maxwell, Jean	K	L.65
1783	Maxwell, John	K	L.271
1760	Maxwell, John	S	B.214/6
----	Maxwell, Mark	K	M.129
1760	Maxwell, Mary	K	K.229
1798	Maxwell, Nimrod	S	A87.88
1751	Maxwell, Robert	K	K.38
1769	Maxwell, Robert	K	L.66/7
1787	Maxwell, Robert	N	M.235
1738	Maxwell, William	K	H.154
1739	Maxwell, William	K	I.11/12
1753	Maxwell, William	K	K.87
1761	Maxwell, William	K	K.264
1782	May, Ann	S	A87.90
1721	May, John	S	A.308/9
1782	May, Jonathan	S	A87.95
1721	May, Thomas, Jr.	S	A.155/7

1725	May, Thomas	S	A.200/2
1777	May, Thomas	S	C.78/80
1792	May, Thomas	N	N.253
1797	Meads, John	S	A88.16
1798	Means, Hugh	N	O.356
1776	Mecottor, William	S	C.28/9
1756	Medcalf (Metcalf), John	K	K.144
1708	Medcalfe, Thomas	N	B.206
1783	Meeks, Joseph	K	M.5
1785	Meers, Robert	N	M.154
1791	Megee, Samuel	S	A88.22
1774	Melchop, George	K	L.151
1749	Meldrom, John	N	G.373
1793	Meldrum, Robert	N	N.347
1795	Meldrum, Sarah	N	O.55
1773	Mellogue, Samuel	K	L.130
1774	Mellowchop, George	K	L.151
1789	Melony, Richard	S	A88.29
1786	Melony, Susanna	S	D.99
1798	Melson, Daniel	S	E.189/90
1785	Melson, John	S	A88.45
1780	Melson, Joseph	S	C.225/6
1791	Melson, William	S	A90.145
1774	Melven, Edmond	K	L.158
1774	Melven, John	K	L.158
1751	Melvin, Edmund	K	K.45/6
1772	Melvin, Phebe	K	L.113
1793	Melvin, Solomon	K	N.64/5
1797	Mendelhall, Benjamin	N	O.226
1749	Mendinhall, Joseph	N	G.348
1774	Menshall, Samuel	K	L.157
1773	Mercer, John	N	K.85
1793	Mercer, Robert	N	N.313
1790	Mercer, Stephen	K	M.246
1799	Merchant, John	K	N.234
1741	Merchant, William	K	I.57
1767	Merchant, William	K	L.38
1795	Meredith, Jacob	K	N.126
1748	Meredith, Job	K	I.230/1
1793	Meredith, Job	K	N.56
1767	Meredith, John	K	L.38

1796	Meredith, Jonathan	K	N.144
1796	Meredith, Joseph	K	N.138
1796	Meredith, Joseph	K	N.137
1775	Meredith, Joshua	K	L.176
1786	Meredith, Levy	K	M.127
1785	Meredith, Luff	K	M.52
1796	Meredith, Martha	K	N.147
1796	Meredith, Nathan	k	N.142
1768	Meredith, Robert	K	L.49
1782	Meredith, Ruth	K	L.231
1776	Meredith, Samuel	K	L.180
1773	Meredith, Wheelor	K	L.144
1797	Meredith, William	K	N.189
1795	Meredith, William	K	N.122
1784	Meres, Andrew	K	M.29
1780	Merick, Sarah	S	A88.71
1721	Meredith, Rees	N	C.341
1775	Meroney, William	K	L.175/6
1787	Merrick, Isaav	K	M.128
1786	Merriss, John	N	M.215
1762	Merydith, Job	K	K.278/9
1775	Messex (Mezicks), Julien	K	A34.230
1781	Messick, George	S	C.250/3
1798	Messick, George	S	A88.128
1779	Messick, Isaac	S	C.331/2
1788	Messick, Obediah	S	A88.128
1759	Metcalfe, Richard	S	B.173/6
1792	Methvinm, Mary	S	D.378
1784	Metten, William	K	M.21
1710	Middleton, James	N	B.227
1798	Middleton, James	S	A88.147
1772	Middleton, John	K	L.121
1721	Miers, John	S	A.148/50
1750	Miers, John	S	A.408/10
1753	Miers, Margery	S	B.57/9
1729	Miers, Mary	S	A.236/7
1775	Miers, Thomas	K	L.169
1797	Mifflin, Andesiak	K	N.169
1787	Mifflin, Benjamin	S	D.145
1796	Mifflin, Mathew	K	N.148
1797	Mifflin, Matthew	K	N.169

1799	Mifflin, Sarah	S	E.198
1790	Mifflin, Walker	K	M.260
1799	Mifflin, Warner	S	N.224/5
1787	Milby, Levin	S	D.155
1779	Milby, Elizabeth	S	C.187
1796	Mileham, Harmon	K	N.144
1798	Mileham, Maryann	K	A35.55
1772	Mileham, Samuel	K	L.113
1784	Mileham, Samuel	K	M.30
1795	Miles, Catherine	N	O.77
1797	Miles, James	N	O.247
1773	Millaway, Joseph	K	L.127
1777	Miller, Alexander	N	K.333
1795	Miller, Andrew	N	O.61
1795	Miller, Andrew	N	O.90
1778	Miller, Bertha	N	L.78
1793	Miller, Conrod	K	N.39/40
1790	Miller, Isaac	N	N.136
1749	Miller, James	N	G.357
1795	Miller, James	K	N.187
1737	Miller, John	K	H.137
1777	Miller, John	K	L.188
1794	Miller, John	K	N.86
1782	Miller, John	S	A88.192
1750	Miller, John	K	K.25
1791	Miller, John	K	N.3
1747	Miller, Joseph	K	I.176
1798	Miller, Joseph	K	N.216
——	Miller, Killen	K	L.170
1729	Miller, Mary	N	Misc.1.353
1780	Miller, Joseph	S	C.323/7
1778	Miller, Peter	S	A88.199
1791	Miller, Peter, Jr.	K	M.261
1767	Miller, Rebecca	K	L.38
1760	Miller, Robert	K	K.233
1787	Miller, Robert	N	M.275
1733	Miller, Robert	S	A.256/8
1793	Miller, Sarah	K	N.60/61
1745	Miller, William	K	I.118
1689	Millington, John	S	AM2013.104
1798	Millis, Ann	K	M.182

1785	Millis, John	K	M.61
1799	Millis, Stephen	K	N.248
1798	Millman, Jonathan	S	A89.5
1785	Millman, Mary	S	D.90/2
1782	Millman, Michael	S	A89.9
1773	Milloway, Ann	K	L.127
1773	Milloway, John	K	L.127
1751	Mills, Edward	S	B.4/5
1749	Mills, George	K	K.7
1745	Mills, John	K	I.110
1703	Mills, Mary	K	B.49
1762	Mills, Sarah	K	K.289/90
1799	Milly, Zadok	S	A88.182
1793	Milman, Peter	S	D.406/7
1775	Milner, William	N	K.211
1771	Milvin, Ann	K	L.97
1798	Milvin, David	K	N.199
1799	Milway, James	K	N.225/6
1796	Minner, Edward	S	E.65/6
1791	Minner, Peter	K	N.5
1797	Minner, Peggy	S	A89.22
1797	Minner, Priscilla	S	A89.23
1777	Minors, Charles	S	A89.24
1799	Minors, George	K	N.231/2
1783	Minshall, Jane	K	L.275
1685	Mitchall, Richard	K	AM2013.52
1786	Mitchell, Catherine	N	M.202
1799	Mitchell, George	S	F.320/3
1799	Mitchell, George	K	N.231/2
1790	Mitchell, James	S	D.318/9
1780	Mitchell, Randal	S	A89.64
1796	Mitchell, Thomas	K	N.148
1774	Mitten, James	S	A89.84
1695	Moalston, Thomas	S	AM2013.172/3
1785	Moffett, John	K	M.87/88
1790	Moleston, William	K	M.255/6
1740	Molleston, Ann	K	I.23/4
1762	Molleston, Henry	K	K.280
1779	Molleston, Henry	K	L.209
1760	Molleston, Jemima	K	K.245/6
1709	Molleston, John	K	B.78

1775	Molleston, Jonathan	K	L.162
1782	Molleston, Sarah	K	L.252
1737	Molleston, William	K	H.142/3
1766	Molleston, William	K	L.12
1772	Molleston, William	K	L.120
1792	Molleston, William	K	N.19
1798	Molleston, William	K	N.210
1799	Molleston, William	K	A35.223/4
1759	Molliston, Mary	S	B.176/7
1727	Molony, Loholen	K	G.3
1728	Monro, William	N	Misc.1.352
1762	Montgomery, Alexander	K	K.301
1785	Montgomery, Ann	N	M.87
1799	Montgomery, James	N	O.458
1778	Montgomery, Martha	N	L.38
1779	Montgomery, Robert	N	L.125
1794	Montgomery, Thomas	N	O.37
1799	Montgomery, Thomas	N	O.508
1789	Montgomery, William	K	M.203
1764	Moor, Abraham	K	K.333/4
1777	Moor, Henniritta	K	L.187/8
1751	Moor, Henry	K	K.42
1735	Moor, Jean	N	Misc.1.355
1767	Moor, Martha	K	L.27
1784	Moore, Alexander	N	M.41
1785	Moore, David	K	M.51
1793	Moore, David	S	E.167
1789	Moore, David	S	A89.96
----	Moore, Elisha	S	D.117
1748	Moore, George	N	G.222
1731	Moore, Henry	K	H.112&115
1784	Moore, Jacob	S	D.48/50
1748	Moore, James	K	I.208
1756	Moore, James	K	K.129
1783	Moore, James	S	A89.119
1761	Moore, Jane (Jean)	K	K.253/4
1797	Moore, Jesse	N	O.208
1747	Moore, John	K	I.260/1
1758	Moore, John	K	K.186
1776	Moore, John	K	L.178
1779	Moore, John, Jr.	K	A36.56/8

1787	Moore, John	N	M.285
1795	Moore, John	N	O.116
1783	Moore, Joseph	K	L.269
1783	Moore., Joshua, Sr.	S	C.289/91
1794	Moore, Margaret	K	N.89
1721	Moore, Mordecai	N	N.57
1788	Moore, Nicholas	N	N.5
1778	Moore, Peter	N	L.114
1796	Moore, Rebecca	N	O.150
1734	Moore, Richard	N	N.63
1748	Moore, Richard	N	G.178
1742	Moore, Richard	K	I.60
1788	Moore, Robert	K	M.181
1790	Moore, Robert	S	A89.138
1761	Moore, Samuel	N	H&I.25
1789	Moore, Samuel	N	N.59
1773	Moore, Samuel	K	L.132/3
1770	Moore, Samuel	K	L.79
1784	Moore, Samuel	K	L.271
1791	Moore, Sarah	S	A89.129
1798	Moore, Sarah	K	N.191
1747	Moore, Thomas	K	I.197
1798	Moore, Thomas	K	N.190
1796	Moore, Thomas	K	N.151
1790	Moore, Thomas	N	N.103
1793	Moore, Thomas	S	D.386/7
1779	Moore, William	S	C.253/4
1783	Moore, William	S	D.32/3
1785	Moore, William, Sr.	S	E.18/19
1792	Moore, William	N	N.268
1743	Moran, Andrew	K	I.73/4
1748	Morey, Thomas	K	A37.34
1754	Morgan, Brian	K	A36.128
1789	Morgan, Daniel	K	M.208
1692	Morgan, David	K	A.5
1793	Morgan, David	K	N.35
1693	Morgan, Edward	S	AM2013.141/2
1727	Morgan, Elizabeth	K	F.26
1760	Morgan, Elizabeth	K	K.238
1722	Morgan, George	K	D.62
1769	Morgan, George	K	L.67

1755	Morgan, George	K	K.117
1770	Morgan, Jacob	K	A36.150
1775	Morgan, Jacob	K	L.176
1748	Morgan, James	K	I.250
1726	Morgan, John	K	F.12
1747	Morgan, David	K	I.182
1794	Morgan, John	N	N.403
1798	Morgan, John	S	A89.196
1727	Morgan, Joshua	K	F.31
1775	Morgan, MarmadukeK	K	L.161
1755	Morgan, Martha	K	K.121
1785	Morgan, Mary	N	M.169
1726	Morgan, Richard	K	F.13
1784	Morgan, Robert	K	M.21
1779	Morgan, Sarah	N	L.171
1794	Morgan, Thomas	K	N.82
1744	Morgan, William	K	I.102
1748	Morgan, William	K	I.213/4
1781	Morgan, William	K	M.96
1725	Morphee, Nicholas	K	F.2
1770	Morris, Aaron	K	L.73
1764	Morris, Absolem	K	K.354
1790	Morris, Absolem	K	M.250
1766	Morris, Bevins	S	B.302/4
1785	Morris, Bevins	S	A90.18
1759	Morris, Cornelius	K	K.207
1782	Morris, Daniel	S	C.321/3
1794	Morris, Dennis	S	D.415/6
1799	Morris, Elizabeth	K	N.248
1796	Morris, Ezekiah (Hezekiah)	S	E.79/80
1745	Morris, Frederick	K	I.114
1790	Morris, George	S	A90.52
1789	Morris, Isaac	S	A90.55
1796	Morris, Isaac	S	E.73/4
1790	Morris, Jacob	S	A90.63/4
1747	Morris, James	K	I.172/3
1750	Morris, James	N	G.389
1783	Morris, James	K	M.124/5
1789	Morris, James	K	M.203
1795	Morris, Jeminah	K	N.128
1792	Morris, Jeremiah	K	N.16

1772	Morris, Jeremiah	K	L.121
1789	Morris, Jesse	K	M.195
1731	Morris, John	K	H.22&47
1749	Morris, John	N	G.331
1790	Morris, John	S	A90.75
1794	Morris, John	S	A90.76
1795	Morris, John	S	A90.77/8
1792	Morris, John	K	N.18
1773	Morris, John	K	L.134
1791	Morris, John	K	N.5
1776	Morris, Joseph	K	L.185
1796	Morris, Joshua	K	N.157
1799	Morris, Nehemiah	S	A90.125
1784	Morris, Richard	K	M.27
1779	Morris, Samuel	N	L.167
1793	Morris, Samuel, Jr.	K	N.50
1798	Morris, Samuel	K	N.223
1799	Morris, Samuel	K	N.248
1791	Morris, Sarah	K	N.2/3
1793	Morris, Susanna	K	N.39/40
1794	Morris, Susannah	K	N.82
1793	Morris, Tamer	S	D.404/5
1774	Morris, Theophilus, Rev.	K	L.149
1725	Morris, William	K	N.167
1774	Morris, William	K	L.149
1794	Morris, William	K	N.79
1797	Morris, William	S	E.151/3
1791	Morris, William	S	A90.145
1793	Morrison, Joseph	S	A90.163/4
1745	Morriss, George	N	Misc.1.358
1778	Morrow, Philip	N	L.84
1786	Morrow, William	N	M.188
1790	Morton, Christianah	N	N.149
1795	Morton, Ebenezer	N	O.48
1785	Morton, Mathias	N	M.125
1771	Morton, Matthias, Sr.	N	M.336
1789	Morton, Robert	N	N.39
1704	Morton, William	K	B.51/2
1785	Mortonson, Joseph	N	M.140
1798	Mortonson, Regina	N	O.415
1795	Mosley, Absolem	S	E.33/4

1750	Mott, Adam	K	K.6/8
1762	Mott, Richbell	K	K.285
1766	Mott, Richard	K	L.21
1692	Mott, Samuel	K	A.3
1688	Mouleston, Thomas	S	AM2013.98
1723	Mounce, Peter	N	Misc.1.353
1786	Mountford, Samuel	S	D.113/4
1785	Muldroh, Andrew	N	M.152
1792	Muldroh, David	N	N.275
1784	Muldroh, Hugh	N	L.437
1749	Mullen, Ann	K	K.8
1792	Mullen (Mutton), William	K	N.15
1778	Mullet, Thomas	K	L.201
1769	Mullett, William	K	L.59
1743	Mullin, James	K	I.72
1729	Mullinex, Penelope	S	A.214/5
1762	Mullinex, William	S	B.250
1702	Mulroney, John	K	B.44
1788	Mumford, Solomon	K	M.168
1776	Muncey, Levey	K	L.179
1738	Muncy, Francis	K	I.3
1758	Munt, Mary	K	K.188/9
1775	Munt, Robert	K	L.171
1770	Murphey, David	K	L.85
1774	Murphey, Esther	K	L.154
1771	Murphey, Thomas	K	L.100
1782	Murphey, Thomas	K	L.232
1760	Murphey, William	K	K.237/8
1793	Murphy, Andrew	K	N.52
1750	Murphy, Archibald	N	G.450
1796	Murphy, Charles	K	N.141
1780	Murphy, Elizabeth	K	L.223
1756	Murphy, Henry	K	K.149
1776	Murphy, John	K	L.181
1797	Murphy, John	K	N.179
1799	Murphy, Margaret	K	L.213
1760	Murphy, Sarah	K	K.241/2
1772	Murphy, Thomas	N	K.37
1796	Murphy, William	K	N.149
1720	Murphly, John	S	A.135/6
1756	Murray, Bryan	K	K.148/9

1795	Murray, James	S	E.21/22
1798	Murray, John	S	A91.16
1778	Murry, Jean	K	L.207
1760	Mustard, John	S	B.203/7
1789	Myers, Stephen	K	M.203

- N -

1787	Nash, Richard	N	M.263
1796	Naudian, Arnold	N	O.182
1766	Naudian, Charles	N	I.364
1794	Naudian, Cornelius	N	N.438
1749	Naudian, Elias	N	G.350
1743	Naws, Edward	S	A.339/41
1787	Neal, Jonathan	K	M.147
1794	Neal, Margaret	S	E.145/6
1793	Needham, Agatha	K	N.57
1756	Needham, Daniel	K	K.154
1769	Needham, Phebee	K	L.53
1795	Needles, Sarah	K	N.121
1791	Needles, Thomas	K	N.10
1795	Needles, Thomas	K	N.121
1787	Neill, Bethia	S	D.150/1
1782	Neill, Hugh	K	L.266/7
1781	Neill, John	S	C.263/5
1748	Nelson, Thomas	N	G.107
1700	Nerring, John Williams	N	Misc.1.366
1775	Nesbit, Mary	N	K.275
1773	Nesbit, William	N	K.71
1742	Nevin, David	N	Misc.1.369
1751	Nevin, Robert	N	G.467
1747	Nevin, William	N	———
1776	New, John	K	L.183
1767	New, Mary	K	L.25
1767	New, Robert	K	L.25
1773	New, William	K	L.125
———	Newbold, Francis, Jr.	S	A91.64
1790	Newbold, John	S	A91.67/8
1789	Newbold, Margaret	S	D.226
1792	Newbold, Thomas	S	A91.70

1792	Newbold, Thomas	S	A91.80
1777	Newbold, William	S	C.104/5
1757	Newcomb, Hester	S	B.148/50
1790	Newcomb, John	K	M.260
1708	Newcomb, William	S	A.68/9
1771	Newel, Charles	N	Misc.1.363
1739	Newell, John	K	I.14
1759	Newell, John	K	K.216
17454	Newell, Joseph	K	I.116
1744	Newell, Thomas	K	I.105
1748	Newell, William	K	I.258/9
1768	Newlin, Joseph	N	H&I.237
1775	Newlin, Pheby	N	K.207
1743	Newnam (Newman), Edward	K	I.86
1799	Newson, Joseph	K	N.238
1733	Newton, George	K	H.70
1703	Newton, Henry	K	B.49
1724	Nicheson (Nickerson), Jeremiah	K	D.67
——	Nicholas, Samuel	K	L.25
1731	Nicholds, Samuel	K	H.18
1763	Nichols, Edmund, Sr.	K	K.320/1
1798	Nichols (Nickels), Joseph	S	E.156
1774	Nichols, Samuel	N	K.170
1794	Nichols, Thomas	N	N.421
1796	Nicholls, Nehemiah	S	E.70
1790	Nicholls, Sarah	S	D.270/1
1708	Nicholson, John	K	B.71
1760	Nickerson, George	K	K.222/3
1756	Nickerson, Joshua	K	K.132/3
1798	Nickols, Daniel	N	O.350
1770	Nicoills, Joseph	K	L.87
1796	Nicolls, Levin	S	A91.95
1794	Nicoson, Abraham	K	N.80
1796	Niles, Samuel	N	O.174
1748	Nillson, Gerard	N	G.117
1796	Nixon, Abraham	K	A38.7
1784	Nixon, Anne	K	M.29
1796	Nixon, Charles	K	N.151
1775	Nixon, James	N	K.244
1751	Nixon, Joseph	K	K.36
1779	Nixon, Thomas	K	L.215/6

1797	Nixon, Thomas, Sr.	K	N.179
1793	Nock, Daniel	K	N.52
1773	Nock, Ezekiel	K	L.145
1724	Nock, Thomas	K	D.68
1782	Nock, Thomas	K	L.254/5
1799	Nock, Thomas	K	N.245/6
1794	Noel, Edward	K	N.89
1750	Norman, Isabel	N	G.449
1747	Norman, Thomas	N	G.60
1788	North, Margaret	K	M.181
1781	North, Richard	K	L.225/6
1784	North, Thomas	K	M.23
1781	North, William	K	L.230
1796	Norwood, Henry	S	A91.115
1786	Norwood, Nathyan	S	A91.116
1796	Nottingham, Chloe	S	A91.117
1750	Nowell, Francis	N	G.451
1730	Nowell, George	K	H.13
1788	Nowell, Henry	K	M.173
1729	Nowell, Sarah	K	H.2
1780	Noxon, Sarah	N	L.186
1748	Nugin, Thomas	N	G.198
1759	Numbers, James	K	K.204
1794	Numbers, Jane	K	N.79
1775	Numbers, John	K	L.176
1790	Numbers, John	K	M.213
1768	Numbers, Peter	K	L.50
1789	Numbers, Sarah	K	M.202
1789	Numbers, Susannah	K	M.209
1775	Numez, Daniel	S	C.1/2
1785	Nuttall, Adam	N	M.107
1789	Nutter, Christopher	S	A91.126/7
1702	Nutter, John	S	A.36/9
1725	Nutter, John	S	A.319/20
1795	Nutter, John	S	A91.131
1795	Nutter, Robert	S	A91.133
1734	Nys, Johannia	K	H.48

- O -

1792	Oakey, Jeangull	S	D.142
1749	Oakford, John	K	K.6/7
1684	Oalson, Lassee	N	———
1770	Oborn, Daniel	N	Misc.1.382
1754	O'Bryan, Dennis	N	Misc.1.379
1747	O'Callaghan, Benjamin	K	I.187/8
1785	O'Day, Henry	S	A91.141
1727	Offley, Caleb	N	Misc.1.373
1755	Offley, David	K	K.119
1716	Offley, Hadahiah	N	C.54
1767	Offley, Michael	N	I.381
1734	Ogle, Elizabeth	N	Misc.1.376
1789	Ogle, George	K	M.213
1793	Ogle, George	K	M.213
1734	Ogle, James	N	Misc.1.378
1771	Ogle, Thomas	N	Misc.1.384
1785	Ogle, Thomas	N	M.119
1699	Ohagitha, Dennish	K	B.36
1786	O'Harra, Henry	N	M.189
1708	Oharrill, Thomas	K	B.70
1797	Oliver, Levi	S	E.139/41
1748	Olliett, Mary	K	I.252
1744	O'Neal, Conn.	K	I.84
1723	O'Neal, Neal	N	Misc.1.353
1789	Onions, Pearson	S	A91.163
1738	Onorton, John	S	A.290/3
1748	Orr, James	K	I.239
1741	O'Shaveling, Owen	N	Misc.1.379
1694	Otto, Wallraven	N	B.25
1779	Otwell, Curtis	S	B.192/201
1775	Otwell, rancis	S	B.559/60
1798	Otwell, William, Jr.	S	E.170/2
1776	Otwell, Urania	S	A91.180
1799	Owen, Ammon	K	N.249
1708	Owen, Lewes	N	Misc.1.371
1780	Owen, Owen	K	L.219
1780	Owen, William	K	L.219
1792	Owens, Amon	K	N.29
1775	Owens, David, Sr.	S	C.4/6

1796	Owens, Ishmael	K	N.143
1787	Owens, Paris	S	D.126
1754	Owens, Robert	N	Misc.1.380
1780	Owens, Robert	S	C.226/9
1791	Owens, Sarah	S	A92.22
1796	Owens, Sarah	K	N.145
1776	Owens, Thomas	N	K.311
1787	Owens, William	S	A92.214
1793	Ozburn, Eunice	K	N.50
1787	Ozburn, Mary	S	A92.31
1738	Ozburn, Mathew	S	A.295/7
1776	Ozburn, Richard	S	A92.33
1765	Ozburn, Thomas	S	B.280/2
1790	Ozburn, Thomas	S	D.319/20
1777	Ozier, John	N	L.51

- P -

1774	Packard, Ann	N	K.185
1774	Packard, Henry	N	K.191
1708	Page, Edward	S	A.65/6
1721	Pain, Fletcher	K	D.50
1725	Pain, John	K	F.9
1692	Palmatary, Robert	K	A.3
1748	Palmatary, Robert	K	I.247
1795	Palmatory, Allen	N	----
1790	Palmatry, Robert	K	M.223
1728	Palmer, Daniel	S	A.230/1
1773	Palmer, John	K	L.128
1780	Palmer, Joseph	S	C.234
1748	Paradue, John	K	I.235
1788	Paradue, Hannah	K	M.168
1759	Paradue, Stephen	K	K.217/8
1727	Pardee, Stephen	K	G.1
1779	Paremore, Matthew	S	A92.89
1683	Park, Edward	K	AM2013.9
1781	Park, John	K	L.230
1768	Park, Ann	K	L.49
1770	Parke, John	K	A39.15/17
1738	Parke, Sarah	K	I.84

1727	Parke, Theodore	K	A39.25/6
1759	Parke, Theodore	K	K.210/11
1766	Parke, Thomas	K	L.21&48
1792	Parke, Thomas	K	N.26
1783	Parker, Alice	S	D.28/9
1785	Parker, Anderson, Jr.	S	A92.53
1793	Parker, Anderson	S	D.388/90
1760	Parker, Anderson	S	B.211/4
1796	Parker, Eli	S	E.95/6
1799	Parker, Elinore	S	A92.182
1767	Parker, John	K	L.39
1784	Parker, John	S	A92.71
1785	Parker, John	S	D.112
1794	Parker, John	K	N.86
1719	Parker, Mathew	S	A.111/3
1694	Parker, Pella	N	A.65
1753	Parker, Peter	N	Misc.1.396
1784	Parker, Peter	S	A92.78
1762	Parker, Sarah	K	K.274/5
1769	Parker, Sarah	K	L.53
1750	Parker, Thomas	K	K.20/21
1773	Parker, Thomas	K	L.132
1788	Parker, Thomas	K	M.168
1798	Parker, Thomas	K	N.215
1797	Parker, William	K	N.173/4
1799	Parker, William	K	N.223
1775	Parkerson, Christopher	K	L.171
1787	Parkerson, Christopher	K	M.165
1775	Parkerson, Thomas	K	L.172
1751	Parkinson, John	N	Misc.1.394
1781	Parmacy, Robert	K	L.230
1796	Parmor (Parmer), Sheldon	S	E.96
1794	Parmore, Joseph	S	A92.86
1796	Parremore, Mary	S	A92.88
1789	Parremore, Patrick	S	A92.91
1698	Parry, William	K	A.23
1790	Parsons, Abraham	K	M.242
1785	Parsons, Jennet	K	M.53/4
1734	Parsons, John	S	A.274/5
1745	Parsons, John	K	I.119
1786	Parsons, Joseph	K	M.121

1790	Parsons, Martha	K	M.246
1790	Parsons, Michael	K	M.259
1793	Partridge, James	N	N.371
1725	Parvis, Richard	K	F.9
1685	Parvis, Robert	K	AM2013.44
1739	Parvis, William	K	H.156
1791	Parvis, William, Jr.	K	N.4
1778	Passmore, Abigail	N	L.47
1795	Passwaters, Richard	S	———
1797	Passwaters, William	S	E.116/17
1749	Paswater, James	K	K.43
1749	Paten, Andrew	K	I.199
1693	Patte, Richard	S	AM2013-A.141/5
1789	Patten, Matthew	N	M.8
1750	Patterson, Charles	N	G.458
1795	Patterson, Hugh	S	E.59
1750	Patterson, John	N	G.421
1788	Patterson, Robert	N	M.338
1785	Patterson, Samuel	N	M.114
1790	Patterson, William	N	N.120
1794	Patterson, William	N	O.4
1793	Pattison, Isaac	K	N.48
1792	Pattison (Patterson), John	K	N.25/26
1793	Pattison, John	K	N.48
1793	Pattison (Patterson), Rachel	K	N.43/44
1738	Patton, Eliner	K	I.2
1789	Patton, Mary	K	M.186
1783	Patton, Robert	K	M.15/16
1727	Paul, William Bunker	N	G.458
1786	Paulson, Andrew	N	M.205
1798	Paulson, Charles	N	O.311
1782	Paulson, John	N	L.286
1728	Payn, Samuel	K	G.21
1759	Payne (Pain), Thomas	K	K.199
1732	Paynter, John, Jr.	S	A.260/1
1793	Paynter, John	S	A92.123
1782	Paynter, Lemuel	S	A92.128
1694	Paynter, Richard	S	AM2013.166
1722	Paynter, Richard	S	A.162/3
1746	Paynter, Richard	S	A.372/3

1767 Paynter, Samuel S B.229/31
1795 Pearce, Benjamin N O.103
1792 Pearce, Charlotte N N.274
1776 Pearce, Isabella K L.183
1795 Pearce, Jacob K N.114
1794 Pearce, John K N.76
1776 Pearce, Joseph K L.181
1790 Pearce, William K M.227
1706 Pearl, Bryan N B.104
1788 Pearsen, Hannah K M.173
1796 Pearson, Elias K N.153
1757 Pearson, John K K.164
1796 Pearson, Joseph K N.153
1795 Pearson, Mary K N.120
1798 Pearson, Richard N O.331
1790 Pearson, Robert K M.228
1735 Pearson, Thomas N Misc.1.390
1746 Pearson, William K I.148
1793 Pearson, William N N.431
1761 Peasley, John K K.267
1798 Pedrick, Joshua N O.410
1789 Peery, Aaron S A92.174/6
1789 Peery, William N N.22
1789 Peirce, Joseph N N.11
1792 Pell, David K N.15
1766 Pell, Haley N Misc.1.404
1786 Pell, Haley N N.181
1795 Pemberton, James K N.128
1734 Pemberton, Joseph S A.273/4
1789 Penal, John K M.187
1796 Pendigrist, Patrick K N.147
1747 Penn, John K I.150/60
1747 Penn, John N G.1
1791 Pennell, John K A39.197/9
1788 Pennington, Benedict S A92.147
1778 Pennington, Mary N L.50
1748 Pennington, William K I.240/1
1784 Pennuel, William K M.20
1797 Penny, Arthur N O.292
1762 Penny, John K K.298/9
1797 Penrose, Mary N O.256

1779	Penton, Philip	S	A92.158
1794	Penton, Ranier	N	N.440
1720	Pepper, Richard	K	D.37
1729	Pepperlo, Joseph	S	A.491/2
1720	Perine, Thomas	K	D.37
1749	Perkins, Caleb	N	G.330
1707	Perkins, Joseph	N	——
1756	Perkins, Thomas	K	K.137
1796	Perkins, Thomas	K	N.160
1706	Penmain, Henry	K	B.56
1760	Perry, Charles	S	B.198/200
1795	Perry, George	K	N.129
1708	Perry, Rowland	S	A.65/6
1758	Perrymore, Philip	K	K.184/5
1789	Peterkin, John	K	M.202
1784	Peterkin, Rhoda	K	M.28/9
1775	Peterkin, Thomas	K	L.174/5
1747	Peteronsmith, Peter	N	Misc.1.393
1763	Peterson, Adam	K	A.40-15
1766	Peterson, Adam	N	H&I.32
1773	Peterson, Adam	N	K.97
1761	Peterson, Andrew	K	K.225
1780	Peterson, Andrew	K	L.221
1784	Peterson, Elizabeth	N	M.40
1720	Peterson, George	N	C.238
1794	Peterson, Grace	N	N.406
1766	Peterson, Hance	N	H&I.146
1795	Peterson, Henry	N	O.99
1788	Peterson, Peter	K	M.173
1694	Peterson, Thomas	K	A.10
1707	Peterson, Thomas	K	B.27
1785	Peterson, Veronica	N	M.176
1772	Petit, Laban	S	A.92
1772	Pettigrew, William	N	K.18
1797	Pettyjohn, Aaron	S	A92.194
1788	Pettyjohn, Hannah	S	D.201/2
1752	Pettyjohn, James, Sr.	S	B.23/7
1733	Pettyjohn, ?	S	A.263/5
1754	Pettyjohn, John	S	B.71/3
1782	Pettyjohn, John	S	A93.8
1751	Pettyjohn, Richard	S	A.429/31

1721 Pettyjohn, Thomas S A.152/3
1782 Pettyjohn, Thomas, Sr. S C.299/300
1749 Pettyjohn, William S A.403/5
1781 Pheady, Randolph K L.229
1798 Phillips, Benjamin S E.206/7
1731 Phillips, Hannah K H.19/20
1760 Phillips, Jacob S B.207/11
1728 Phillips, John K G.21
1729 Phillips, John K G.34/5
1772 Phillips, John, Sr. S K.21
1795 Phillips, John, Sr. S E.45/8
1798 Phillips, Sarah S E.185/7
1755 Phillips, Thomas N Misc.1.400
1749 Phillips, William K K.11
1790 Phillips, William, Sr. N N.108
1778 Phippen, Lott S A93.65
1793 Pickeral, Littleton K N.43
1774 Pickeral, William K L.153
1729 Pickerell, William K G.34/5
1775 Pickerell, Youell K L.162
1792 Pierce, Isaac N N.286
1795 Pierce, Jean K N.114
1793 Pierce, John N N.380
1786 Pierce, Jonathan S A93.73
1744 Pierce, Joseph K I.95
1782 Pierce, Joseph N L.357
1791 Pierce, Levi N N.188
1718 Pierce, Phillip N Misc.1.389
1744 Pierce, Robert K I.95
1792 Pierce (Piece), Timothy, Sr. N N.240
1774 Pierce, William S B.528/30
1793 Pierce, William K N.64
1745 Piles, James S A.373/4
1701 Piles, William S A.28/30
1733 Pindor, Alexander K H.42
1786 Piper, John S D.103/4
1776 Piper, Susannah N K.317
1795 Platt, Samuel, Jr. N O.110
1799 Platt, Samuel N O.434
1774 Pleasanton, David K L.152
1795 Pleasanton, David K N.118

1795	Pleasanton, Deborah	K	A40.104
1749	Pleasanton, John	K	K.88
1791	Pleasanton, Jonathan	K	M.264
1790	Pleasanton, Letitia	K	M.250
1795	Pleasanton, Letitia	K	N.118
1788	Pleasanton, Nathaniel	K	M.173
1788	Pleasanton, Nathaniel	K	A40.130
1795	Pleasanton, Rachel	K	N.118
1796	Plowman, Josiah	K	N.147
1727	Plum, George	N	Misc.1.399
1749	Poillion, John	K	A40.148
1749	Poition, Ann	K	K.3
1792	Polk, Avery	S	A93.105
1784	Polk, Charles	S	D.62
1795	Polk, Charles	S	E.53/4
1784	Polk, Clement	S	D.57/8
1796	Polk, Daniel	K	N.147
1796	Polk, Daniel	K	N.152
1798	Polk, Daniel	S	A93.113
1795	Polk, David	S	A93.115
1779	Polk (Pollock), David	S	A93.172
1799	Polk, Elizabeth	S	A93.116
1797	Polk, Emanuel (Manuel)	S	E.138/9
1791	Polk, Ephraim	S	D.343/4
1789	Polk, James	S	A93.122
1788	Polk, John	S	A93.127/8
1792	Polk, John	S	A93.129
1784	Polk, John	S	A93.124
1784	Polk, John	S	A93.125
1779	Polk (Pollock), John	S	C.205/9
1788	Polk, John	S	D.181/2
1790	Polk, Joshua	S	D.309/10
1777	Polk, Leah	S	A93.139
1797	Polk, Leah	S	E.119/20
1796	Polk, Margaret	K	N.151/2
1799	Polk, Maria	K	N.223
1799	Polk, Maria	K	N.245
1789	Polk, Mary	S	E.45
1792	Polk, Nelly	S	A93.149
1782	Polk, Roger	S	A93.150
1783	Polk, Sarah	S	A93.151

1794	Polk, William	S	A93.162
1784	Polk, William	S	A93.155
1789	Polk, William	S	D.197/99
1791	Polk, William	S	D.227/8
1797	Pollock, Margaret	S	A93.176/7
1782	Pollock (Polk), Priscilla	S	A93.178
1798	Polson, William	S	E.178
1719	Ponder, John	S	A.107/9
1787	Ponder, John	S	D.152/3
1794	Pool, Major	S	D.408
1788	Poole, William	N	M.329
1698	Pooll, William	N	B.73
1798	Poor, Henry	K	N.207/8
1772	Poor, Mary	S	B.532/4
1761	Pope, William	K	K.267
1784	Purter, Alexander	N	L.441
1751	Porter, David	N	G.456
1795	Porter, Johas	N	O.59
1763	Porter, John	N	Misc.1.401
1788	Porter, Mary	S	D.188
1766	Porter, Patrick	N	Misc.1.402
1693	Porter, Robert	K	A.5
1767	Porter, Robert	N	O.222
1781	Porter, Thomas	K	L.229
1775	Porter, William	K	L.161
1780	Porter, William	K	L.219/20
1774	Postles, Thomas	S	B.532/4
1742	Potter, Abraham	S	A.331/3
1789	Potter, Comfort	S	D.205/6
1785	Potter, Edmond	K	M.71
1747	Potter, James	K	I.174
1756	Potter, James	K	K.140/1
1780	Potter, James	K	L.215/6
1795	Potter, John	K	N.125
1749	Potter, Mary	K	K.11
1756	Potter, Parismus	K	K.140
1767	Paulson, Margaret	N	H&I.203
1720	Paulson, Paul	N	C.260
1748	Paulson, Peter	N	G.139
1771	Paulson, William	K	A41.21
1747	Poultney, Francis	K	A.41&22

1730	Pound, Samuel	K	H.8
1723	Powell, John	K	D.64
1782	Powell, John	K	L.264/5
1776	Powell, Joseph	K	L.177
1762	Powell, Nicholas	K	K.284
1791	Power, Abraha	K	N.1
1781	Paynter, John	S	C.265/6
1780	Paynter, Nathaniel	S	C.221/3
1776	Paynter, William	S	B.546/7
1781	Paynter, William	S	C.256/9
1761	Pratt, Dinah	K	K.258/9
1794	Pratt, Fredirec	K	N.88
1796	Pratt, George	K	N.150
1785	Pratt, Luke	K	M.52
1788	Pratt, Mary	K	M.173
1775	Pratt, Mary	K	L.161&320
1789	Pratt, Michael	N	N.47
1752	Pratt, Thomas	K	K.79
1772	Prettyman, Comfort	S	B.251/2
1777	Prettyman, Elizabeth	S	C.76/8
1767	Prettyman, Isaac	S	B.319/21
1799	Prettyman, John	S	E.249/50
1745	Prettyman, John	S	----
1724	Prettyman, John, Sr.	S	A.177/8
1784	Prettyman, Perry	S	A94.93
1721	Prettyman, Robert	S	A.154/5
1769	Prettyman, Robert	S	B.364/6
1792	Prettyman, Robert, Sr.	S	A94.101
1792	Prettyman, Robert	S	A94.102
1793	Prettyman, Robert	S	A94.103
1719	Prettyman, Thomas, Sr.	S	A.108/9
1762	Prettyman, Thomas	S	B.242/4
1765	Prettyman, Thomas	S	B.278/80
1790	Prettyman, Thomas	S	D.314/6
1772	Prettyman, William	S	B.350
1766	Prettyman, William	S	B.308/11
1748	Prettyman, William	S	A.400/2
1780	Prettyman, William	S	A94.126
1744	Price, Elizabeth	S	A.338/9
1786	Price, Elizabeth	S	A94.136
1778	Price, James	K	L.198

1746 Price, John K I.123/4
1776 Price, Joseph K L.178
1766 Price, Joseph, Jr. K L.18
1797 Price, Joseph K N.174
1786 Price, Magdalin S A94.138
1784 Price, Mary S A94.139
1793 Price, Mary N N.335
1796 Price, Sarah N O.169
1737 Price, Thomas S A.311/3
1745 Price, Thomas S A.363/4
1792 Price, William S D.348/9
1795 Price, William N O.118
1794 Price, William S A94.145
1790 Pride, Anna S D.269/70
1793 Pride, James S A94.147
1790 Pride, John S D.318
1790 Pride, William S A94.152
1796 Prider, Rachel S E.109/11
1747 Priest, Henry N G.36
1687 Prime, Hannah N ——
1776 Primrose, John K L.181
1747 Prior (Pryor), Hannah K I.170/1
1747 Prior, Jacob K I.166
1740 Prior (Pryor), John K I.12
1785 Prole, John N M.147
1788 Pryor, Elizabeth K M.174/5
1785 Pryor, John K M.46/8
1791 Pryor, John N N.223
1797 Pryor, John K N.172/3
1789 Pryor, John K M.194
1798 Pryor, Joseph K M.170
1791 Pugh, Jacob N N.209
1746 Pugh, John N Misc.1.391
1765 Pugh, Roger K L.9
1770 Pugh, Roger K L.78
1771 Pugh, William K L.96
1782 Pullet, William S A92.128
1788 Purden, Andrew K M.169
1776 Purden, James K L.180
1767 Purden, John K L.32/33
1757 Purdon, Andrew K K.164

1771	Pusey, Margaret	N	Misc.1.405
1738	Pusley, Thomas	K	H.151
1729	Pussey, Caleb	K	H.106
1728	Pusy, Caleb	K	G.21/2
1789	Pyle, David	N	N.33

- Q -

1783	Quenanault, Paul	K	L.273
1790	Quillen, Elizabeth	K	M.260
1781	Quillen, Joseph	K	L.230
1777	Quillen, Thomas	K	L.197
1799	Quillen, Thomas	K	N.229
1773	Quilling, John	K	L.125
1797	Quilling, John	K	N.185/6
1741	Quilling, Thomas	K	I.59

- R -

1730	Rackliff, Mary	S	A.248/50
1757	Rakes, Nicholas	K	K.171
1779	Rakes, Weston	K	L.209
1769	Ralph, Edwards	K	L.53
1782	Ralph, Mitchell	S	A94.182
1769	Ralph, Sarah	K	L.61
1787	Ralph, William	S	A94.184
1784	Raly, Philip	K	M.21
1748	Rash, Ambrose	K	I.248/9
1769	Rash, James	K	L.52/3
1771	Rash, James	K	L.98
1761	Rash, John	K	K.251
1778	Rash, Joseph	K	L.203/4
1755	Rash, Samuel	K	K.115
1757	Rash, Samuel	K	A42.74
1782	Rasin, Benjamin	K	L.251
1791	Rasin, Philip	K	N.48
1782	Ratlidge, John	K	A42.102
1773	Rattledge, John	K	L.138/9
1771	Raymond, John	K	L.104

1746	Raymond, Jonathan	K	I.45
1771	Raymond, Jonathan	K	L.96/7
1758	Raymond, Mary	K	K.180./1
1793	Raymond, Mary	K	A42.167
1758	Raymond, Presley	K	K.164&184
1793	Raymond, Presley	K	N.37
1776	Ratledge, Thomas	K	L.185
1681	Rawlings, John	K	A.1
1735	Rawlings, John	K	H.93
1766	Razer, Peter	S	B.311/3
1790	Read, Allen	S	A95.3
1713	Read, George	N	B.182
1786	Read, James	K	M.96
1797	Read, Jesse	S	A95.5
1796	Read, Job	S	A95.6
1790	Read, Thomas	N	N.264
1772	Read (Reed), Walter	K	L.112
1794	Reading, Hester	N	O.47
1778	Reading, Philip Rev.	N	L.106
1712	Reall, Jean	N	B.232
1799	Records, Levin	S	E.251
1792	Redden, Charles	S	A95.10
1798	Redden, William	S	A95.18
1772	Reddick, Benjamin	K	L.115
1762	Reddick, Robert, Sr.	K	K.272
1729	Redman, Jane	K	G.31
1774	Redman, John	N	K.125
1748	Redman, Joshua	K	I.202
1701	Redman, Thomas	K	B.42
1742	Reece (Rice), Evan	N	Misc.1.409
1771	Reece, Lewis	N	Misc.1.422
1798	Reed, Edmond	S	E.243/5
1757	Reed, James	S	B.138/40
1784	Reed, James	K	M..20
1790	Reed, James	K	A42.194
1795	Reed, James	K	N.110
1785	Reed, James	K	M.20
1785	Reed, John	S	D.76
1792	Reed, John, Sr.	K	N.29
1789	Reed, John, Jr.	S	A95.35
1793	Reed, Mathew	S	D.392/3

1741	Reed, William	S	A.324/5
1765	Rees, Abel	K	L.9
1778	Rees, Daniel	N	L.118
1758	Rees, David	K	A42.237
1759	Rees, David	K	K.218
1750	Rees(e), David	K	K.30
1762	Rees, David	N	K.53
1763	Rees, Ephraim	K	K.317/8
1737	Rees, Evan	K	H.140
1760	Rees, Even	K	K.249
1770	Rees, Jane	K	A42.243/4
1757	Rees, Jeremiah	K	K.156
1795	Rees, Jeremiah	K	N.128
1728	Rees, John	K	B.65
1769	Rees, John	K	L.58/9
1756	Rees, Margaret	K	K.143/4
1729	Rees, Martha W.	K	G.34&H.66
1785	Rees, Martha	K	M.20
1734	Rees, Mary	N	Misc.1.412
1774	Rees, Rees	N	K.160
1784	Rees, Robert	K	A43.26
1785	Rees, Robert	K	A43.27
1770	Rees, Sarah	K	A43.32
1794	Rees, Thomas	K	N.110
1784	Rees, William	K	M.24
1785	Rees, William	K	M.60
1749	Rees, William	K	K.12/3
1749	Reese, David	K	K.6
1792	Reese, Jeremiah, Jr.	K	N.29
1790	Register, Henry	K	M.257
1774	Register, Jeremiah	K	L.152
1734	Register, John	K	H.52
1784	Register, Robert	K	M.21
1708	Register, William	K	B.70
1719	Register, William	K	D.16
1747	Rehue (Reyhoe), Powell	K	I.187
1799	Reiley, Laurence	S	E.210/12
1757	Reily, Hugh	K	K.157/8
1796	Rench, James	K	N.184
1732	Renold (Renelds), Elizabeth	K	H.56
1791	Revel, John	K	M.265/6

1790	Reynalds, Eleanor	K	M.245
1742	Reynalds, John	K	I.48
1760	Reynalls, Henry	K	K.249
1728	Reynalls, John, Sr.	K	H.61
1736	Reynals, Daniel	K	H.147
1768	Reynolds, Catherine	K	K.322
1700	Reynolds, Francis	K	B.39
1734	Reynolds, George	K	H.104
1792	Reynolds, Henry	N	N.287
1795	Reynolds, Jane	N	O.93
1745	Reynolds, John	K	I.111
1749	Reynolds, John	N	G.316
1784	Reynolds, John	N	L.432
1791	Reynolds, John	K	A43.108
1785	Reynolds, Jordan	K	M.20
1708	Reynolds, Richard	N	B.162
1779	Reynolds, Richard	N	L.174
1758	Reynolds, Robert	K	K.179
1798	Reynolds, Robert	K	——
1774	Reynolds, Samuel	K	L.154
1775	Reynolds, Thomas	N	K.259
1777	Reynolds, William	N	Misc.417
1774	Rhodes, Benjamin	N	K.110
1781	Rhodes, John	K	L.230
1782	Rhodes, John	K	L.231
1782	Rhodes, Mary	K	L.259
1781	Rhodes, William	K	L.248/9
1782	Rhodes, William	K	L.231
1787	Riccords, John	S	A95.171
1790	Rice, Elizabeth	N	N.101
1783	Rice, Evan	N	L.405
1782	Rice, George	N	L.277
1798	Rice, William	N	O.371
1791	Rich, Edward	K	N.6
1779	Rich, William	K	L.213
1796	Richards, D.	S	E.99/100
1769	Richards, Elizabeth	K	L.51
1765	Richards, Henry	K	L.3
1781	Richards, Isaac	S	D.62
1784	Richards, James	S	A95.82/3
1790	Richards, John	S	D.302/4

1704	Richards, John, Sr.	S	A.47/50
1784	Richards, Joseph	S	A95.89
1775	Richards, Joshua	S	B.550/3
1774	Richards, Mary	K	A43.154
1684	Richards, Robert	S	AM2013.26
1732	Richardson, Anna	K	H.64&103
1777	Richardson, Azariah	K	L.193
1718	Richardson, Benjamin	N	G.131
1703	Richardson, John, Sr.	K	B.50
1710	Richardson, John	N	B.223
1750	Richardson, John	N	G.392
1791	Richardson, Letitia	N	N.206
1731	Richardson, Richard	K	H.15/17
1774	Richardson, Richard	K	A42.169
1742	Richardson, Richard	K	A43.168
1797	Richardson, Richardson	N	O.266
1757	Richardson, Robert	N	Misc.1.413
1794	Richardson, Sarah	N	N.412
1793	Richardson, Sarah	S	A95.103
1747	Richardson, Stephen	K	I.164
1750	Richee, Samuel	K	K.29
1750	Richmond, Ann	K	A43.174
1739	Richmond (Richman), Martha	K	H.157
1737	Richmond (Richman), Michael	K	H.132
1792	Rickards (Ricords), Charles	S	A95.106
1799	Rickards, Elias	S	E.217/8
1798	Rickards, George	S	E.166/7
1793	Rickards, John	S	A95.124
1797	Rickards, John	S	A95.127
1790	Rickards, Jones	S	D.261/3
1798	Rickards, Mary	S	A95.135
1781	Rickards, Michael	S	C.262/3
1791	Rickards, William	S	D.332/3
1793	Rickards, William	S	D.405/6
1799	Rickards, William, Jr.	S	E.195/6
1791	Ricketts, Reece	S	A95.155
1766	Ricords, Ann	S	B.312/4
1793	Ricords, Benjamin	S	D.388
1795	Ricords, Esther	S	E.187/8
1776	Ricords, John	S	C.58/9
1772	Ricords, Joseph	S	B.509/10

1753	Ricords, Samuel	S	B.46/7
1792	Rider, Betty	S	D.365/6
1783	Rider, George	S	D.29/30
1792	Rider, John	S	D.375/6
1790	Rider, Wilson	S	D.261/3
1788	Ridge, William	K	M.178
1788	Ridgely, Charles, Jr.	K	M.176
1755	Ridgely, Nicholas	K	K.103
1731	Ridley, Isaac	K	H.17
1769	Ridley, Isaac	K	L.61
1748	Rie, Christopher	N	G.278
1784	Riggin, Joshua	S	A96.26
1784	Riggins, James	S	A96.26
1688	Riggs, George	S	AM2013.90
1771	Riggs, John	S	A96.28
1785	Riggs, Peter	S	A96.32
1773	Riley, John	S	A96.41
1785	Riley (Rieley), Lawrence	K	M.67
1771	Riley, Thomas	S	B.428/30
1774	Ringgold, Thomas	K	L.149
1773	Ringgold, William	K	L.110
1745	Rinkin, William, Sr.	N	Misc.1.41
1771	Roach, John	K	L.91
1795	Roach, John	K	N.113
1791	Roach, Levi	S	A96.65
1751	Roach, Nathaniel	K	K.37
1694	Roades, Elizabeth	S	AM2013.155
1769	Roades, John	S	B.373/5
1771	Roades, John	S	A96.76
1687	Roads (Roades), John	S	H.10/2
1759	Roanny, Peter	K	K.218
1789	Robbins, Josiah	S	A96.101
1740	Robbinson, William	K	I.48
1733	Robbison, George	K	H.67/8
1748	Robbison, John	K	I.193/4
1780	Roberts, Alexander	S	C.229/30
1782	Roberts, Francis	S	A96.83
1785	Roberts, Joseph	S	D.84
1785	Roberts, Thomas	K	M.90
1786	Roberts, Thomas	K	M.127
1795	Roberts, William	S	E.43

1797	Roberts, William	S	A96.93
1798	Robertson, Alexander	K	N.218/9
1777	Robeson, Perry	N	K.377
1787	Robinson, Abraham	N	M.257
1786	Robinson, Alexander	S	A96.104
1787	Robinson, Ananias	S	D.141/2
1760	Robinson, Asa	K	K.250/1
1794	Robinson, Benjamin	N	O.20
1761	Robinson, Edward	N	I.543
1748	Robinson, Francis	N	G.288
1784	Robinson, George	N	M.47
1793	Robinson, George	N	N.327
1766	Robinson, George	K	L.112
1733	Robinson, James	K	H.67/8
1726	Robinson, James	N	Misc.1.408
1790	Robinson, James	N	N.128
1708	Robinson, John	K	B.65
1782	Robinson, John	K	L.257/8
1772	Robinson, John	K	----
1782	Robinson, John	K	L.232
1784	Robinson, John	K	M.20
1796	Robinson, John	K	N.157
1789	Robinson, John	S	D.224/5
1798	Robinson, John	N	O.398
1748	Robinson, Jonas	N	G.221
1788	Robinson, Jonathan	N	M.305
1785	Robinson, Jordan	K	M.20
1777	Robinson, Jordan	K	L.189
1797	Robinson (Robison), Joseph	S	E.142/3
1798	Robinson, Joseph	K	N.215/6
1784	Robinson, Joshua	S	D.108/9
1786	Robinson, Joshua	S	D.50/1
1769	Robinson, Lawrence	K	L.50
1793	Robinson, Margaret	N	N.328
1774	Robinson, Mary	K	L.156
1784	Robinson, Parker	S	D.63/5
1777	Robinson, Perry	S	C.88/9
1798	Robinson, Polly	S	A96.170
1773	Robinson, Rachel	K	L.137
1787	Robinson, Robert	N	N.249
1747	Robinson (Robisson), Samuel	K	I.177/8

1774	Robinson, Samuel	K	L.167
1795	Robinson, Samuel	K	N.125
1796	Robinson, Samuel	K	A46.87
1791	Robinson, Sarah	N	N.190
1798	Robinson, Thomas	N	O.421
1788	Robinson, Thomas	S	F.82/6
1790	Robinson, Thomas	S	D.291/2
1748	Robinson, Valentine	N	G.185
1757	Robinson, William	S	B.223/6
1778	Robinson, William	S	C.346/7
1783	Robinson, William	S	D.31/2
1797	Robinson, William	S	A96.193
1764	Robisson, Daniel	K	K.335/6
1718	Rock, Patrick	K	D.4
1720	Rodeney, Anthony	K	D.19
1745	Rodeney, Caesar	K	I.111
1708	Rodeney, William	K	B.65
1744	Rodes, Joseph, Sr.	N	N.142
1760	Rodgers, Thomas	N	Misc.1.415
1784	Rodney, Caesar	K	L.238/42
1744	Rodney, Daniel	K	I.96
1764	Rodney, Daniel	K	K.244
1781	Rodney, Margaret	K	L.226
1770	Rodney, William	S	———
1787	Rodney, William	K	M.155/7
1781	Roe, Caesar	K	M.126
1791	Roe, Samuel	K	M.265
1798	Roe, Thomas	K	N.199
1784	Roe, William	K	M.27
1796	Rogers, Agnes	S	E.90
1796	Rogers, Christopher	S	E.95
1797	Rogers, Comfort	S	E.116
1798	Rogers, Edward	K	N.217
1794	Rogers, John	S	E.7
1799	Rogers, Joseph	K	N.225
1761	Rogers, Roger	K	K.298
1700	Rogers, Thomas	K	B.36
1782	Roley, James	K	L.268
1771	Rolph, William	K	L.193
1760	Rork, William	K	K.246
1758	Rose, Ephraim	K	A42.237

1761	Rose, James	K	K.253
1739	Rositor, John	K	I.13
1762	Ross, Andrew	K	K.292/3
1798	Ross, Edward	S	A97.81/2
1764	Ross, John	K	K.344
1786	Ross, Levey	K	M.126
1787	Ross, Levi	K	M.166
1797	Ross, Matthew	S	A97.86
1787	Ross, Nathaniel	K	M.140
1794	Ross, Roberts, Sr.	S	E.16/7
1765	Ross, Samuel	K	L.5
1768	Ross, William	K	L.43
1795	Rotheram, Joseph	N	O.81
1787	Rothwell, Benjamin	N	M.234
1757	Rothwell, John	N	N.166
1777	Rothwell, Lydia	N	K.378
1772	Rothwell, Thomas	N	K.31
1791	Rothwell, William	N	N.200
1792	Rouse, John	S	D.362
1792	Rouse, John	N	N.248
1755	Rowan, William	K	K.120
1767	Rowe, James	K	L.22
1798	Rowen, John	K	N.200/1
1787	Rowland, Alice	S	D.147/8
1767	Rowland, David	N	Misc.2.27
1780	Rowland, Elizabeth	S	A97.107
1744	Rowland, Hugh	K	I.96
1727	Rowland, Samuel	S	A.219/21
1788	Rowland, Samuel	S	A97.117
1792	Rowland, Samuel	S	D.363/4
1766	Rowland, Samuiel, Jr.	S	B.296/8
1727	Ruluf, Deborah	K	G.9
1782	Rumford, Jonathan	N	L.307
1780	Russ, Robert	K	L.231
1734	Russel, George	K	H.63/4
1797	Russel, Jane	S	A97.134
1790	Russel, JOhn	S	A97.137
1796	Russel, Joseph	S	A97.143
1774	Russel, Katherine	S	A97.144
1786	Russel, Philip	S	A97.148
1791	Russell, Henry	K	M.271

1795	Russell, James	N	O.131
176	Russell, John	S	B.239/41
1736	Russell, Joseph	S	A.285/8
1768	Russell, Joseph	S	B.346/8
1769	Russell, Joseph	K	L.52/3
1798	Russell, Margaret	N	O.321
1794	Russell, Samuel	S	E.15/6
1749	Russell, William	K	K.7/8
1779	Russell, William	K	L.22
1791	Russell, William	K	M.271
1784	Russom, James	S	A97.156
1772	Russum, Peter	K	L.119
1795	Russum, Peter	K	N.131
1784	Rust, Jonathan	S	A97.165
1798	Rust, Jonathan	S	A97.166
1794	Rust, Peter	S	E.15
1793	Rust, William	S	A97.172
1767	Ruth, John	K	L.37
1748	Ruth, Samuel	N	G.233
1792	Ruth, Samuel, Sr.	N	N.280
1767	Rutherford, William	K	L.30
1771	Rutter, John	K	L.96
1748	Rutter, Philip	K	I.203
1750	Ryan, Owen	N	G.438
1777	Ryland, Mary	N	Misc.1.421
1767	Ryon, John	K	L.34

- S -

1728	Sallindine, William	K	G.16
1765	Salmon, Benjamin	S	A.97
1778	Salmon, James	S	C.152/4
1768	Salmon, William	S	A.98.1
1778	Salmons, Agnes	S	C.329/30
1757	Samples, Elias	K	K.178
1729	Samuels, John	K	G.32
1720	Sanderson, Jane	S	A.129/30
1757	Sap, Isaac	K	K.170
1772	Sapp, Henry	K	L.128
1750	Sapp, William	K	K.31

1785	Saterfield, Nathaniel, Sr.	K	M.68/9
1787	Sauce, Richard	N	M.230
1788	Saulsburg, ——	K	M.179
1798	Saunders, Jenny	S	E.168/9
1783	Saunders, Paul	K	L.271
1774	Saunders, Robert	K	L.157
1790	Saunders, Silos	S	A98.20
1862	Savage, John	K	K.279
1786	Savage, Robinson	S	D.106/7
1792	Savin, William	K	N.30
1794	Savin, William	K	A45.33
1706	Sawyer, Thomas	N	B.120
1773	Saxton, Andrew	K	L.128
1796	Saxton, George	K	N.144
1790	Saxton, Prudence	K	M.227/8
1799	Saxton, William	K	N.233
1779	Say, Mary	S	C.185/6
1796	Scales, William	K	N.259
1788	Schee, Harmonus	N	M.351
1776	Schoalfield, Benjamin, Sr.	S	C.44/5
1776	Schoalfield (Schofield), Bridget	S	A98.32
——	Schofield, Joseph	S	——
1755	Scot, James	K	K.109/10
1788	Scot, John	K	L.198
1777	Scott, Thomas	N	K.368
1788	Scott, Thomas	N	M.350
1750	Scott, William	N	G.438
1792	Scotten, Richard	K	N.13/14
1784	Scotten, Thomas	K	M.21
1788	Scotten, Thomas, Sr.	K	M.176
1775	Scotton, James	K	——
1790	Scotten, John	K	M.248
1786	Scotten, Nathan	K	M.110
1790	Scotton, Nathan	K	M.245
1799	Scotton, William	K	N.227
1791	Scouvenant, Nicholas	S	D.325/6
1791	Scronders, James	K	M.169
1730	Scudder, David	S	A.246/8
1771	Scudder, Jonathan	S	B.431/3
1785	Scull, Sarah	N	M.111
1797	Scully, John Burton	K	A45.108/9

1790	Scurlog, John	K	M.249
1788	Scurry, Thomas	N	M.323
1694	Seamon, Joseph	K	N.89
1794	Seccondiron, Sarah	N	N.400
1717	Secttown (Sealtown), James	S	A.122/4
1758	See, Derrick	N	Misc.1.442
1776	See, Isaac	N	K.297
1785	See, John	N	M.123
1793	See, Richard	N	N.312
1795	See, Wiliam	N	O.120
1799	Seears, William	K	N.239
1759	Seeds, William	K	K.217
1771	Seenea, Owen	K	L.103
1796	Sellars, Nicholas	N	O.146
1798	Semons, Gilbert	K	N.190
1708	Senew, Torich	S	A.442/3
1788	Serril, John	N	M.298
1797	Severson, James	K	N.180
1750	Severson, John	K	K.35
1763	Severson, John	K	K.314/5
1728	Seymour, Ebenezer	S	A.305/6
1795	Shahan (Sheborn), David, Sr.	K	N.123
1684	Shaltham, Jacob	S	AM2013.33
1797	Shane, James	K	N.187
1796	Shane, Mary	K	N.151
1748	Shane, Thomas	N	G.104
1740	Shankland, John	S	A.313/9
1794	Shankland, Samuel	S	A98.60
1731	Shankland, William W., Sr.	S	A.250/3
1759	Shankmire, Peter	K	K.197/8
1765	Sharp, Adam	K	L.7
1780	Sharp, Elizabeth	S	C.244/6
1700	Sharp, George	K	B.38
1798	Sharp, Joseph	S	E.180/7
1793	Sharp, Joshua	S	A98.89/90
1736	Sharp, Richard	S	A.283/4
1731	Sharp, Thomas	K	H.21
1790	Sharp, William	S	D.274/5
1763	Sharpless, Joseph	K	K.320
1720	Sharpley, Adam	N	C.207
1788	Sharpley, Daniel	N	M.333

1796	Shaver, Ann	S	E.98
1788	Shaver, Isaac	S	A98.101
1791	Shaver, Levin	S	A98.103
1771	Shaw, Ephraim	K	L.89
1780	Shaw, James	N	L.213
1733	Shaw, Joshua	K	H.51
1789	Shaw, Joshua	K	M.211
1781	Shaw, Richard	K	L.247/8
1789	Shaw, Samuel	K	M.210
1713	Shaw, Thomas	N	C.15
1768	Shaw, Thomas	K	L.50
1756	Shaw, William	K	K.126
1789	Shaw, William	K	M.210
1788	Shay, Dennis	K	M.178
1796	Shea, Elizabeth	K	N.151
1714	Sheffer, Isaac	N	C.19
1769	Shelley, Moses	K	L.69
1786	Shelpman, Alice	S	D.102
1777	Shelpman, Isaac	S	C.66/7
1776	Shelpman, Jacob	S	C.34/5
1732	Shennan, Samuel	N	Misc.1.429
1790	Shepard, Easter (Hester)	K	M.250/1
1764	Shepard, Samuel	K	K.253
1709	Shepherd, John	K	C.79
1709	Shepherd, John	K	C.82
1792	Shepherd, Richard	N	N.261
1786	Shepherd, Thomas	K	M.110
1790	Shepherd, Thomas	K	M.251
1790	Sheppard, Esther	K	A45.230
1799	Shepperd, Benjamin	K	N.227
1798	Shepperd, John	K	N.222
1766	Sherer, John	N	H&I.153
1761	Sherman, Thomas	S	B.229/31
1709	Sherrer, William	K	B.77
1763	Sherwood, Hannah	K	K.308
1734	Sherwood, James	K	H.85
1784	Shield, Luke	S	A98.113
1792	Shields, Robert	N	N.251
1797	Shipley, Rebecca	N	O.215
1789	Shipley, Thomas	N	N.68
1769	Shipley, William	N	H&I.241

1794 Shipley, William N O.28
1758 Shirly, William K K.177
1777 Shockley, John S A98.138
1784 Shockley, Levin S A98.141
1798 Shockley, Mary S A98.143
1733 Shockley, William K H.102
1786 Shoel, Andrew N M.214
1790 Shoemaker, John K M.229
1729 Sholand, Trustrom N Misc.1.428
1796 Short, Abraham S A98.152
1781 Short, Abraham N L.246
1788 Short, Abraham S D.182/3
1748 Short, Adam, Sr. N G.181
1799 Short, Adam S A98.154
1799 Short, Adam S E.229/30
1796 Short, Adam, Sr. S D.51/0
1799 Short, Betty S A100.191
1788 Short, Elizabeth S D.111/2
1794 Short, Jonathan S A99.6
1751 Short, Martha N G.481
1789 Short, Marg(a)ret S D.24/5
1789 Short, Phillip S D.227/8
1793 Short, Thomas N N.349
1759 Shrick, Mathias N Misc.1.440
1721 Shurley, Richard K D.50
1695 Shurly, Roger K A.13
1737 Shurmer, Benjamin K H.137/8
1737 Shurmer, Benjamin K H.146/7
1764 Shurmer, William K K.336
1787 Shurmizer, John N M.274
1784 Silevan (Sullivan), William S D.68/9
1756 Silliven (Sullivan), William K K.150
1772 Silsbee, Nathaniel N K.23
1789 Silsbee, Nathaniel N N.51
1751 Silsbee, Samuel N G.485
1722 Sim, Margaret K D.61
1781 Simmons, Daniel K A46.50
1772 Simmons, Elizabeth K L.119
1689 Simons, John S AM2013.103
1708 Simons, Stephen K B.68/9
1736 Simons, Stephen K H.131

1751	Simonton, John	S	A.437/9
1791	Simonton, John	N	N.202
1771	Simonton, Margaret	S	B.435/7
1694	Simpkins, Michael	K	A.10
1762	Simple, Caleb	K	K.275
1789	Simpler, Margaret	S	D.230/1
1786	Simpler, Paul	S	D.95/6
1780	Simpler, Philip	S	A99.58
1781	Simpler, Susannah	S	C.274/5
1784	Simpson, James	N	M.18
1775	Simpson, John	K	L.160
1790	Simpson, John	K	M.260
1753	Simpson, Margaret	S	B.59/61
1765	Simpson, Moses	K	L.5
1793	Simpson, Peter	S	D.396
1780	Simpsom, Thomas	K	L.216
1757	Simpson, William	K	K.171
1770	Sims, Henrietta	S	A99.196
1730	Simson, James	S	A.246/8
1708	Sinnexen, Brewer	N	B.205
1788	Sipple, Caleb	K	M.166
1770	Sipple, Caleb, Jr.	K	L.84
1752	Sipple, Christopher	K	K.52
1771	Sipple, Christopher	K	L.89
1785	Sipple, Elijah	K	M.52
1795	Sipple, Elijah	K	N.126
1784	Sipple, Garret	K	M.21
1785	Sipple, Garret, Jr.	K	M.69
1752	Sipple, John	K	K.82
1795	Sipple, John	K	N.134/5
1797	Sipple, John	K	N.185
1780	Sipple, Jonathan	K	A46.148/9
1788	Sipple, Jonathan	K	M.180
1793	Sipple, Martinus	K	N.60
1777	Sipple, Silvey	K	L.190
1798	Sipple, Sylvia	K	N.214
1798	Sipple, Thomas	K	N.196/7
1762	Sipple, Waitman	K	K.276
1772	Sipple, Waitman, Sr.	K	L.115
1784	Sipple, William	K	M.25/6
1790	Sirman, Elizabeth	S	D.280/1

1780	Sinman, George	S	A99.76
1772	Sinman, Job	S	C.180/1
1784	Sinman, John	S	A99.81
1776	Skeer, Laurence	N	K.331
1794	Skewes, James	K	N.112
1759	Skidmore, Henry	S	B.188/90
1796	Skidmore, Henry	S	A.99.99
1762	Skidmore, John	K	K.277
1708	Skidmore, Joseph	K	B.62
1760	Skidmore, Mary	K	K.224
1771	Skidmore, Samuel	K	L.94
1728	Skidmore, Thomas	K	A46.202
1744	Skidmore, Thomas	K	I.103
1783	Skidmore, Thomas	S	D.8/9
1696	Skidmore, Thomas	K	A.18
1767	Skidmore, Thomas	K	L.25
1770	Skidmore, Thomas	K	L.79
1760	Skidmore, Thomas	K	K.228
1784	Skillington, Elijah	K	M.20
1794	Skiner, William	K	N.89
1758	Skinner, William	K	K.190
1792	Skinner, William	K	A46.216
1691	Skrika, John Mattson	N	Misc.1.425
1792	Skulley (Scully), John Burton	K	N.24/5
1726	Slater, John	K	G.2
1780	Slater, John	N	L.228
1745	Slater, Thomas	K	I.114/5
1790	Slator, Jonathan	K	M.242
17669	Slaught, John	K	L.54
1759	Slaughter, John	K	K.206
1791	Slaughter, Jonathan	K	A46.223
1791	Slay, George	K	M.276
1785	Slayter, Mary	N	M.134
1770	Sleighter, George	K	L.69
1774	Slocom, Benjamin	K	L.159
1771	Smalley, John	K	L.89
1797	Smalley, John, Sr.	K	N.169
1795	Smith, Alexander	S	E.19
1793	Smith, Allen	S	A99.108/9
1783	Smith, Benjamin	K	L.269
1756	Smith, Benjamin	K	K.127

1785	Smith, Benjamin	K	M.46
1759	Smith, Betty (Bette)	S	B.180/4
1793	Smith, Charles	K	N.38
1791	Smith, Curtis	S	D.346/7
1769	Smith, Daniel	K	L.55
1794	Smith, Daniel, Sr.	K	N.93/4
1795	Smith, Daniel	K	N.124
1720	Smith, Daniel	K	D.21
1727	Smith, Daniel	K	G.8
1719	Smith, David	K	D.9
1777	Smith, David	S	A99.124
1753	Smith, David	S	B.54/7
1775	Smith, Denton	K	L.175
1750	Smith, Elizabeth	K	K.26/7
1751	Smith, Elizabeth	K	K.39
1785	Smith, Francis	N	M.151
1784	Smith, George	N	M.12
1778	Smith, George	S	C.140/2
1793	Smith, George	S	D.397
1788	Smith, George	K	M.169
1790	Smith, George	K	M.217
1770	Smith, Henrietta	K	L.86
1768	Smith, Henry	K	A47.48
1776	Smith, Henry	S	C.42/3
1754	Smith, Henry	K	K.100
1755	Smith, Henry	K	K.101
1771	Smith, Holliday	K	O.139/40
1796	Smith, Hugh	N	O.165
1778	Smith, Isaac	K	L.200
1781	Smith, Isaac	S	C.259/62
1797	Smith, Jacob	K	N.175
1789	Smith, Jacob	K	M.211
1783	Smith, James	K	M.15
1761	Smith, James	K	K.267
1766	Smith, James	K	L.23
1770	Smith, James, Jr.	K	L.85
1788	Smith, James	K	M.182
1792	Smith, James	K	N.23
1788	Smith, James	N	N.1
1799	Smith, Job	S	E.204/6
1798	Smith, Job, Sr.	S	E.174/6

1684 Smith, John N A.66
1708 Smith, John, Sr. N B.158
1722 Smith, John S A.166/7
1758 Smith, John S B.184/7
1760 Smith, John N Misc.1.437
1790 Smith, John S D.312/3
1796 Smith, John S E.104/5
1783 Smith, John S A99.168
1719 Smith, John K D.13
1745 Smith, John K A47.71
1748 Smith, John K I.236/7
1758 Smith, John K K.190
1768 Smith, John K L.44/5
1748 Smith, John K I.230
1783 Smith, John K L.276
1791 Smith, John K M.269
1788 Smith, Jonathan S D.186/7
1793 Smith, John K N.62
1798 Smith, Joseph K N.222
1775 Smith, Joseph K L.170/1
1761 Smith, Mark K K.259
1749 Smith, Mark K I.267
1766 Smith, Mark, Jr. K L.15
1766 Smith, Martha K L.23
1797 Smith, Mary K N.175
1695 Smith, Mary N B.38
1757 Smith, Mary N Misc.1.441
1778 Smith, Mary S C.137/9
1784 Smith, Mary S D.35/6
1786 Smith, Mary S D.109
1790 Smith, Mary S D.361/2
1798 Smith, Mary S E.169/70
1798 Smith, Mary K N.203
1799 Smith, Mary S E.235/6
1698 Smith, Maurice K B.30
1793 Smith, Nathaniel K N.62
1708 Smith, Nicholas N B.202
1744 Smith, Nightingale K I.95
1797 Smith, Noah K N.173
1796 Smith, Obediah S E.76/7
1748 Smith, Philip N G.208

1785	Smith, Philip	K	M.82/3
1790	Smith, Philip	K	M.217
1770	Smith, Rebecca	K	L.71/2
1713	Smith, Robert	N	C.17
1788	Smith, Robert	K	M.180/1
1794	Smith, Robert	K	N.110
1796	Smith, Robert	K	N.153
1791	Smith, Samuel	S	A106.4
1730	Smith, Samuel	K	G.36/7
1789	Smith, Samuel	K	M.183
1746	Smith, Samuel	K	I.143
1760	Smith, Sarah	K	K.250
1744	Smith, Solomon	K	I.76
1791	Smith, Solomon	K	M.273
1750	Smith, Thomas	K	K.26
1751	Smith, Thomas	K	K.47
1784	Smith, Thomas	K	M.36
1795	Smith, Thomas	K	N.123/4
1789	Smith, Thomas	S	D.421/2
1719	Smith, Thomas	S	A.109/11
1737	Smith, Thomas	N	Misc.1.432
1751	Smith, Thomas	K	K.47
1767	Smith, Thomas	K	A47.179/80
1756	Smith, William	K	K.152/3
1773	Smith, William	K	L.125
1788	Smith, William	K	M.179
1770	Smith, William	K	L.70
1770	Smith, William	L	L.75
1782	Snipe, Joseph	K	A47.227
1799	Snipe, Joseph	K	M.244
1794	Snipe, Joseph	K	N.111
1798	Snow, Anthony	K	N.222
1744	Snow, Elisha	K	K.53/4
1763	Snow, Elisha	K	K.305
1791	Snow, Isaac	K	M.275
1792	Snow, Isaac	K	N.19
1748	Snow, Isaac	K	I.251
1796	Snow, James	K	N.156
1766	Snow, James	K	L.10
1738	Snow, John	K	I.1
1761	Snow, John	K	K.256

1782	Snow, John	K	L.232
1788	Snow, John	K	M.170
1792	Snow, John	K	N.26
1796	Snow, John	K	N.144
1757	Snow, John	K	K.160/1
1773	Snow, John	K	A48.16
1779	Snow, Joseph	K	L.213
1744	Snow, Joshua	K	I.93/4
1752	Snow, Mary	K	K.56
1793	Snow, Silas	K	N.59
1775	Snow, William, Jr.	K	L.172
1744	Snowden, Isaac	K	I.84/5
1782	Soden, ---	K	L.260
1795	Soner, Robert	K	N.117
1748	Sonney, Jemina	N	Misc.1.436
1799	Soper, Samuel	K	N.230
1741	Sorath, William	K	I.57
1758	Souden (Sowden), Henry	N	Misc.1.443
1730	Southard, Benjamin	K	H.6
1768	Southard, Benjamin	K	L.44
1684	Southren, Edward	S	AM2013.32
1796	Soward, Eleanor	K	N.160
1776	Soward, George	K	L.179
1771	Soeder, Henry	K	----
1798	Spackman, George	N	O.417
1791	Spear, John	K	N.4
1776	Speer, Isabel	N	K.280
1768	Speer (Sphear), John	K	L.39
1791	Spence, James	S	D.357
1789	Spence, John	S	D.222/3
1772	Spence, John	K	L.105
1773	Spence, John	K	L.136
1773	Spence, Mary	K	L.136
1797	Spence, Patrick	K	N.187/8
1785	Spencer,Betsy	S	----
1778	Spencer, Catherine	S	A11.49
1778	Spencer, Donovan	S	C.134/7
1772	Spencer, Ebenezer	S	A100.52
1716	Spencer, Henry	S	A.89/91
1794	Spencer, Isaiah	K	N.76
1793	Spencer, John	K	N.49

1766	Spencer, John	S	A100.56
1772	Spencer, John	S	A100.58
1784	Spencer, John	S	A100.59
1773	Spencer, John	S	A100.60
1770	Spencer, Levi	S	B.394/6
1798	Spencer, Nathan	S	E.177
1772	Spencer, Samuel	S	B.462/7
1688	Spencer, William	S	AM2013.94
1765	Spencer, William	N	Misc.1.446
1690	Spencer, William, Jr.	S	AM2013.113
1779	Spencer, William	K	L.211
1783	Spencer, William	K	L.276
1792	Sprague, Paul	K	N.32
1796	Springer, Charles	N	O.163
1781	Springer, Gabriel	N	L.250
1753	Springer, John, Jr.	N	Misc.1.438
1772	Springer, John	N	K.35
1792	Springer, John	N	N.269
1799	Springer, Joseph, Sr.	N	O.446
1790	Springer, Lydia	N	N.155
1790	Springer, Mary	N	N.107
1776	Springer, Solomon	N	K.303
1694	Spooner, Charles	S	AM2013.168
1798	Spruance, Henry	K	N.199
1783	Spruance, John	K	M.17
1787	Spruance, John	K	M.160/1
1764	Spry, John (Joseph)	K	K.349/50
1685	Spry, Thomas	N	A.69
1786	Staats, Abraham	N	M.221
1793	Staats, Amy	N	N.331
1787	Staats, Ann	N	M.242
1785	Staats, Isaac	N	M.158
1790	Stafford, Elijah	K	A48.126/7
1776	Stafford, Henry	S	C.49/50
1791	Stafford, James	S	A100.100
1797	Stafford, Thomas	S	E.145
1743	Stalcop, Andrew	N	Misc.1.434
1747	Stalcop, John	N	G.140
1751	Stalcop, John	N	----
1778	Stalcop, Peter	N	L.14
1710	Stallcop, Peter	N	B.193

1708 Stanley, Christopher N B.151
1748 Stanley, John N G.210
1796 Stant, Charles K N.145
1799 Stant, Zadok K N.228
1769 Stanton, Elizabeth K L.55/6
1765 Stanton, John K L.6
1734 Stanton (Stenton), Jonathan K H.59/60
1773 Stanton, Matthias K L.142
1751 Stanton, Stephen K K.44
1696 Stapleford, Sarah K N.154
1793 Stapleford, Thomas S A100.108/9
1796 Stapler, Jemina N O.175
1793 Stapler, John N N.351
1797 Stapler, Stephen N O.298
1708 Stapleton, William, Sr. S A.60/1
1683 Starker, Andrew K AM2013.5
1703 Starkey, Edward K B.47/8
1787 Starling, James K M.133
1732 Starling, John N Misc.1.431
1794 Starling, John K N.88
1788 Starr, Bethia S A100.113
1785 Starr, Catherin(e) S D.77/8
1799 Starr, Isaac, Jr. N O.503
1790 Starr, Mary K M.253
1784 Starr, Nathaniel S D.46/7
1790 Starr, Samuel K M.221
1786 Starr, Samuel K M.120
1794 Start, Elijah K N.111
1768 Start, James K L.50
1792 Staten, Hillard K N.33
1774 Staton, Elisabeth S B.524/5
1773 Staton, Jehu K L.125
1788 Stayton, Nehemiah S D.172
1796 Stedham, Ann K A49.13/15
1712 Stedham, Asmund N B.237
1787 Stedham, Henry N M.253
1776 Stedham, Jonas N K.307
1792 Stedham, Margery N N.271
1797 Stedham, Thomas K N.185
1795 Stedham, Thomas K N.122
1686 Stedham (Stiddom), Timon N A.73

1796	Steel, Allen	N	O.193
1783	Steel, Allexander	N	L.404
1772	Steel, Daniel	S	B.459/60
1777	Steel, Hugh	N	K.384
1751	Steel, James	N	G.468
1741	Steel, James	K	I.38/40
1788	Steel, James	K	M.168
1784	Steel, John	N	M.23
1783	Steel, Joseph	K	L.270
1770	Steel, Mary	K	L.85
1709	Steel, William	K	C.81
1773	Steel, William	N	K.60
1779	Steel, William	S	C.217/9
1790	Steele, James	S	A100.140
1780	Steele, Margaret	N	L.208
1788	Steele, Prisgrove	S	A100.144
1797	Steele, Samuel	S	A100.145
1789	Steen, Christopher	S	A100.149
1775	Stellman, John	K	L.160
1784	Stephenson, Eli	S	A100.154
1773	Stephenson, Hannah	S	B.511/3
1776	Stephenson, Jannett	S	E.162/3
1763	Stephenson (Stepenson), Jeames (James)	S	B.345/6
1784	Stephenson, Jonathan	S	A100.161
1782	Stephenson, Robert	S	A100.164
1747	Stephenson, Robert	K	L.169
1782	Stephenson, Samuel	S	A100.165
1777	Stevans, George	K	L.187
1748	Stevens, Daniel	K	I.200/1
1746	Stevens, Daniel	K	I.130
1796	Stevens, Daniel	K	N.143
1694	Stevens, Henry	K	A.15
1744	Stevens, Henry	K	I.100
1789	Stevens, Henry	K	M.196/8
1798	Stevens, Isaac	S	E.162/3
1733	Stevens, John	K	H.66
1768	Stevens, John	K	L.48
1769	Stevens, John	K	L.57
1748	Stevens, Letitia	K	I.204
1797	Stevens, Luke	S	A100.168
1716	Stevens, Mathew	S	A.96/8

1782	Stevens, Nathan	K	L.231
1783	Stevens, William	S	A100.172
1708	Stevenson, Henry	K	B.73
1794	Stevenson, James	N	O.39
1790	Stevenson, Robert	S	D.293/4
1777	Steward, Catherine	K	L.194
——	Steward (Stewart), James	K	L.197
1790	Steward, Moses	S	D.263/4
1775	Steward (Stewart), Thomas	K	L.169
1793	Steward, Thomas	K	N.64
1788	Stewart, Alexander	N	M.325
1787	Stewart, Ann	N	M.255
1794	Stewart, Charles	K	N.112
1776	Stewart, David	N	K.324
1793	Stewart, David	N	N.362
1794	Stewart, Elizabeth	S	A100.182
1773	Stewart, James	K	L.129
1774	Stewart, James	N	K.137
1788	Stewart, James, Sr.	N	M.339
1786	Stewart (Stuart), Jean	K	M.103
1772	Stewart, John	N	K.42
1786	Stewart (Stuart), John	K	M.92
1769	Stewart, John	K	L.50
1754	Stewart, John	K	K.104
1776	Stewart, Margaret	N	K.283
1780	Stewart, Mary	K	L.214/5
1788	Stewart, Moses	K	M.171
1772	Stewart, Samuel, Jr.	N	K.11
1773	Stewart, Samuel	N	K.80
1786	Stewart, Samuel	N	M.195
1792	Stewart, Samuel	N	N.233
1698	Stidham, Christian	N	B.75
1759	Stidham, Henry	N	Misc.1.444
1795	Stidham, John	N	O.115
1777	Stidham, Peter	N	K.385
1721	Stidham, amuel	N	C.327
1767	Stidham, Timothy	N	K.114
1753	Stiles, John	K	A49.23
1774	Stilly, Jacob	N	K.114
1797	Stilwell, Mary	S	E.125/6
1759	Stinson, Jean (Jane)	K	K.200

1683	Stocker, Andrew	S	AM2013.5
1798	Stockley, Ann	S	A100.191
1782	Stockley, Cornelius	S	A100.195/6
1788	Stockley, Elijah	S	A101.2
1784	Stockley, Jacob	S	A101.9
1797	Stockley, Jacob	S	A101.10
1771	Stockley, John	S	B.424/6
1789	Stockley, Mary	S	A100.22
1793	Stockley, Nathaniel	S	A101.27
1775	Stockley, Oliver	S	A101.30
1745	Stockley, Oliver	S	A.366/7
1785	Stockley, Painter	S	D.92/3
1772	Stockley, William, Jr.	S	B.437/9
1749	Stockly, Joseph	S	A.414
1778	Stockton, Benjamin	N	L.58
1782	Stokely, Benjamin	K	L.231
1695	Stone, Basil	K	A.10
1747	Stone, James	K	I.168/9
1775	Stoop, Christopher	N	K.199
1788	Stoops, Sarah	K	M.172
1751	Storey, James	K	K.37
1787	Storie, Jodhua	N	M.233
1773	Srory, Francis	K	L.127
1782	Story, Marmaduke	K	L.243/4
1764	Story, Peter	K	K.343
1734	Stout, Benjamin, Sr.	N	Misc.1.431
1741	Stout, Benjamin	K	I.31
1795	Stout, Jacob, Sr.	K	N.121
1781	Stout, Immanuel	K	L.228
1764	Stout, Peter	K	K.342
1798	Stradley, Caleb	K	N.202
1777	Stradley, Dill	K	L.194
1767	Stradley, John	K	L.36
1796	Stradly, Absalom	K	N.156
1788	Stradly, Samuel	K	M.173
1790	Stradly, Thomas	K	M.250
1746	Strange, Jonathan	N	G.285
1798	Stratten, Thomas	K	N.192
1774	Stratton, Jacob	K	L.158
1764	Stratton, Thomas	K	K.345/6

1750	Stretcher, Frenwick	S	A.434/5
1753	Strickland, William	K	K.86
1797	Strong, Samuel	K	N.167
1772	Stuart, Charles	K	L.122
1782	Stuart, Charles	K	A49.91&93
1774	Stuart, Daniel	S	B.502/3
1783	Stuart, Daniel	K	L.270
1799	Stuart, George, Jr.	K	N.226
1797	Stuart, George	K	N.16
1770	Stuart (Steward), Hugh	K	L.75/6
1799	Stuart, James	K	N.226
1798	Stuart, James	K	A49.98
1756	Stuart, John	S	B.124/8
1795	Stuart (Stewart), John	K	N.128
1782	Stuart, Mary	K	L.231
1799	Stuart, Mary	S	A101.10
1772	Stuart, Moses	K	L.120
1781	Stuart, Sarah	K	L.238
1781	Stuart, Sarah	K	L.229
1776	Stuart, William	S	C.43/4
1773	Studham, John	K	L.139
1721	Sturges, Jonathan	K	D.45
1748	Sturges, Richard	N	G.199
1797	Sturgis, Shadrack	S	A101.10
1787	Sturgis, Stokely	K	M.137/8
1752	Styles, John	K	K.55
1756	Sudrey, John	K	K.132
1783	Sullivan, David	K	L.273
1766	Sullivan, Jeremiah	N	Misc.1.447
1796	Sullivan, Mary	K	N.151
1727	Sullyvan, Cornelius	K	——
1770	Sumner, John	K	L.76/7
1769	Summers, Laurence	N	Misc.1.449
1751	Summers (Somers), Rosannah	K	K.30
1749	Summers, Thomas	K	K.1
1777	Summers, William	K	L.192/3
1792	Summerville, Mary	N	N.377
1727	Sumption, Anthony	K	F.24
1777	Sundergill, Joshua	K	L.186
1785	Sundergill, Lambert	K	M.61

1790	Sunders, Jacob	K	M.251
1789	Sutton, Edward	K	M.198
1776	Sutton, John	K	L.180
1750	Swallow, George	K	K.30/1
1768	Swallow, George	K	L.47
1786	Swallow, John	K	M.101
1708	Swan, Richard	K	B.74
1756	Swancey, Barbara	K	K.147
1693	Sweatman, William	S	A.13/4
1719	Swett, Benjamin	N	C.169
1775	Swett, Benjamin	N	K.201
1742	Swift, William	K	K.17/18
1780	Swiggett, James	S	C.344/5
1749	Syddle, James	K	K.17
1687	Sykes, James	S	AM2013.87/8
1730	Sykes, James	N	Misc.1.427
1792	Sykes, James	K	N.16/17
1748	Sympson (Simpson), William	K	I.250

- T -

1787	Taggart, James	K	M.148
1790	Tarr, Azariah	K	M.260
1791	Tate, Ann	N	N.168
1782	Tate, William	N	L.274
1798	Tatmen, Delight	S	A101.105
1779	Tatman, Lowden (Louder)	S	A101.106
1787	Tatmen, Mitchell	S	A101.107
1790	Tatnall, Edward	N	N.94
1799	Taught, Elizabeth	K	N.239
1790	Taylor, Abraham	N	N.96
1761	Taylor, Anr.	K	K.269
1791	Taylor, Benjamin	K	M.272
1773	Taylor, Francis	K	L.140
1773	Taylor, Francis	K	L.142
1775	Taylor, George	N	K.228
1783	Taylor, George	N	L.356
1792	Taylor, Hugh	S	D.372/3
1760	Taylor, Jacob	N	Misc.1.459

1748	Taylor, James	K	I.228
1685	Taylor, John	N	A.67
1695	Taylor, John	N	B.49
1722	Taylor, John	N	Misc.1.451
1752	Taylor, John	K	K.80/1
1778	Taylor, John	N	L.20
1785	Taylor, John	S	A101.119
1786	Taylor, John	S	D.122/3
1791	Taylor, John	N	N.178
1795	Taylor, John	K	N.110
1799	Taylor, John	K	N.227/8
1796	Taylor, Leurenah	K	N.140
1788	Taylor, Richard	N	M.308
1788	Taylor, Tandy	S	A101.126
1748	Taylor, Thomas	K	D.39/40
1747	Taylor, William	K	I.196/7
1750	Taylor, William	N	G.394
1787	Taylor, William	K	M.219
1782	Teague, Sally	K	L.230
1776	Teat, Robert	K	L.178
----	Tepen (Tippin), Thomas	K	K.195/6
1797	Teppin, Thomas	K	N.162
1790	Tharp, John	S	A101.142
1775	Tharp (Thorp), Nathan	S	A101.141
1733	Thistlewood, William	K	H.38
1748	Thomas, Daniel	K	I.233
1771	Thomas, Daniel	K	A50.43
1787	Thomas, Daniel	K	M.129
1748	Thomas, David	N	G.204
1772	Thomas, David	N	K.46
1776	Thomas, David	N	K.314
1794	Thomas, David	N	N.429
1737	Thomas, Elias	N	Misc.1.453
176	Thomas, George	K	L.38
1796	Thomas, Isaac	N	O.96
1726	Thomas, John	K	F.20
1712	Thomas, John	N	B.234
1778	Thomas, Jonathan	K	L.204
1762	Thomas, Joseph	N	H&I.253
1769	Thomas, Joseph	N	N.265
1798	Thomas, Joseph, Jr.	N	O.318

1781	Thomas, Josiah	N	L.230
1718	Thomas, Lewis	N	G.128
1797	Thomas, Luke	S	E.157/9
1797	Thomas, Margaret	N	O.238
1753	Thomas, Richard	N	Misc.1.457
1774	Thomas, Thomas	N	K.161
1746	Thomas, Thomas	K	I.127
1790	Thomas, William	K	M.22
1798	Thomas, William	K	N.193/4
1748	Thomas, Zachiras	N	G.166
1707	Thomason, Powell	N	B.172
1767	Thompson, Hannah	N	Misc.1.465
1791	Thompson, Jacob	K	M.262
1783	Thompson, James	N	L.324
1798	Thompson, Jethro	K	N.193
1733	Thompson, John	K	H.98
1788	Thompson, John	N	O.79
1788	Thompson, John	N	M.342
1758	Thompson, Joseph	K	K.182/3
1767	Thompson, Joseph	K	L.35
1771	Thompson, Rachel	K	L.186
1775	Thompson, Richard, Sr.	N	K.273
1773	Thompson, Robert	K	L.130
1799	Thompson, Robert	K	N.223
1796	Thompson, Stewart	N	O.203
1749	Thompson, Thomas	K	I.256
1785	Thompson, William	N	M.86
1731	Thomson, Alice	N	Misc.1.453
1718	Thomson, Andrew	S	A.446/7
1761	Thomson, Martha	K	K.261
1795	Thomson, Mary	N	O.50
1699	Thomson, Walter	K	B.35/6
1748	Thony, John Daniel	N	G.115
1793	Thorne, Sydenham	K	N.41
1791	Thoroughgood, John	S	D.321/2
1835	Thoroughgood, Paul	S	C.183/5
1732	Thorpe, Hannah	K	H.35
1707	Thorrold, Timothy	K	B.59
1750	Throp, Abigail	K	K.22
1748	Throp (Thorp), Mark	K	I.219
1748	Throp, Samuel	K	I.220

1788	Tibbit, Mary	K	M.167
1781	Tilgham, Elijah	S	A101.188
——	Till, Thomas	S	A101.197
1785	Tilney, Stringer	S	D.79/80
1710	Tilton, John	N	B.208
1746	Tilton, John	K	I.140
1748	Tilton, John	K	I.248
1754	Tilton, Joseph	K	K.93
1719	Tilton, Mary	K	D.13
1797	Tilton, Sabrah	K	N.186/7
1766	Tilton, Sarah	K	L.21
1789	Tilton, Thomas	K	M.207
1797	Timblin, Sarah	K	N.173
1791	Timmons, Aaron	S	D.351
1796	Timmons, John, Sr.	S	E.86/8
1786	Timmons, John	S	D.111
1792	Tinch, Samuel	K	N.10
1776	Tindall, Charles	S	A102.9
1797	Tindall, Elizabeth	K	N.184
1799	Tingle, Parthense	S	E.240/2
1720	Toas, Daniel	K	D.22
1708	Tobias, Tunis	K	B.68
1758	Tobin, Cornelius	K	K.183
1775	Tobin, Rachel	N	K.246
1753	Toland, John	N	Misc.1.455
1692	Toltwood, Henry	K	A.4
1747	Tomblin, John	K	I.166/7
1792	Tomlin, John	K	N.12
1763	Tomlin (Tublin), Joseph	K	K.301/2
1756	Tomlin, Nathaniel	K	K.134
1757	Tomlinson, James	K	K.267
1775	Tomlinson, John	N	K.251
1786	Tomlinson, Joseph	K	M.122
1797	Tomlinson, Richard	K	N.165
1794	Tomlinson, Sarah	K	N.87/8
1785	Tomlinson, Thomas	K	M.86/7
1745	Tompson, Jethro	K	I.19/20
1763	Tompson, John	K	K.303
1698	Tomson, Urbanus	K	B.29
1763	Toogood, Hugh	K	L.227
1760	Tool, Clay	K	K.248/9

1793	Toppin, John	N	N.382
1760	Torbert, Hugh	K	K.233/4
1781	Torbert, Peter	K	L.227
1772	Townsend, Charles	K	L.118/9
----	Townsend, Coster	S	A102.48
1745	Townsend, Elisabeth	S	A.490/1
1798	Townsend, Isaac	S	A102.52
1785	Townsend, James	K	N.68
1793	Townsend, Jeremiah	K	N.63/4
1788	Townsend, Jesse	S	D.166
1795	Townsend, Job	S	A102.60
1739	Townsend, John	K	H.155
1744	Townsend, John	K	I.206
1786	Townsend, Julian	S	A102.62
1791	Townsend, Littleton	S	D.327
1787	Townsend, Luke	S	D.138/9
1784	Townsend, Mary	K	M.36
1773	Townsend, Solomon	S	B.481/2
1759	Townsend, Stephen	S	B.190/4
1786	Townsend, Stephen	S	D.115
1737	Townsend, William	S	A.284/5
1795	Townsend, William	K	N.96
1744	Trail, James	K	I.79/80
1765	Train, Esther	K	L.7
1768	Train, Esther	K	L.43
1768	Train, Hamilton	K	L.45
1764	Train, James	K	K.233
1781	Train, James	K	M.173
1737	Train, Roger	K	H.124
1764	Transberg, Ann Catharin	N	Misc.1.460
1748	Transberg, Peter	N	G.196
1685	Trayle, Robert	S	AM2013.29/30
1785	Treasures, Richard	K	M.52
1786	Tree, Daniel	S	A102.95
1789	Trepett, William	K	M.229
1784	Trial, John	K	M.36
1774	Trigar, Zebedee	K	L.150
1774	Trippet, Caleb	K	L.419
1761	Trippet, Daniel	K	K.269
1775	Trippet, Govey	K	L.169
1738	Trippet, John	K	H.149

1744	Trippet, William	K	I.90
1708	Trombalt (Trumell), Michael	N	B.149
1722	Trood, Henry	K	D.62
1788	Truax, Benjamin	K	M.167
1730	Truax, Cornelius	N	N.62
1798	Truax, Henry H.	K	N.216/7
1766	Truax (Trevax), Jacob	N	Misc.1.463
1774	Truax, Mary	N	K.126
1773	Truitt, Benjamin	S	B.484/5
1777	Truitt, Benjamin	S	C.65
1796	Truitt, Betty	S	A102.104
1781	Truitt, Elijah	S	A102.107
1787	Truitt, James	S	D.136
1744	Truitt, Henry	K	I.107/8
1784	Truitt, John	S	A102.134/5
1795	Truitt, John, Sr.	S	A102.136
1786	Truitt, Joseph	S	A102.143
1795	Truitt, Leah	S	A102.149
1790	Truitt, Martha	K	M.245
1784	Truitt, Micage	S	A101.151
1776	Truitt, Micajah	S	C.35/7
1790	Truitt, Peter	S	D.309
1757	Truitt, Samuel	S	B.140/3
1784	Truitt, Sarah	S	A105.158
1772	Truitt, Solomon	S	B.441/5
1799	Truitt, Southern	K	N.234
1790	Truitt, William	K	M.243/4
1797	Truitt, Zadock	K	N.164
1798	Truitt, Zadok	S	A102.164
1796	Trumble, Joseph	N	O.183
1777	Tweedy, David	N	L.91
1778	Triggs, Mary	N	L.34
1796	Tubbs, David	S	E.90
1798	Tubbs, Elizabeth	S	A102.108
1797	Tubman, Aninias	K	N.179
1764	Tucker, John	K	L.2
1799	Tucker, John	K	N.209
1720	Tuilly, Robert	K	D.34
1790	Tull, Joshua	S	D.306
1798	Tull, Levin	S	A102.176
1788	Tull, Noble	S	A102.178

1796	Tull, Sarah	S	E.97
1795	Tull, William	S	E.24/25
1749	Tull, William	S	A.411/2
1797	Tully, James	S	A102.188/9
1788	Tully, Sarah	K	M.173
1787	Tumblin, Covil	K	M.136
1732	Tumblin, Judah	K	H.105
1798	Tumblin, Ruth	K	N.212
1797	Tumblin, Sarah	K	N.173
1795	Tumblinson, Cory	K	N.136/7
1776	Tunnell, William	S	C.37/8
1748	Turley, William	K	K.2
1789	Turlington, Sarah	S	D.226
1789	Turly, Richard	K	M.204/5
1791	Turly, William	K	M.276
1771	Turner, Andrew	N	Misc.1.466
1769	Turner, Charity	S	B.371/3
1785	Turner, Ephraim	S	A103.13
1799	Turner, Eunice	S	A103.14
1790	Turner, Isaac	N	N.90
1797	Turner, Jehu	K	N.163/4
1789	Turner, James	S	A103.17
1748	Turner, John	N	G.205
1750	Turner, Joseph	S	A.431/2
1777	Turner, Lazarus	S	A103.20
1798	Turner, Levin	S	A103.22
1789	Turner, Martin	K	M.210
1771	Turner, Nathan	S	B.417/9
1777	Turner, Nicholas	S	C.110/2
1770	Turner, Samuel	K	L.74
1716	Turner (Tournier), Thomas	N	C.85
1789	Turner, William	S	D.240/1
1771	Turner, William	S	B.430/1
1795	Turpin, Charles	S	A103.28
1784	Turpin, Elizabeth	S	D.43/44
1784	Turpin, James	S	A103.30
1784	Turpin, John	S	D.43
1785	Turpin, Joseph	S	D.88/9
1784	Turpin, Mary	S	D.44/5
1776	Turpin, Solomon	S	C.89/90
1785	Turpin, Solomon	S	A103.36

1789	Turpin, William	S	A103.37
1746	Tussey, Charles (Elias)	N	Misc.1.454
1716	Tussey, Gertrude	N	C.57
1772	Tussey, William	N	K.1
1741	Tuthill, Charles	K	I.58
1746	Tybout, James	K	I.135
1746	Tybout, Rachel	K	I.135/6
1788	Tygart, James	K	M.169
1752	Tyndle, William	K	K.25

- U -

1765	Underhay, Heneritte	K	L.3
1759	Underwood, Benjamin	N	Misc.1.469
1785	Underwood, John	N	M.70
1758	Underwood, Richard, Sr.	K	K.181/2
1765	Underwood, Richard	K	A51.196
1773	Underwood, Richard	K	L.128
1722	Underwood, Samuel, Sr.	N	Misc.1.468
1796	Underwood, Samuel	N	O.148
1785	Underwood, Sarah	N	M.96
1750	Underwood, Thomas	K	A16.229
1772	Uptegrave, John	K	L.113
1748	Uptegrave, Joseph	K	I.211
1748	Uptegrave, Rachel	K	I.186
1716	Urinson, Christian	N	C.60
1690	Urinson, Urin	N	Misc.1.467
1750	Ussher, Mary	K	K.211

- V -

1775	Vail, John	N	K.222
1778	Van Bebber, Henry	N	L.8
1733	Vab Bebber, Jacob	N	Misc.1.485
1733	Van Bebber, Mary	N	Misc.1.486
1782	Vanbebber, Mary	N	L.263&359
1774	Van Bibber, William	N	K.193
1785	Vanburkalow, Peter	K	M.42
1713	Van Burkloe, Reynier Hammens	M	C.16

1747	Vanbuskirk, John	K	I.163
1739	Vance, Alexander	K	I.26
1738	Vance, James	K	I.6/7
1727	Vance, John	N	I.476
1797	Vance, Joseph	N	O.262
1748	Van Coolen, John	N	G.226
1727	Vancoolin (Vanquilon), John	N	Misc.1.475
1770	Vanderford, John	K	L.69
1772	Vandeford (Vandevore), Matthew	K	L.121
1747	Vanderford, Thomas	K	I.175
1767	Vanderford, Thomas	K	L.24
1780	Vandegrift, Abraham	N	L.200
1754	Vandegrift, Jacob	N	Misc.1.495
1750	Vandegrift, Leonard	N	G.432
1695	Vanderculine, Reynier	N	Misc.1.470
1695	Vanderculine, Zacharias	N	B.2
1718	Vandervare, William	N	C.236
1699	Vandeveer, Jacob	N	B.79
1784	Vandever, Breata	N	L.434
1712	Van Dever, Cornelius	N	B.253/4
1783	Vandever, Peter	N	L.350
1787	Vandevere, John	K	A51.230
1747	Vandike, Abraham	N	Misc.1.493
1730	Vandike, Andreas	N	Misc.1.484
1747	Vandike, Elizabeth	N	G.39
1762	Vandike, Henry	N	Misc.2.2
1727	Vandike, Isaac	N	Misc.1.479
1772	Vandike, Jacob	N	K.8
1759	Vandike, John	N	Misc.2.1
1755	Vandike, Nicholas	N	Misc.1.496
1760	Vandike, William	N	Misc.1.499
1733	Vandiver, Jacob	N	Misc.1.488
1750	Vandivere, Philip	N	G.414
1776	Vandyke, Daniel	K	L.176
1798	Vandyke, David	N	O.379
1776	Vandyke, Elizabeth	N	K.292
1788	Vandyke, James	K	M.181
1729	Vandyke, Nicholas	N	Misc.1.481
1791	Vandyke, Rachel	N	N.204
1776	Vangaskin, John, Sr.	K	L.179
1781	Vangaskin, John, Jr.	K	L.222

Year	Name		Reference
1783	Vangaskin, John, Sr.	K	A51.242/4
1783	Vangaskin, Sarah	K	M.18
1726	Vangaso, John	K	F.33
1787	Vangezelle, John	N	M.268
1717	Vangosoll, Cornelius	N	C.126
1782	VanHazel, John	K	L.232
1778	Vanhorn, Elizabeth	N	L.13
1780	Vanhorn, Isaac	N	L.212
1794	Vanhorn, Jacob	N	O.43
1796	Vanhorn, Paul	N	O.205
1788	Vanhoy, Abraham, Jr.	K	M.172
1743	Vankirk (Venkirk), Art	S	A.344/5
1782	Vankirk (Vinkirk), Barnard	S	C.315/17
1792	Vanleuveneigh, Catherine	N	N.298
1759	Vanleuveneigh, Samuel	N	Misc.1.497
1775	Vanleuvenigh, Jacob	N	K.234
1789	Vanleuvenigh, Zachariah	N	N.15
1754	Vanlewveneigh, John	N	Misc.1.494
1745	Vanluveneigh, Philip	N	Misc.1.492
1792	Vannatta, Samuel	K	N.165/6
1757	Vannette (Venatta), James	K	K.154/5
1799	Vanpelt, Joseph	K	N.239
1753	Vansandt, Albert	N	N.141
1788	Vansandt, George	N	N.4
1795	Vansant, Jean	K	N.121
1799	Vansant, John	N	O.490
1796	Vansant, William	K	N.137
1776	Vanwinckle, Jacob	K	L.185
1781	Vanwinckle, Jacob	K	L.225
1796	Vanwinckle, Jonas	K	N.140
1781	Vanwinckle, Mary	K	L.225
1752	Vanwinkle, Simon	K	K.50/1
1748	Vanwye, Jacob	K	I.210
1715	Vardamon, John	N	Misc.1.472
1792	Vaughan, Ann	S	A102.59
1782	Vaughan, Edward	S	C.292/3
1724	Vaughan, Elizabeth	K	D.67
1781	Vaughan, Ephraim	S	A103.63
1797	Vaughan, Jonathan	S	E.122
1788	Vaughan, Jonathan	S	A103.67
1791	Vaughan, Joseph	S	A103.7

1786	Vaughan, Nathaniel	S	A103.81
1784	Vaughan, William	S	D.51/2
1794	Vaughan, William	S	D.423/4
1775	Vaughan, William	S	B.543/4
1765	Veagle, Nicholas	S	B.288/91
1783	Veal, Jean	N	L.318
1782	Veal, John	N	L.268
1797	Veazey, Robert	N	O.254
1790	Veazey, William	N	N.113
1786	Veazey, William	S	A103.94
1734	Veight, Garret	N	K.224
1789	Venatta, Ruth	K	M.211
1797	Venoi, Abraham	K	N.181
1797	Venoi, Sarah	K	N.163
1798	Vent, Jane	S	A103.101/2
1790	Vent, James	S	A103.100
1796	Vent, Mary	S	A103.104
1799	Verdmon, Christopher	S	A103.107
1684	Verhoofe, Cornelius	S	AM2013.11/13
1784	Verner, John	N	M.2
1719	Vessey, Robert	K	D.15
1772	Viccory, John	K	L.111/12
1797	Viccory, Waitman	K	N.164
1772	Vickery, Walter	K	L.121
1786	Vickory, Hezekiah	K	M.117
1793	Vincent, Daniel	K	N.63
1795	Vincent, James	K	N.127
1795	Vincent, James	K	M.134
1798	Vincent, Jethro	K	N.202
1689	Vines, John	S	AM2013.109
1689	Vines, John	S	A.9/10
1795	Vinson, Bathsheba	K	N.128
1798	Vinson, Charles	S	A103.145
1792	Vinson, Daniel	S	D.373
1793	Vinson, Elijah	S	A103.150
1797	Vinson, George	S	E.122
1798	Vinson, Jethro	K	N.220
1792	Vinson, Newbold	S	D.386
1778	Virden, Absalom	K	L.206
1786	Virden, Eleanor	K	N.101
1773	Virden, Hugh	S	B.496/7

1769	Virden, John, Sr.	K	L.56/7
1785	Virden, John	K	M.39/40
1796	Virden, Marnix	s	B.496/7
1793	Virden, Peter	K	N.55
1791	Virden, William	K	N.7/8
1787	Virdin, Alexander	K	M.132
1776	Virdin, Daniel	K	L.180
1787	Virdin, Eleanor	K	M.132
1796	Virdin, John	K	N.160
1768	Vn Bebber, Jacob	N	Misc.2.4
1737	Von Burkelow, Daniel	N	Misc.1.490
1790	Voshal, James	K	N.147
1780	Voshall, Levi	K	L.216/7
1796	Voshall, Obediah	K	N.147

- W -

1796	Wade, William	K	N.150
1694	Waddle, Thomas	K	A.9
1794	Wails (Wales), Levin	S	A62.198
1794	Wainwright, John	S	A104.5
1779	Wainwright, Levin	K	L.209
1782	Walker, Agnes	K	L.269
1786	Walker, Ann	K	M.105/7
1787	Walker, Jacob	S	D.101
1789	Walker, Jacob	S	A104.16
1756	Walker, James	S	B.117/9
----	Walker (Wolker), Jean	K	K.24
1687	Walker, John	N	A.87
1707	Walker, John	K	B.59
1708	Walker, John	K	B.69
1788	Walker, John	S	D.179/81
1777	Walker, John	K	L.189
1793	Walker, John	K	N.39
1747	Walker, John	K	I.190/1
1780	Walker, Leah	S	A104.31
1791	Walker, Ralph	N	N.196
1684	Walker, Richard	K	AM2013.35
1727	Walker, Richard	K	F.25
1749	Walker, Robert	K	I.254

1785	Walker, Robert	K	M.85
1749	Walker, Samuel	K	K.2
1798	Walker, Tamer	S	E.174
1731	Walker, Thomas	S	A.253/5
1697	Walker, Wilbrough	N	B,68
1794	Walker, William	K	L.159
1769	Walker, William	K	L.54
1770	Wallace, Agnes	K	L.79
1794	Wallace, Alice	S	D.409
1786	Wallace, Benjamin	S	D.120/1
1772	Wallace, Benjamin	K	L.105
1797	Wallace, Benjamin	N	N.154
1755	Wallace, Barbara	K	K.122
1798	Wallace, Carbin	K	N.217/8
1720	Wallace, Charles	N	——
1751	Wallace, David	K	K.40/1
1790	Wallace, David	K	M.230/1
1787	Wallace, George	S	D.127
1779	Wallace, Hannah	K	L.213
1787	Wallace, Hannah	N	M.286
1797	Wallace, James	K	N.163
1721	Wallace, John	N	C.309
1756	Wallace, Joshua	K	K.142
1763	Wallace, Josiah	K	K.311
1785	Wallace, Mary	K	M.36
1762	Wallace, Mathhew	K	K.291/2
1772	Wallace, Reuben	K	L.110
1781	Wallace, Robert	S	C.272/4
1798	Wallace, Sarah	K	N.200
1777	Wallace, Solomon	K	L.190/1
1761	Wallace, Thomas	K	K.25/60
1792	Wallace, William	K	A54.17
1764	Wallace, William	K	K.338
1779	Wallace, William	K	L.211
1781	Wallace, William	K	A53.18&30
1783	Wallace, William	K	L.276
1789	Wallace, William	K	M.212
1767	Wallace, William	K	L.38
1797	Waller, Ann	S	E.140/2
1791	Waller, Charles	S	A104.57
1773	Waller, John	S	B.492/4

1776	Waller, Nathaniel, Sr.	S	C.15/6
1786	Waller, Nathaniel, Sr.	S	D.110
1784	Waller, Richard	S	D.62/3
1776	Waller, William, Sr.	S	C.33/4
1718	Wallis, James	K	D.38
1798	Walls, John Milton	K	N.194/5
1896	Walls, Levin	S	A104.100
1794	Walls, Thomas	S	D.414/5
1776	Walls, William	S	C.59/60
1701	Walmsley, John	K	B.43
1708	Walraven, Gisbort	N	B.147
1764	Walraven, John	N	Misc.2.7
1791	Walraven, Justa	N	N.224
1712	Walraven, Peter	N	B.19
1764	Walraven, Swain	N	Misc.2.10
1799	Walter, Mitchell	S	A104.124
1780	Walter, Peleg	S	C.231
1798	Walter, Sally	S	A101.126
1793	Walters, William	K	N.62
1729	Waltham, John	S	A.236/7
1788	Walton, Ann	K	M.174
1787	Walton, Bagwell	K	M.141
1791	Walton, David	K	M.269
1729	Walton, George	S	A.104/6
1796	Walton, George	S	E.91/3
1798	Walton, George	K	N.197
1763	Walton, George	K	K.319
1707	Walton, John	S	A.209/13
1745	Walton, John	S	A.365/6
1751	Walton, John	S	A.436/7
1783	Walton, John	K	L.274/5
1793	Walton, Luke	S	A104.153
1799	Walton, Mary	S	A104.154
1712	Walton, Matthew	N	B.229/30
1740	Walton, Matthew	N	Misc.1.104
1791	Walton, Nancy	K	M.269
1785	Walton, Samuel	S	A104.103/4
1752	Walton, William	K	K.79
1797	Walton, William	K	N.168
1734	Walton, William	K	H.43/4
1764	Wann, Christopher	K	K.346

1775	Waples, Abigail	S	B.538/40
1796	Waples, Ann	S	A104.168
1796	Waples, Burton	S	E102.3
1797	Waples, Burton	S	A104.172/3
1778	Waples, Cornelius	S	A104.178/9
1775	Waples, Dirickson	S	B.541/3
1776	Waples, Dirickson	S	A104.83
1785	Waples, Eli	S	A97.176
1796	Waples, Elihu	S	A105.13
1785	Waples, Elizabeth	S	D.85/6
1785	Waples, John	S	A67.43
1757	Waples, Marg(a)ret	S	B.158/60
1785	Waples, Marg(a)ret	S	D.70
1796	Waples, Mary	S	A105.13
1784	Waples, Patience	S	D.67/8
1757	Waples, Paul	S	B.133/5
1796	Waples, Peter	S	A105.39/40
1775	Waples, Stockley	S	A105.52
1775	Waples, Temperance	S	C.9/10
1746	Waples, William	S	A.381/3
1774	Waples, William	S	B.500/1
1791	Ward, James	S	D.333/4
1796	Ward, John	K	N.150
1752	Ward, Joseph	K	K.63/4
1719	Ward, Thomas	N	Misc.2.20
1790	Ware, Ann	K	M.254/5
1781	Ware, John	K	L.227
1792	Ware, William	K	N.39
1793	Ware, William, Sr.	K	A53.111& 116/119
1799	Ware, William, Sr.	K	A53.112& 114/115
1780	Warks, Elizabeth	N	L.190
1684	Warner, Edmond	K	AM2013.19
1789	Warner, Mankin	K	M.212
1783	Warnock, Robert	N	L.370
1772	Warren, Benjamin	K	L.112
1773	Warren (Warring), Lodwick	S	A105.112
1799	Warren, Margaret	S	A105.118
1776	Warren, Robert	S	C.26/7
1799	Warren, Samuel	S	E.249/50

1750	Warren, Thomas	K	K.28
1796	Warren, Wrixam	S	E.67/9
1798	Warren, Zipporah	K	N.198
1785	Warrington, Benjamin	S	A105.145
1791	Warrington, Benjamin	S	D.350/1
1784	Warrington, Elizabeth	K	M.50/1
1773	Warrington, Jacob	K	L.143
----	Warrington, Jacob	S	A105.150
1785	Warrington, Joseph	S	A105.155
1779	Warrington, Joseph	S	C.177/9
1762	Warrington, Mary	S	B.252/4
1787	Warrington, Sarah	S	A105.164
1727	Warrington, Stephen	S	A.159/62
1751	Warrington, Thomas	S	B.14/17
1783	Warrington, William	S	C.310/2
1796	Warrington, William	S	A91.112
1793	Warwick, Jeremiah	S	A105.178
1782	Water, Thomas	K	L.251
1794	Waters, William	K	N.84
1734	Watkins, Peter	K	H.100
1774	Watkins, Peter	K	L.155
1793	Watkins, Robert	K	N.49
1799	Watkins, Samuel	K	N.227
1728	Watkins, Samuel	K	G.11
1792	Watkins, Thomas	K	N.33
1794	Watson, David	S	A106.3/4
1753	Watson, Hugh	N	Misc.2.12
1732	Watson, John	K	H.48
1779	Watson, John	S	A106.19
1789	Watson, John	S	A86.20
1793	Watson, John	S	A106.22
1779	Watson, Luke	S	A106.29
1708	Watson, Luke	S	A.440/1
1776	Watson, Margaret	N	K.316
1777	Watson, Pryor	K	L.187
1785	Watson, Purnol	S	A106.34
1794	Watson, Rachel	S	A106.36/7
1755	Watson, Thomas	K	K.111/12
1746	Watson, Wiliam	K	I.138
1773	Watt, Robert	N	K.93
1778	Watt, Robert	N	L.16

1686	Wattkings, John	N	A.70
1768	Watts, John	K	L.40
1784	Watts, John	K	M.35
1794	Wattson, Bethuel	S	E.132/4
1797	Wattson, Betsy	S	A105.193
1773	Wattson, Isaac	S	B.476/8
1705	Wattson, Luke	S	A.52/4
1797	Wattson, Luke	S	A106.30
1781	Wattson, William	S	C.283/5
1786	Wattson, William	S	D.98
1767	Wattson, William	N	H&I.250
1782	Way, Caleb	N	L.265
1785	Way, Francis	N	M.82
1774	Way, John	N	K.111
1797	Weaver, John	K	N.163
1687	Webb, Isack	K	AM2013.77
1748	Webb, John	N	G.169
1760	Webb, John	K	L.195 & 204/5
1749	Webb, Jonas	S	A.399/400
1793	Webb, Obediah	S	A106.73
1795	Webb, Rhoda	N	O.114
1708	Webb, Robert	K	D.59
1778	Webb, Thomas	K	L.199
1747	Webster, John	N	G.71
1754	Webster, Timothy	N	Misc.2.11
1786	Welber, John	K	M.109
1792	Welch, Pennington	S	A106.90
1687	Welch, William	N	A.83
1788	Weldin, Isaac	N	M.348
1774	Weldin, John	N	K.124
1787	Weldin, Sarah	N	M.292
1746	Weldon, Isaac	N	Misc.2.13
1752	Weldon, Joseph	K	K.55
1766	Weldon, William	N	H&I.144
1684	Welley, James	K	AM2013.24
1797	Wells, Benjamin	K	N.170
1771	Wells, Elizabeth	K	L.104
----	Wells, George	K	H.49
1781	Wells (Walls), George	K	L.227
1775	Wells, James, Sr.	K	L.176

1733	Wells, John	K	H.86
1747	Wells, John	K	I.167/8
1721	Wells, John	K	D.46
1787	Wells, Lydia	K	M.140
1790	Wells, Mary	K	M.237
1793	Wells, Mary	K	N.49
1767	Wells, Richard	K	L.29/30
1788	Wells, Richard	K	M.173
1732	Wells, Thomas, Jr.	K	H.97/8
1767	Wells, Thomas	K	L.38
1793	Wells, Thomas	S	D.397/8
1762	Wells, William	K	K.27
1790	Wells, William	K	M.217
1793	Wells, William	K	N.49
1778	Welsh, John	N	L.110
1787	Wert, Martin	N	M.261
1798	Wesley, Mary	S	E.147/8
1775	West, Benjamin	K	L.172
1777	West, Benjamin	S	A106.103
1774	West, Comfort	S	B.504/5
1762	West, David	K	K.278
1751	West, Elizabeth	S	B.11/14
1790	West, Ezekiel	S	D.310/11
1789	West, George	S	D.237/8
1776	West, George	S	A106.122
1797	West, George	S	A106.123
1775	West, John	S	A106.142
1781	West, John	K	L.246
1786	West, John	K	M.122/4
1789	West, John	S	D.237/8
1797	West, John	S	E.130/1
1768	West, Joseph	S	B.348/50
1785	West, Joseph	S	D.90
1779	West, Joseph	K	L.214
1776	West, Joseph	S	A106.152
1791	West, Joseph	N	N.139
1787	West, Joseph	K	M.132
1776	West, Lewis	S	A106.156
1779	West, Margaret	S	A106.157
1772	West, Peter	S	B.391/2
1737	West, Robert	S	A.333/5

1784	West, Robert	S	D.40/1
1721	West, Sarah	N	C.298
1777	West, Thomas, Sr.	S	C.108/10
1755	West, Thomas	K	K.120
1766	West, William	K	L.17
1778	West, William	N	L.97
1771	West, Wrixam	S	B.422/6
1728	Westbury, Thomas	K	G.14
1747	Westbury, William	K	I.191/2
1780	Westley, John	S	A107.2
1784	Westley, Richard	S	A107.3
1765	Wharton, Augustus	K	L.2
1786	Wharton, Baker	S	A107.8
1791	Wharton, David	S	A107.13
1789	Wharton, Garret	K	M.208
1788	Wharton, George	S	A107.16
1778	Wharton, Hinman, Sr.	S	C.146/8
1782	Wharton, Isiah	K	L.242/3
1787	Wharton, Isiah	K	M.155
1791	Wharton, Jonathan	S	D.328/9
1744	Wharton, Rixon	K	I.108
1798	Wharton, Sipple	K	N.192
1776	Wharton, William	S	C.46/8
1793	Wharton, William	K	N.41
1789	Wharton, Wrixam	S	A107.38
1791	Whaley, Charles, Sr.	S	D.324/5
1798	Whaley, John	K	N.219
1783	Whealer (Wheeler), William	S	D.16/7
1770	Wheelar, Elizabeth	K	L.82
1721	Wheeldon, Joseph	N	C.334
1788	Wheeler, John	S	D.169/70
1723	Wheeler, John	K	D.62
1730	Wheeler, John	K	H.5
1748	Wheeler, Joshua	K	I.242
1791	Wheeler, Lemuel	K	M.267
1762	Wheeler, Samuel	K	K.298
1722	Wheeler, William	K	D.62
1782	Wheeler, William	K	L.266
1774	Wheeler, William	K	L.157/8
1783	Wheelor, William	K	M.17
1783	Wheldin, Joseph	N	L.373

1795	Whitacre, Elizabeth	K	N.118
1775	Whitacre, Isaac	K	----
1767	Whitacre, William	K	L.38
1741	Whitaker (Whitacre), Anna	K	I.54/5
1793	Whitaker, Henry	K	N.112
1725	Whitaker, Moses	K	F.1
1763	White, Andrew	K	K.330/1
1783	White, Anne	S	D.20/1
1786	White, Ansley	S	D.79
1750	White, Benjamin	S	A.423/4
1797	White, Benjamin	K	N.189
1709	White, Benjamin	K	C.81
1727	White, Benjamin	K	F.28
1787	White, Catherine	S	D.143/4
1794	White, Deborah	N	N.442
1789	White, Elizabeth	K	M.212
1795	White, Gilbert	K	N.135
1792	White, George	S	A107.59
1792	White, Isaac	S	A107.61
1797	White, Isabella	K	N.174
1774	White, Jacob	S	B.515/20
1763	White, James	S	B.272/5
1784	White, James	K	M.27/38
1788	White, James	K	M.167
1745	White, John	N	Misc.2.14
1768	White, John	N	H&I.191
1773	White, John	K	L.140
1786	White, John	K	M.95
1797	White, John	K	N.170
1798	White, Joseph	N	O.427
1690	White, Magnus	N	----
1797	White, Margaret	K	N.166
1797	White, Mary	K	N.166
1735	White, Moses	N	Misc.2.22
1798	White, Paul	S	A107.61
1794	White, Richard	K	N.75
1782	White, Robert	K	L.231
1747	White, Robert	K	I.149
1790	White, Robert	S	D.267/8
1769	White, Sarah	K	L.63
1786	White, Stephen	K	M.95

1795	White, Thomas	K	N.115/7
1723	White, William, Sr.	S	A.172/4
1736	White, William	K	H.127
1762	White, William	K	K.293/4
1778	White, William	K	L.198
1788	White, William	K	A54.172
1793	White, William	K	N.38
1794	White, William	K	N.86
1794	White, William	K	A54.176
1796	White, William	K	A54.173/5
1720	White, Wrixam	S	A.127/8
1778	White, Wrixam	S	C.162/4
1795	Whiteart (Whitchart), Henry	K	N.118
1730	Whitehart, Elizabeth	K	H.13&66
1778	Whitehart, Grace	K	L.206
1730	Whitehart, James	K	H.14
1732	Whitehart, Richard	K	H.100
1701	Whitehart, Richard	K	B.44
1791	Whitehart, Solomon	K	M.274
1762	Whitehart, Solomon	K	K.285/6
1707	Whitehart, William	K	B.60
1692	Whitehall, William	K	A.3
1725	Whitehead, Isaiah	K	F.5
1758	Whitehead, Isiah	K	K.193
1748	Whitehead, Joseph	K	I.242
1796	Whitehead, Lemuel	K	N.147
1795	Whitel, William	K	N.98
1781	Whitelock, Isaac	N	L.223
1793	Whitelock, Sarah	N	N.340
1780	Whitesett, Thomas	S	A97.107
1767	Whiteside, Arthur	S	B.343
1741	Whiteside, John	K	I.44
1747	Whiteside, Peter	K	I.197/8
1748	Whithart (Whitehart), James	K	I.223/4
1748	Whithart, Samuel	K	I.224
1762	Withart (Whitehart), Sarah	K	K.300/1
1728	Whitman, Joshua	K	G.18&H.66
1728	Whitman, Samuel	K	G.22
1783	Whitman, Samuel	K	L.270/1
1733	Whitman, Samuel	K	H.73
1767	Whittet, William	N	H&I.201

1773	Whittington, John	K	L.137
1684	Whitwell, Francis	K	AM2013.20
1780	Whorton, Charles, Sr.	s	C.342/3
1792	Whorton, Daniel	S	D.371/2
1709	Whyte, James	K	C.80
1790	Wiatt, Boaz	K	M.271
1790	Wiatt, William, Sr.	K	M.240
1798	Wiggins, Charles	K	N.217
1759	Wilcot, Josias	K	K.209
1718	Wilcox, Stephen	N	C.123
1795	Wilcuts, Caleb	K	N.108
1794	Wilcuts, David	K	N.82
1796	Wilcuts, Josiah	K	N.154
1797	Wilcuts, Nancy	K	N.162
1796	Wilcutts, Levin	K	N.153
1740	Wild, Joshua	K	H.156
1786	Wild, Richard	N	M.194
1789	Wild, Robert	N	N.17
1795	Wildgoos, Thomas	S	E.43/4
1786	Wildgoose, Jesse	S	A107.107
1763	Wilds, John	K	K.328
1794	Wiley (Willey), Andrew	S	D.408/9
1798	Wiley, Ann	S	E.172
1773	Wiley, John	K	L.141
1797	Wilkerson, Henry	K	N.165
1789	Wilkins, James	S	D.243
1790	Wilkinson, Isabella	K	M.260
1781	Wilkinson, James	K	L.237
1742	Willcocks, John	K	I.41
1792	Willey, Absalom	S	A107.121
1784	Willey, Aisle	K	M.32/3
1793	Willey, Ezekiel	S	A107.123
1751	Williams, Aaron	K	K.39
1790	Williams, Aaron	S	A107.140/2
1795	Williams, Andrew	S	E.10
1785	Williams, Ann	S	A107.145
1792	Williams, Benjamin	K	N.21/2
1774	Williams, Bethuel	S	B.505/6
1790	Williams, Charles	S	D.282/3
1790	Williams, Charles	N	O.460
1785	Williams, Christopher	K	M.57

1776	Williams, David	S	C.50/3
1794	Williams, David	S	E.2/3
1787	Williams, David	N	M.244
1771	Williams, Deborah	K	L.105
1773	Williams, Deborah	K	L.144
1790	Williams, Deborah	N	N.154
1686	Williams, Dirk	N	A.75
1683	Williams, Edward	K	AM2013.10
1778	Williams, Eleanor	K	L.206
1784	Williams, Elijah	S	A107.164
1767	Williams, Francis, Sr.	S	A.134/5
1729	Williams, Griffeth	K	H.4
1695	Williams, Henry	N	B.16
1708	Williams, Henry	N	B.162
1724	Williams, Henry	S	A.170/1
1798	Williams, Isaac	S	A107.175
1773	Williams, Isaiah	K	L.144
1791	Williams, Jacob	K	M.264/5
1796	Williams, James	K	N.143
1759	Williams, James	K	K.204
1767	Williams, James	K	L.25
1722	Williams, James	N	Misc.2.22
1729	Williams, James	K	H.7
1797	Williams, James	K	N.164
1744	Williams, Jean	K	I.101
1785	Williams, John	S	A107.190
1792	Williams, John	K	A55.100
1722	Williams, John	S	A.143/5
1758	Williams, John	S	B.14/6
1787	Williams, John	S	D.154/5
1789	Williams, John	S	D.225
1777	Williams, John, Sr.	K	L.194
1769	Williams, John	K	L.54
1769	Williams, John	K	L.69
1774	Williams, John	K	L.151
1796	Williams, Jonathan	S	E.85/6
1786	Williams, Joseph	S	D.130/1
1782	Williams, Lewis	K	L.231
1750	Williams, Lewis	K	K.87
1798	Williams, Martha	N	O.398
1695	Williams, Mary	N	B.33

1781	Williams, Mary	N	L.239
1740	Williams, Mary	S	A.301/2
1725	williams, Morgan	S	A.193/5
1794	Williams, Morgan	S	D.413/4
1795	Williams, Morgan	S	E.22/3
1789	Williams, Nathaniel	N	N.29
1757	Williams, Nicholas	S	B.146/8
1698	Williams, Patrick	S	———
1709	Williams, Reynear	K	C.82
1745	Williams, Reynear	K	I.125
1793	Williams, Reynear	K	N.53
1698	Williams, Richard	S	A.24/6
1721	Williams, Richard	S	A.134/5
1770	Williams, Richard	K	I.73
1796	Williams, Robert	S	E.93
1741	Williams, Rodger (Roger)	N	Misc.2.15
1729	Williams, Samuel	K	H.64
1780	Williams, Sarah	K	A55.154
1794	Williams, Spencer	S	E.9/10
1797	Williams, Stephen	S	A108.50
1744	Williams, Thomas	K	K.58
1783	Williams, Thomas	K	A55.169
1791	Williams, Ward	K	N.4
1790	Williams, William	K	M.254
1729	Williams, William	N	O.493
1783	Williams, William	N	L.387
1799	Williams, William	N	O.493
1773	Williamson, Jacob	K	L.144
1794	Willin (Willing), Thomas	S	D.423
1795	Willis, Israel	S	E.27/8
1789	Willoughby (Willoby), Eleanor	K	M.193
1795	Willoughby (Willoby), Job	K	N.122
1752	Wills, Hugh	K	K.80
1763	Willson, Elisabeth	K	K.32
1763	Willson, James	K	K.315
1748	Willson, John, Jr.	K	I.234/5
1697	Willson, John	K	B.31
1748	Willson, John, Sr.	K	I.225
1781	Willson, John	K	L.236
1797	Willson, John	S	E.114/5
1747	Willson, Jonathan	K	I.190

1770	Willson, Martha	K	L.78
1772	Willson, Moses	S	B.457/9
1757	Willson, Robert	K	K.167
1766	Willson, William	S	B291.3
1722	Willson, William	K	D.56
1719	Willson, William	K	D.12
1770	Willson, William, Sr.	K	L.69
1705	Wilson, Abel	K	B.52
1705	Wilson, Ann	K	B.53
1778	Wilson, Ann	K	F.206
1755	Wilson, Daniel	S	B.112/4
1756	Wilson, George	K	K.148
1788	Wilson, George	K	M.177/8
1798	Wilson, Hosea	K	N.218
1732	Wilson, Hugh	K	B.41
1786	Wilson, James	K	M.122
1792	Wilson, John	K	N.12
1732	Wilson (Willson), John	K	H.30
1767	Wilson, John	K	L.26
1791	Wilson, Joseph	K	M.269
1705	Wilson, Mathew	K	B.52
1790	Wilson, Matthew	S	D.295/6
1794	Wilson, Nathan	K	N.88
1700	Wilson, Richard	K	B.38/9
1723	Wilson, Richard	K	D.63
1737	Wilson, Samuel	N	Misc.2.21
1787	Wilson, Samuel	K	M.147/8
1796	Wilson, Susannah	K	N.151
1793	Wilson, Temperance	S	D.406
1732	Wilson, Thomas	S	A.227/9
1783	Wilson, Thomas	N	L.314
1763	Wilson, Thomas	K	K.310
1794	Wilson, Thomas Rodney	K	N.86
1732	Wilson, Thomas	K	H.101
1736	Wilson, Thomas	K	H.136
1756	Wilson, William	K	K.137/8
1791	Wilson, William	S	A108.135
1794	Wilson, William	S	A108.136
1746	Wilson, William	K	F.134
1797	Wilson, William	K	N.174
1778	Wilson, William, Sr.	S	C.182/3

1778 Wilson, William N L.71
1730 Wiltbanck, Abraham S A.245/6
1761 Wiltbanck, Abraham S B.234/7
1724 Wiltbanck, Cornelius S A.174/7
1741 Wiltbanck, Cornelius S A.321/3
1693 Wiltbanck, Halmanius (Hermanis) S AM2013.14
1708 Wiltbanck, Isaac S A.59/60
1792 Wiltbanck, John S D.366/71
1795 Wiltbanck, Mary S E.28/30
1771 Wiltbanck, Naomy S B.419/20
1779 Windell, David N L.149
1787 Windol, Thomas K M.83
1783 Windsor, James S A106.166
1795 Windsor, Jesse S A108.169
1794 Windsor, Joseph S A108.170
1775 Windsor, Philip S C.13/15
1789 Windsor, Philip S D.243
1787 Windul, Jonathan K M.131
1790 Winford, Alexander K M.223
1790 Wingate, John S D.272/3
1709 Winghouse, Morris Vander (Moorits Vanwidwenhuysen) N Misc.1.471
1786 Winsmore, Robert K M.110
1721 Winsmore, Thomas K D.47
1788 Winsmore, Valentine K M.167
1686 Winsmore, William K C.88
1787 Winsmore, William K M.158/9
1748 Winterton, Ralph K I.212
1793 Wirt, Frederick N N.379
1790 Wirt, Mary N N.125
1797 With, Thomas K N.171
1709 Withe, James N B.191
1781 Witherspoon, Flora N L.244
1718 Witherspoon, Robert N C.142
1738 Woddle, David K H.151
1779 Wolbough, Peter N L.169
1797 Wolfe, Benjamin S E.142
1785 Wolfe, Francis S D.84/5
1799 Wolfe, Mary S E.220/1
1797 Wolfe, Reece S E.124/5
1716 Wolfe, Russ S A.88/9

1772 Wollaston, Jeremiah N K.51
1796 Wollaston, Thomas N O.186
1750 Wollaston, William N G.377
1781 Wood, James S C.256
1791 Wood, John N N.170
1792 Wood, John S A109.46
1755 Wood, John, Jr. K L.172
1787 Wood, John K M.131
1791 Wood, John N N.170
1721 Wood, Joseph N C.361
1771 Wood, Joseph K L.104
1787 Wood, Joseph K M.158
1769 Wood, Martha S B.354/6
1793 Wood, Nathan N N.369
1778 Wood, Nicholas N L.18
1732 Wood, Robert K H.36
1782 Wood, Robert K L.258/9
1781 Wood, William N L.237
1790 Woodcock, Elizabeth K M.216
1785 Woodcraft, William, Jr. S A109.48
1749 Woodell, Mary N G.354
1796 Woodell, Mary K N.188/9
1792 Wooderson, William N N.305
1748 Woodland, Catherine N G.176
1750 Woodle, Joseph K K.34/5
1749 Woodley, Edward K I.225
1792 Woodrop, Daniel K N.27
1744 Woodward, Anthony S A.367/9
1773 Woolf, Rees S B.491/2
1757 Woolf, William S B.194/6
1784 Wooten, Benjamin S A109.51
1796 Wooten, Isaac S E.82/3
1748 Wootten, Robert K A56.126
1777 Wootton (Wooten), John, Jr. S A109.58
1698 Word, Patrick K B.32
1792 Worknott, Alexander K N.33
1778 Worms, Daniel N L.10
1726 Worrall, James K F.17/18
1734 Worrall, James K A56.140
1745 Worrell, Joseph K I.117

1789	Worth, Jonathan	K	M.211
1792	Wott, John	N	N.290
1744	Wrath, William	K	A56.144
1786	Wright, Comfort	S	A100.77
1796	Wright, Ezekiel	S	E.111
1791	Wright, George	N	N.201
1785	Wright, Jeremiah	S	A109.84
1752	Wright, John	S	B.41/3
1798	Wright, John	N	O.340
1799	Wright, Joshua	S	A109.90
1795	Wright, Nathaniel	S	A109.95
1791	Wright, Fretwell	S	D.344/5
1781	Wright, Sarah	K	L.229
1778	Wright, Solomon	S	A109.101
1798	Wright, William	K	N.220
1798	Wright, William	S	E.183
1709	Wrotten, William	K	M.211
1799	Wyatt, John	S	A109.112/4
1770	Wyatt, Maryann	K	L.79
1792	Wyatt, William	K	A56.179
1778	Wydelott, Thomas	S	C.169/70
1754	Wynkoop, Abraham	S	B.20/2
1766	Wynkoop, Esther	K	L.13/14
1778	Wynkoop, Mary	N	L.43
1755	Wynkoop, Thomas	S	B.114/6
1769	Wynn, Benjamin	K	L.68
1799	Wyth, William	K	A56.188

- Y -

1792	Yarnall, Elizabeth	N	N.284
1749	Yarnall, John	N	G.346
1799	Yarnall, John	N	O.501
1720	Yaw, Jasper	N	C.211
1775	Yaw, Thomas	S	A109.128
1795	York, Samuel	K	N.127
1794	Young, David	K	N.87
1696	Young, Jacob	N	B.66
1781	Young, John	S	A109.130

1688	Young, Mary	S	----
1790	Young, Preston	K	M.242/3
1789	Young, Robert	S	D.135/6
1799	Young, Robert	S	A109.142
1729	Young, Thomas	K	H.3
1777	Young, Wells	K	L.197
1792	Young, William	S	A91.80
1782	Younger, Thomas	K	L.231

- Z -

1782	Zebley, John	N	L.354
1778	Zelefro, Joseph	K	L.206

A Bibliography of Some Material Related to This Book

Clark, Raymond B., Jr. *Kent County, Delaware, Wills and Administrations, 1680-1800: An Index*. Maryland and Delaware Genealogy Magazine, St. Michael's, Maryland, 1985.

Colonial Dames of America. *A Calendar of Delaware Wills, New Castle County, Delaware, 1682-1800*. New York, 1910. Reprinted in 1992 by Heritage Books, Inc., Bowie, Maryland.

Daughters of the American Revolution of Delaware. *Old Bible Records and Other Genealogical Data*. 13 volumes. Typed and bound. Only three sets exist.

Delaware Genealogical Society. *Delaware Genealogical Research Guide*. Wilmington, Delaware. 1989.

deValinger, Leon, Jr. *Calendar of Kent County, Delaware Probate Records, 1680-1800*. Dover: Public Archives Commission, 1944.

deValinger, Leon, Jr. *Calendar of Sussex County, Delaware Probate Records, 1680-1800*. Dover: Delaware Public Archives Commission, 1964. Reprinted in 1993 by Heritage Books, Inc., Bowie, Maryland.

Division of Historical and Cultural Affairs. *Delaware Archives*. Halls of Records, Dover, Delaware, 1976.

Gehring, Charles T. *New York Historical Manuscripts: Dutch*. Volumes XX-XXI. (Delaware Papers: English Period). Baltimore: Genealogical Publishing Co., Inc., 1977.

Reed, H. Clay, and Reed, Marion Bjornson. *A Bibliography of Delaware through 1960*. Newark: 1966.

Virdin, Donald Odell. *New Castle County, Delaware Wills and Estates, 1682-1800*. Maryland and Delaware Genealogy Magazine, St. Michael's, Maryland, 1982.

Weinberg, Allen, and Slattery, Thomas E. *Warrants and Surveys of the Province of Pennsylvania Including the Three Lower Counties, 1759*. Philadelphia: City of Philadelphia, Department of Records, 1965.

Other books by the author:

The Virdins of Delaware and Related Families
Some Pioneer Delaware Families
Delaware Bible Records, Volume 2
Delaware Bible Records, Volume 3
Delaware Bible Records, Volume 5
Pennsylvania Genealogies And Family Histories: A Bibliography of Books about Pennsylvania Families
Maryland and Delaware Genealogies and Family Histories
Virginia Genealogies and Family Histories: A Bibliography of Books about Virginia Families
Civil War Correspondence of Judge Thomas Goldsborough Odell
CD: The Civil War Correspondence of Judge Thomas Goldsborough Odell

New England Family Histories and Genealogies: States of New Hampshire and Vermont
Texas Family Histories and Genealogies
New England Family Histories: State of Connecticut

Other books by Lu Verne V. Hall and Donald O. Virdin:

New England Family Histories and Genealogies: States of New Hampshire and Vermont
Texas Family Histories and Genealogies
New England Family Histories: State of Connecticut

New England Family Histories and Genealogies: States of Maine and Rhode Island
New England Family Histories and Genealogies: Miscellaneous New England States
CD: The Civil War Correspondence of Judge Thomas Goldsborough Odell
CD: Delaware Bible Records, Volumes 1-4

www.ingramcontent.com/pod-product-compliance
Lightning Source LLC
LaVergne TN
LVHW050636100826
845148LV00011B/1883

* 9 7 8 0 7 8 8 4 0 0 2 0 9 *